Introducing town planning

Series: Exploring Town Planning

Series editor Clara Greed

Volume I *Introducing Town Planning*   **2nd edition**
Volume II *Implementing Town Planning*
Volume III *Investigating Town Planning*
Volume IV *An Introduction to Urban Design*

Introducing town planning

2nd Edition

Clara H. Greed

Series: Exploring Town Planning

Series Editor: Clara H. Greed

Longman

Addison Wesley Longman Limited
Edinburgh Gate, Harlow
Essex, CM20 2JE, England
and Associated Companies throughout the world

© Addison Wesley Longman Limited 1993
© Addison Wesley Longman Limited 1996

First published 1993
Second edition 1996

British Library Cataloguing in Publication Data
A catalogue entry for this title is available from the British Library.

ISBN 0–582–29300–6

Set by 8 in 10/11pt New Baskerville
Produced through Longman Malaysia, GPS

Contents

List of tables and figures   vii

Preface   ix

Acknowledgements   xi

Part I   The planning and development framework   1

   1   The scope and nature of town planning   3
   2   The organisation of planning and the
     development process   20
   3   The property professions and the role of the
     planners   43

Part II   The evolution of modern town planning   63

   4   Urbanisation and the industrial revolution   65
   5   Reaction and reform   81
   6   The development of state intervention in the
     first half of the twentieth century   101
   7   Reaction and rethink: the development of
     town planning in the second half of the
     twentieth century   120

Part III   The visual and design aspects of planning   145

   8   The historical development of town planning   147
   9   Urban and rural conservation   165
  10   Development and design control   189

Part IV   The social aspects of planning   215

  11   Urban social perspectives on planning   217
  12   An alternative viewpoint and unresolved issues   242

   Appendices I   Guidance for students   265
          II   Traditional vernacular architectural
             styles   274

Bibliography   276

Index   293

List of tables and figures

Tables

3.1 Membership of the professional bodies as at
January 1995   53
4.1 Population of England and Wales, 1801–1901
(millions)   69
4.2 Urban growth, 1801–1901   69
4.3 Socio economic groupings   76
4.4 Social grading scale   77
4.5 Surrey occupational class scale   77
8.1 Chronological development of architectural styles   151

Figures

2.1 The levels of town and country planning   22
2.2 The process of property development   35
5.1 Ebenezer Howard's 'three magnets'   92
5.2 Howard's conception of the Garden City and its
rural belt   93
5.3 The neighbourhood ward of Howard's Garden City   95
6.1 The New Towns of Britain   117
9.1 Areas of rural control   177
11.1 Three social ecology models   228

Preface

This book is intended as a relatively simple introduction to town and country planning, rather than a polemical or academic analysis of the subject. It is chiefly aimed at students studying for the various built environment professions, but it is hoped it will be of interest to a wider range of general readers too. The book should be seen as a compendium of topics grouped into four main sections, which may be read sequentially, or dipped into as need arises. Although there are some strands which run throughout the book, for example on the scope and nature of town planning, it is not intended to be strongly thematic, nor strictly chronological in structure. Rather the aim is to juxtapose the main elements of the subject – namely the physical, social, legal, economic, visual and environmental dimensions – in an accessible manner, within the framework of discussing different aspects of town planning. Indeed, these components are seldom separated out in the real world of planning practice, or the built environment itself. The structure of the book is informed by the author's experience as a chartered town planner, and from teaching introductory planning courses within the Faculty of the Built Environment at the University of the West of England to a range of different student groups, including those enrolled on surveying, estate management and housing courses, as well as those taking town planning as their main subject.

Whilst *Introducing Town Planning* covers and updates material currently found on many introductory courses, emphasis has also been put, throughout, upon incorporating, to a limited extent, a gender perspective to reflect modern syllabus demands, and student interest. To avoid possible confusion, it must be pointed out that a deeper, more discursive inquiry into town planning from this perspective is the subject of another book by the author entitled *Women and Planning: Creating Gendered Realities* (Greed, 1994). This is aimed at more advanced readers, already familiar with the rudiments of town planning, including students on a postgraduate planning course, the wider academic community and established practitioners.

Those who wish to pursue particular aspects of town

planning touched upon in *Introducing Town Planning* in more detail will find that cross references are given to later volumes in this series in which fuller coverage is given to a range of topics. Volume II consists of contributions from planning practitioners, edited as a collection by the present author, and entitled *Implementing Town Planning*. This looks at different aspects of the implementation process (introduced in Part I of this present Volume), such as the procedural and legal context; the commercial property development perspective; and the social implications of policy implementation, all illustrated with case studies. Emphasis is put upon the planning gain and betterment controversy, which is only touched upon in the present volume, and upon the role of negotiation and planning appeal procedures in resolving conflict. Volume II is intended for intermediate and final year students, and all those who already have an understanding of the basics of town planning, and are interested in planning advice. Volume III *Investigating Town Planning* consists of a series of contributions, also edited by the present author, each of which seeks to discuss, in greater depth, the different manifestations and types of 'planning' which together make up what in Britain we call 'town planning'. For example, economic planning, planning for housing, EC urban policy, and environmental planning. Volume III is more reflective, and discursive in approach, and is aimed at more advanced undergraduate students, post graduates, and those in the profession who are interested in the changing nature of the town planning discourse. Further volumes are being produced by collaborative teams of planners, designers and architects on *Urban Design*, dealing with both theory and practice, under the joint editorship of Clara Greed, of the University of West of England, Bristol, and Marion Roberts of the University of Westminster, London.

Clara Greed
Bristol, 1995

Acknowledgements

I would like to thank Professor Alison Ravetz of Leeds Polytechnic and Robin Tetlow of Oldfield King Planning Consultants, Bristol, for their advice and comments on the whole book, also Lydia Lambert and Judith Porter of Woodspring District Planning Department, Avon for their suggestions in respect of Chapter 10. I would like to thank the students of Bristol Polytechnic (now University of the West of England), Faculty of the Built Environment, for their inspiration, and staff for their advice including Peter Fidler, John Manley, Andrew May, Bill Cousins and others.

Acknowledgements and thanks for the use of Figures are as follows:

Figure 2.2 also appears modified in *Antipode*, 24, 1:16–28 (see Greed, 1992), Blackwell Publishers, Cambridge, Mass.

Trustees of Ebenezer Howard's estate, the Town and Country Planning Association, for the use of Figures 5.1, 5.2 and 5.3 from *Garden Cities of Tomorrow*, originally published 1898.

The Royal Town Planning Institute (produced jointly with Bristol and Leeds Polytechnics) and Tony Hathway for use of Figure 6.1; The British New Towns, which is taken from *The RTPI Distance Learning Unit, Block I, Unit 4, Planning History*.

Thanks to Rosemary Burton, the late Tony Scrase and Martin Chick for the use of Figure 9.1 Areas of Rural Control, previously published in *Agricultural Diversification and the Planning System*, Pickup (UWE) University of West of England, 1990, and Burton (1991).

Thanks to Chauncy D. Harris, Professor Emeritus, University of Chicago, and the American Academy of Political and Social Science for the use of Figure 11.1 Three Social Ecology Diagrams.

Thanks to John Allinson, Hugh Barton, Nick Oatley and David Ludlow of UWE for additional information incorporated into the second edition.

PART I

The planning and development framework

Chapter 1

The scope and nature of town planning

Britain is highly urbanised and yet contains substantial areas of open countryside between the towns and cities. The United Kingdom has a population of 57·2 million, but over 76 per cent of the total 24 410 000 hectares of land is agricultural (*Social Trends*, OPCS, 1995).[1] Levels of traffic flow, congestion and urban overcrowding are relatively low, considering the size of the population. A major contributory factor is the operation of the statutory town planning system, which has sought to control urban development. In spite of undoubted achievements, many people are, nevertheless, of the view that town planning policy has been ineffective and misdirected, and that more could have been achieved with better policy. Many take the view that town planning imposes unnecessary restrictions on the property market and on individual citizens' freedom, with little of benefit to show in return.

Whatever one's opinion of town planning, it is important to know about it, because planning policy affects everyone in their daily lives as members of society. It directly affects professionals involved in the world of property development, as nearly all types of new property development require planning permission before they can go ahead. Whilst in recent years the government has sought to speed up the planning system it has not removed it. Many private developers support the need for town planning, because it is seen as providing a framework within which the market can operate. But they may question the objectives upon which it is based, or the way it is administered.

Planning is not a straightforward subject in which there is one right answer or a fixed set of rules; it all depends on what one wants to achieve, and on the answer to the question 'How do you want to live?' (DOE, 1972a). It is often argued that increased government intervention and control through the town planning system would provide a better alternative to the market. But many people feel that the official planning system does not provide what they want, either. Planners have a long way to go yet towards solving the problems of existing towns and cities, or creating ideal urban communities for the future. Therefore, in this introductory town planning book, the emphasis is upon the importance of taking into account the 'social aspects of planning' when dealing with the physical realities and practicalities of urban land use and development.

Changing circumstances and attitudes behind the evolution of town planning practice will be discussed. The shift will be highlighted from the confident, idealistic, approach in the post-war reconstruction period (1945–52), during which the modern planning system was established, to the more commercial, market-led emphasis which predominated in the 1980s, particularly among the increasing number of planners working in the private sector and to the environmental consciousness of the 1990s, which has led to the greening of planning policy. Questions are raised about the traditional 'top down' approach to planning 'for' people which is based on the idea that the planner 'knows best'. This has been challenged in recent years by community groups who want more consultation so that the planners plan 'with' people. The existence of strong undercurrents of dissatisfaction with the planning system is acknowledged, expressed variously by the residents of towns and cities, by the developers and by those professionals who are concerned with architectural design and the environment. The criticisms of urban sociologists and of so-called 'minorities' are also taken into account, from ethnic groups, women and working-class communities to the elderly (not mutually exclusive categories), who have questioned what they see as the social bias and political naivety evident in the so-called 'objectivity' of the planning process. The general public holds misleading stereotypes of what a planner 'is', a tendency which has not been helped by generalised application of the term to a range of property professionals and politicians who are not planners at all.

There is often a certain amount of consumer resistance from students beginning to study the subject, particularly from those intending to enter the more private sector-orientated property professions such as surveying and estate management. Many people see the planner as a man 'waiting for something to turn down' (unlike Dickens's Micawber, who was always waiting for something to turn up), a negative image fuelled by media representations of the planner. This book proposes that town planners perform a constructive role in enabling, rather than hindering, development and urban renewal, and that they occasionally make urban social problems better rather than worse. It *is* worth 'Believing in Planning' – a slogan which the Royal Town Planning Institute (RTPI, the main professional body) used in the early 1990s, and many would see it as a vital and essential aspect of modern government. There is room for improvement, and ways will be discussed which might make it better. In fairness, planners are dealing with complex issues to which there is often no one simple solution that will please everyone. On the other hand, when planners do get it right, no one seems to notice. For example, everyone takes the Green Belts (protected zones encircling cities) which cover over 12 per cent of the land surface of England alone, for granted. One elderly planner remarked that his greatest lifetime achievement could be judged by what had *not* been built as a result of his efforts. In particular he had prevented two conurbations joining up in a continuous sprawl.

What is town planning and why study it?

What is town planning?

Towns and cities are not God-given or 'natural'. They are the result of centuries of decision-making by individual owners and developers, and of government intervention. Whilst topography and geography do play a part, they do not absolutely 'determine' development. The nature of towns and cities, to a considerable extent, is dependent on who shouts the loudest, and who has the greatest influence over policy. Town planning is to do with property and land, and therefore with money and power. Therefore it is inevitably a highly political activity, inextricably linked with the prevailing economic system, and reflective, in policy-making, of the booms and slumps which are an enduring characteristic of the property market. Planners are not free agents: they are operating not in a vacuum but within a complex political situation at central and local government levels which reflects these social forces.

Here is one traditional definition: 'Town planning is the art and the science of ordering the land-uses and siting the buildings and communication routes so as to secure the maximum level of economy, convenience and beauty' (Keeble, 1969). This sounds plausible, but the situation is not so straightforward. The statement was originally made by a prominent post-war town planner famous for his books on how to build complete new towns from scratch. Many of his ideas were later rendered out of date by the unexpected rate of growth of car ownership towns and cities, and by wider social and political changes in the context of town planning. Whilst this approach to urban design was an important phase during post-war reconstruction in the

1940s, it was based on a simplistic 'master plan' blueprint approach, best suited to planning New Towns on greenfield sites (undeveloped land) which is no longer appropriate today. However, the desire to build new communities, particularly visionary Utopian settlements, remains a continuing theme in the development of town planning theory. But much less than 5 per cent of the population of Britain has ever lived in New Towns; no new ones have been started by the government since the 1970s, and most of the existing ones have now been de-designated (Potter, 1989).

In contrast, some modern pundits of town planning would argue that it should not necessarily be defined as a subject, concerned with a range of identifiable physical land use topics or design policies, but should be seen rather as a process, or a methodology. Senior town planners, particularly in local government, are primarily strategic managers whose skills are particularly valued because their professional perspective enables them to take the broader view, to see the connections between a diverse range of issues and topics: an attitude of mind essential to the understanding and planning of whole cities. Indeed, some senior planners progress from town planning departments to become chief executives and corporate managers in local government.

It is a very debatable question what planning really is and by inference whether town planning is a real profession (such as architecture or civil engineering) or a composite of subjects, put together for various administrative and political reasons, which nonetheless exudes a certain mystique but does not hold water when subjected to detailed investigation (as discussed at length in Reade, 1987, and Healey *et al.*, 1988). Nevertheless, regardless of its somewhat questionable theoretical underpinnings, town planning does exist as a major bureaucratic function of local government, and as an important component of the professional activities of the private-sector property development world.

Another criticism of the traditional definition is that new development represents less than 3 per cent of the total building stock each year (DOE, 1995; JFCCI, 1991), even though much of southern England, for example, has until relatively recently been in the grip of a property boom. Nowadays much of the work of the land use professions, including planning, is concerned with existing rather than new development. For example, the chartered surveyor may spend more time dealing with the transfer, letting the management of existing property than on putting through new development schemes (Marriott, 1989; Cadman *et al.*, 1990; Scarrett, 1983; Stapleton, 1986; Burke and Taylor, 1990). Urban conservation and the preservation of historic buildings and areas have become a major preoccupation of town planning. In the public sector in recent years there has been a drastic decline in the building of council housing, most of the new-build social housing development being undertaken by housing associations. Maintenance and refurbishment of existing stock is a major aspect of the construction industry.

There is a related confusion in that it is sometimes assumed by new students that town planners (like housing managers) are chiefly involved in the provision of council housing. Whilst over 70 per cent of all urban development is residential, to town planners housing is only one land use among several equally important others such as industrial, office and retail uses. Roads and related car parking areas alone can take up to 40 per cent of the total of Central Business District (CBD) land in cities. In dealing with housing development, planners have been more concerned with matters related to land allocation and capacity, the design of the layout and the effect of increased numbers of cars on their transportation policies than, relatively speaking, with whether it is public or private development.

Likewise one should not overestimate the powers, or the culpability, of the planners in dealing with urban problems. Under the present statutory planning system planners have some powers over land use and development, but they have limited powers over the transport systems which connect the land uses. There is tremendous pressure from the green movement for better public transport and thus more sustainable cities, but planners are acutely aware of their limited powers over those bodies which provide public transport, and of the demands of the populace to retain car usage in cities. For many out in the suburbs (where a substantial proportion of the urban population lives), cars may be the only realistic means to get to work, to reach out of town retail centres, and to get young children to school, in existing cities which are characterised by highly dispersed land use patterns.

Why study it?

Many students are attracted to town planning because they have a vocation to leave the world a better place than they found it. Some may be concerned with 'green' issues, and see planning as a means to that end. Others, particularly mature students, may have experienced the problems of inner-city living and have specific changes in mind which they would like to bring about by becoming town planners. Town planning, although categorised as one of the land use professions, has much in common with the other welfare professions found within local and central government structures, also linking across strongly to the realms of social policy and political science – although in the final analysis it is concerned with 'spatial' (physical) land use and design issues.

Other students, particularly those who are intending to follow a career in the private sector, may not like the subject, but realise it is necessary, if only (as some students admit) to understand how to beat the system from a developer's viewpoint. But many surveying and construction students do have a fascination with the subject and possess social and environmental awareness. Once students begin to understand the subject they may become quite keen on coming up with their own solutions, saying enthusiastically in tutorial discussions, 'The government ought to do something,' as if it were just a matter of realising what is needed, without appreciating the problems and tortuous paths involved in getting policy accepted and implemented on the ground. Sometimes their confidence and ideas outstrip their knowledge, but, as has often been said, 'You can't plan for something unless you understand it first.' (Regrettably, so-called planners have done so.) Well-intentioned policies, motivated by the best of social intentions, can lead to monumental disasters unless they are accompanied by a well-informed understanding of the nature and complexity of the problems and issues at which they are directed. Therefore, in parallel with looking at the planning system, the changing characteristics of the built environment and the nature of urban society itself will be explored. If planners have no idea of how ordinary people live, then they cannot plan for them.

Those entering the private property sector may believe that their property development decisions will be, relatively speaking, more straightforward than those of the planners, as they will not have to worry about all the social and environmental factors which make a planner's job so difficult. The opposite is often the case. It is easy to ride on the crest of a wave and make a good investment decision which reflects current trends, but the bottom can fall out of established markets, as occurred in the recession of the 1990s. Wiser people in the private sector look into the future to see what is going to be the next property development 'opportunity' coming over the horizon, such as the demand for retirement housing due to the growing number of elderly people. To do so effectively they need to draw on the same research sources, and apply the same fields of expertise and levels of understanding to the urban situation, as the planners. Many of the large firms of chartered surveyors have their own in-house teams of planning and market researchers, and there is a thriving

Society of Property Researchers which draws much of its membership from the private sector.

Markets tend to go in cycles of boom and slump. Foolish is the society or government which bases its land use strategy on such a lottery. Moreover the fact that something is financially viable or profitable does not of itself mean that it is 'good'. Social and economic needs are often at odds with each other. However, whether planners are working for the public or the private sector of development, there are certain common requirements which have to be adhered to, to make a scheme work. After all, both groups are planning in response to the 'same' needs, even if one group has more of an eye to financial viability of the scheme than the other. The private sector has to take account of social factors, too, for if people do not like a development they will 'vote with their feet' and not put money into it. Whether planning is initiated in the public or in the private sector (and it is increasingly the latter), the decision-makers still need to be aware of these wider social constraints.

Most people see a need for some measure of state intervention in the economy and in the built environment. Government policy is still based on the 'mixed economy', a combination of state control and free enterprise *laissez-faire* (literally 'allow [them] to do') which means a free-for-all property market (Lavender, 1990). So there is a measure of planning, but there is also private ownership of property and an active property market. This is a mid-way position compared with the situation which existed until recently in Eastern Europe, where there was no private ownership of land and therefore no property market or land values. Under such a regime the planner's role was not to control the private sector in response to democratic demands but to replace these elements with state policy, usually implemented by means of Five Year Plans (see Rydin, 1993 for coverage of the economic dimensions of planning, and see Volumes II and III of this series).

In Britain it has traditionally been considered vital for government to take over the provision of non-profit-making – but nonetheless essential – urban amenities and infrastructure, and to provide for those who could not afford to meet their needs through the market. In recent years there has been a breakdown in this consensus, and a more market-oriented, profit-making emphasis has been applied to public services. However affluent people are at an individual level, they still need certain social goods and services such as roads, sewers, fire brigades, local facilities: all this is sometimes aptly called 'social capital' (Saunders, 1979). Otherwise one ends up with a situation, as in some parts of North America, where people have enormous houses but no main drainage and every house has its private septic tank. It may be more economical and in society's and industry's interest to provide these utility services on a non-profit-making basis to reap the returns in the long run (Cullingworth, 1993).

The scope of town planning

Many people's first contact with the planners is in seeking planning permission, perhaps for an ill-fated house extension. Planning law and its enforcement, through what is known as development control, are a major aspect of town planning. But this law is not an end in itself: it is one of the means by which planning policy can be put into effect and made a reality. Some students, especially if they have had contacts with estate agency, housing associations or building firms, may think town planning means the development of new housing estates on greenfield sites. They may expect it to deal primarily with standards and rules about the size of plots, road widths, and the overall layout. These are important aspects of town planning but only part of it. Much of the planners' work consists of dealing with already developed older sites where the objective may be to incorporate existing buildings into the proposed new scheme. On such sites it may be impossible to apply exact 'standards' in respect of car parking or densities. The planners' job is to be flexible in applying planning standards when negotiating with the developer in order to get the best solution possible within a difficult situation. Whilst much of town planning from the developers' perspective appears to be to do with planning law and the details of site development, one of the main aspects of the town planner's work is the production of city-wide development plans that determine which sites can be built upon in the first place. Development plans cover all types and aspects of land use and development, both urban and rural. The strategic level of town planning probably influences people's lives more than detailed site-specific aspects, but it is relatively 'invisible' to the average citizen, or taken for granted – until they are adversely affected.

There is a tendency in the more commercially orientated land use professions such as surveying for practitioners to have little patience with the 'airy-fairy' policy level of town planning, which they may see as time-consuming and over-ambitious; they want to get on with the 'nitty-gritty' of site development and layout. When deciding on the merits of a particular scheme, town planners look at the wider context and consider the social, economic, environmental and political aspects, because their 'client' is society, whilst surveyors tend to look at a particular site more in isolation and consider how they can get the best financial return from it for their client. Likewise housing managers may be more interested in the social, sociological or even socialist aspects of urban development, seeing the social needs of people rather than the built environment as the focus of their attention. Both these groups are often more concerned with the details of site layout than with the city-wide, macro-level implications of their proposals. Architects, on the other hand, may see only the building design and forget the people altogether. Civil engineers, especially highway engineers, may be obsessed with technical responses to current problems, without addressing the wider long-term social implications, and may insist on rigid standards with little regard to the wider environmental and visual consequences. Cities are shaped by all these professional perspectives in a process of negotiation and consultation.

The 'macro', city-wide policy level is linked to the 'micro' site level of town planning. Every time a new housing estate is built on the edge of the city for commuters working in central area offices, the car journeys generated by the new development will add to the rush-hour congestion in the centre. The next 'little' site development may be the straw that breaks the camel's back, leading to the need for new roads and increased car parking provision in the Central Business District of the city. Planners, therefore, have to retain a broader perspective and a more critical attitude towards new development than the private-sector developer, whose horizons may be limited to the boundaries of the site under development, and the cost factor. Trying to solve the traffic problem by building yet more roads and car parks, without considering *why* the cars are travelling in the first place, is a superficial strategy. If everyone is heading for the central-area offices from the suburbs, the way to solve at least some of the parking problem might be to decentralise certain types of office development out to the suburbs, or encourage middle-class inner-city housing.

Town planning is not an unchanging subject. Planning policies reflect changing viewpoints and fashions as to what is 'right' at a particular time in a particular place – often with amazing swings in opinion, as evidenced by the present condemnation of modern architecture, and the return to traditional styles and an emphasis on conservation. But once a policy is agreed upon and implemented anyone who contravenes it by building the 'wrong' building in the 'wrong' place will soon find themselves subject to the full force of the law. It can be a criminal offence to go against an enforcement notice. Town planning policies may seem to be based on opinion (or waffle, as some misinformed students see it), theories and ideas, but nevertheless they are the basis of policies which act as constraints on what can and cannot be built. Therefore most people involved in the private sector of property development treat the planning system as a force to be reckoned with, whatever their personal views on the subject may be. The Town and Country Planning Act, 1990, plus the Planning and Compensation Act, 1991, which introduced further modications, together form the basis of the present planning system. A new Act does not mean that all planning policy changes overnight. Rather it means that the format and 'presentation' of the planning system have been updated and improved, but the objectives and content of planning policy in different areas will not necessarily have changed. In addition to the British planning systems, nowadays, development proposals must conform to the requirements of European-wide, EC regulations and directives as explained more fully in Volume III, adding another level of control and policy change. For example, the 1995 Environment Act brings into force in the UK a wide range of 'green' planning regulations, some of which derive from EC directives (Ball and Ball, 1995; Lane and Peto, 1995).

Planning is for people?

The 'social aspects of planning' should not be seen as a euphemism for 'urban problems', because issues such as leisure, entertainment and recreation are also 'social' issues of great concern to the modern town planner. This is not another, separate subject from the physical aspects, because most social uses generate demand for physical land use, space and design. 'Planning is for people' (Broady, 1968), and there is still a lot of truth in this overused phrase. Some development professionals operate as if planning were purely for the benefit of the buildings, or for cars, and as if property itself were there primarily for profit and not for use by human beings. Therefore, development plans nowadays not only include policies for all the main land uses and types of development but will also take into account, in the policy-making process, broader social, economic and environmental trends in the area. Likewise, in this book, emphasis will be put upon explaining the social issues affecting urban areas, the political context, and the urban theories which have informed policy.

   At a purely pragmatic level politicians need to be aware of the implications of social change and the needs of 'special' groups in drawing up planning policy, if only to avoid social unrest, dissatisfaction and the costs of enforcing law and order. The inner city has become a major planning issue in recent years. Planners would be foolish to ignore the implications of urban poverty, environmental deprivation and ethnic issues in drawing up plans for sensitive urban areas. Developing community relations and undertaking public participation and consultation are important aspects of good town planning practice. Almost worse than disregarding the social aspects of planning is wrongly defining the groups being planned for. Groups of town planners in local government have been keen to justify their power by claiming that they are planning *for* the working class (an elitist idea in itself) when in reality neither the working class nor any other class has been particularly happy with the end results. Planners have been criticised for operating on the basis of outdated stereotypes of who constitute the working class. Increasing numbers of people work in the newer service industries and high-technology areas, and a substantial number of the work force are self-employed. Traditional industrial workers (predominantly male) are far outnumbered by women office workers as the largest single occupational group (*Social Trends*, OPCS, 1995; Crompton and Sanderson, 1990), and town planning must take into account their transport needs as commuters. Therefore, at the outset of the discussion of the development of industrial, urbanised society in Chapter 4, the definition of social class will be considered.

Even if planners disregard the social aspects, purely physical town planning inevitably has effects on people's daily existence through the way in which they encounter the built environment in their daily lives, and can worsen their quality of life. Society is highly urbanised, with over 80 per cent of the population living in towns and cities (OPCS, 1995). To return to the definition of town planning – 'to secure the maximum level of economy, convenience and beauty' (Keeble, 1969) – one must ask: for whom? A planner's job is not a happy one, as not all members of the urban population have the same needs or requirements, and planners can hope only to please some of the people some of the time, rather than all the people all the time. Planning for the 'average man' may in reality lead planners to ignore the real needs of large sectors of the population. Planning may be for people, but some people seem to get their needs taken into account more than others as 'normal'.

The needs of different groups in urban society may be unavoidably at odds with one another. What is practical for car drivers may be very unpractical for people who travel chiefly on foot or by public transport. Whilst around 70 per cent of households own a car, and over 20 per cent own two or more

(OPCS, 1995; Mawhinney, 1995), it does not follow that everyone in a household is going to have equal access to the use of the family car during the day time. It is quite normal for the head of the household to take the car to work with him and leave it in the car park all day, whilst other members of the family who have to travel too, do without. Many people are too young, too poor, or too old to drive. Over 80 per cent of single pensioner households, most of whom are female, do not have the use of a car. Nationally over 80 per cent of males, and around 50 per cent of females are 'drivers' (i.e. hold a licence) but only 15 per cent of women have the use of a car during the daytime, and 75 per cent of all car journeys are still made by men. But, interestingly, 75 per cent of *all* journeys are not by car (i.e. they involve walking, public transport, cycling, etc.: cf. RTPI, 1991). To plan for the motor car as if it were the main means of transport for everyone is an extremely biased approach. There are considerable differences in the land use and transport needs of people in respect of their age, gender (WGSG, 1984; Little *et al.*, 1988), income, disability, mobility and ethnicity (racial issues: Ahmed, 1989, and see *Community Network*, 1989).

This debate has been raised in the opening chapter because how one defines the role of planning – as physical or social – affects how one judges it and what one expects from it. Town planning today is still influenced by its antecedents in architecture, civil engineering, surveying and estate management: all 'straightforward' physical disciplines concerned with 'ordering the land uses' in a logical and scientific manner (Ratcliffe, 1981, Chapter I). The creation of logically planned cities can become an end in itself, 'Legoland', in which the people are almost seen as an irritating extra. Likewise the preservation of the countryside and good rural estate management may be seen as considerably hindered by the influx of hordes of townies with their cars and caravans. The sociological perspective is relatively recent and by no means widespread, particularly in respect of rural planning issues. Nowadays many planners seek to adopt a more balanced and socially sensitive approach, and to accept the importance of the people for whom it is all 'for', but to acknowledge that good traditional physical planning is also needed. Attention to traditional urban design can enhance the quality of the environment, and is seen by some environmental psychologists as an important factor in the well-being of people, enabling everyone to live their lives more effectively. It should be noted that this book centres upon urban issues, that is 'town planning', but rural issues will be included in respect of exploring the position of the inter-relationship between the urban and rural situation: after all, the official name of the subject of this book, as reflected in the names of relevant Acts of Parliament, is 'town and country planning'. However, it might be argued that this compartmentalisation is outdated, because the new wave of environmental planning has begun to redraw the boundaries as global environmental and ecological issues overarch both town and countryside, and transcend traditional demarcations.

Summary of contents

Objectives

This book is aimed at students entering the land use professions who are studying town planning at an introductory level, and covers the scope and nature of the subject as a whole rather than concentrating in detail on individual aspects. However, it is also intended that the book should be of interest to a wider range of readers who are interested in town planning for professional or community-related reasons. Therefore guidance and tasks for students are presented in Appendix I, in relation to each chapter. As indicated, the book seeks to combine the *physical* and *social* aspects of planning, reflecting the trend of existing introductory courses and increasingly of planning practice itself. The book also seeks to introduce students to the *visual* design aspects, the *legal* and institutional context of planning. In practice all these elements are linked and inseparable components of modern town planning. It combines a presentation of the reasons behind planning (the theoretical and historical context) at an elementary level with an introduction to the practical aspects of how the system works. Where relevant, aspects of planning law are introduced, but with reference to planning law books, so as to provide guidance for students who need to pursue particular aspects for a project or tutorial presentation. The visual and design aspects of planning are included, because they have been an important element in shaping towns and cities in the past, when planning was more closely linked with architectural civic design. They remain crucial today in respect of the emphasis on conservation policy and in relation to development control.

Students, and the public, are often daunted by the range of books, at different levels, which are available on the subject of town planning. But there does not seem to be one book which combines all the aspects which are usually found on an introductory course, in which the practical and physical aspects of planning are combined with the social and discursive elements required nowadays on many courses. Many of the books which deal with the social aspects, although excellent, are written in a manner and at a depth which is more appropriate to postgraduate study than to students who want to absorb the main arguments within the context of a busy schedule of studying, perhaps, ten other subjects on the course. This book seeks to present the current debates and issues in an accessible manner, alongside essential background material. It incorporates material from a wide range of relevant realms – namely town planning itself, urban sociology, urban geography, housing, urban design, surveying and estate management – highlighting the aspects relevant to the theme under discussion. As explained in the preface, the book should be seen as a compendium for the beginner rather than as a polemical or analytical work, although certain critical themes and perspectives must, of necessity, be included in a book on such a controversial subject as town planning.

Readers should note, as explained in the Preface, that this book is the first in a series exploring different aspects of town planning. Cross-references are given to chapters in other Volumes in the series, where a more detailed and discursive treatment of the topic in question may be found. For example, Volume II centres upon implementation and expands many of the themes introduced in Part I of the present volume. Volume III covers both the environmental and economic dimensions of town planning in greater depth, whilst Volume IV centres upon urban design. However, for the newcomer to the subject, this present introductory volume should provide adequate coverage in its own right, and readers are strongly advised to complete this volume, to get the whole picture, before attempting to tackle more advanced material in later volumes.

Agenda

The book is divided into four parts, which should ideally be read sequentially but may be read separately if desired. Chapter 1 looks at the scope and nature of town planning within the context of the process of property development. As can be seen, this chapter defines and discusses the subject of town planning, and seeks to show why it is of relevance to the reader, and worth studying. Chapter 2 deals with the organisational framework of town planning, and its context within the development process. Chapter 3 considers the nature and contribution of the main land use professions, and examines the different roles ascribed to the town planner.

In Part II the evolution of modern town planning is traced, from its beginnings in the nineteenth century up to the present day. In Chapter 4 the nature of industrialisation, urbanisation and social change in the nineteenth century, which called forth the need for town planning is described, incorporating a discussion of both urban physical factors and social aspects, such as the development of the modern class structure. In Chapter 5 the reaction to these changes, which took the form of reforming legislation, the development of town planning theory, and the creation of model planned communities, is charted. The main theories and ideas from this era are discussed, as their influence continues to shape the nature of modern town planning. Much of what people think of as natural is the result of particular theories of what towns 'ought' to be like. One may consider it perfectly ordinary that most people in England live in small houses, normally of two storeys, with front and back gardens, but one only has to travel to the Continent to see that many more people in France, Italy and parts of Germany live in blocks of flats (apartments) at a higher density, in closer proximity to the city centre, and thus have less suburban development around their cities. One of the reasons for this difference is the predominance of the influence in Britain of the ideas of Ebenezer Howard (1898, reprinted 1960), the promoter of the Garden City idea. Although this section is predominantly chronological, space is also used to link the past with the present where appropriate, particularly in respect of the social dimensions of urban society (which are developed further in Chapter 11), in order to introduce the student to these dimensions in a gradual manner.

Chapter 6 looks at the development of town planning in the first half of the twentieth century, which culminated in the extensive programme of legislation in the post-Second World War reconstruction period 1945–52, at which time the foundations of the system in operation today were laid. This period was imbued with a spirit of optimism as manifested, architecturally, in Le Corbusier's work and the modern movement, and, politically, in the creation of the British welfare state. In Chapter 7 the development of town planning over the last forty years is discussed in relation to the accompanying criticism and reaction to state intervention in the built environment. The predominant themes and issues of each decade are highlighted.

Part III is devoted to the visual and design aspects of town planning. Planning is not 'only' to do with the 'big' city-wide issues of land use and development but also to do with all the 'little' matters of design, appearance and convenience. Whilst nowadays planning is often related to economic and functional issues, historically it was concerned more with design, and townscape in the *beaux arts* tradition. Firstly, Chapter 8 investigates the historical development of townscape before the nineteenth century. Georgian and Victorian buildings and street patterns comprise substantial elements of many urban areas, and are the subject of conservation policy. Each historical period is described briefly rather than in great detail, but key books are cited for further reading.

In Chapter 9 conservation, both rural and urban, is looked at more closely, as it has been such a key issue in late twentieth-century town planning. Urban conservation is discussed first, with explanations of such matters as 'Listed Buildings' and 'Conservation Areas'. This leads on to an explanation of the history, legislation and policies related to rural conservation. The last part of this chapter brings the discussion up to the present by considering the policy and control dimensions of environmental planning, with reference to the development of the green movement, the role of Europe in relation to EIA (Environmental Impact Assessment controls) and the concern for sustainability. Also in this section, a topic, which has always been part of the traditional town and country planning control, but which may also be seen as a component of the modern sustainability green agenda, namely mineral extraction, will be included because it is an issue of continuing importance in strategic planning policy formulation.

In Chapter 10 the design theme is continued, in respect of the scope and nature of development control in town planning. Planning law provides considerable powers to shape the physical appearance and design of the built environment, and thus determine the land use and development structure of towns and cities. This chapter includes an introduction to the 'nitty-gritty' of how the development control system works, as to planning application forms, the Use Classes Order and the General Development Order. Secondly this chapter looks, at an introductory level, at the question of design standards, layouts, densities and the factors to be taken into account in the development of a residential site.

The final section, Part IV, is more reflective and critical of the nature of the planning system as discussed in the preceding chapters. Planners have frequently been criticised for ignoring the social implications of their physical land use policy-making activities. Chapter 11 looks at the development of the main social theories which have sought to explain the nature of urban society and in turn have affected town planning policy, and at the alleged social consequences and implications of town planning, continuing the themes raised earlier. Much of the social theory discussed is a manifestation of changing political attitudes and unrest among different community groups within the urban situation.

The last chapter, Chapter 12, reinforces the fact that town planning is, in the final analysis, all about 'How do you want to live?' It centres on the recent widespread challenge to conventional town planning brought about by the 'women and planning' movement, reappraising the 'social aspects' theories from this perspective and discussing the issue in relation to the different land uses and types of development which affect our towns and cities. This theme, to a lesser extent, is to be found throughout the book. The topic is used as an illustration of how planning legislation and policy can be used, within the statutory framework, to bring about change. This section links the legal, physical, social and design aspects of planning. As stated in the preface, the book aims to deal with women and planning not in great detail but simply as one aspect of the subject (albeit having implications for all other planning topics), since the author presents a deeper analytical treatment elsewhere (Greed, 1994). The last section of Chapter 12 presents the student with a concluding critique of town planning, identifies unresolved issues of current importance, and invites readers to develop their own views on the future.

Notes

1. The United Kingdom is defined as England, Wales, Scotland and Northern Ireland (94 201 square miles). (One hectare = 2·471 acres, and 0·405 ha = 1 acre. There are 640 acres in a square mile.) Great Britain (or Britain) means England, Scotland and Wales but not Ireland, the Channel Isles or the Isle of Man. The British Isles consist of all the United Kingdom plus all of Ireland and the other islands. The planning Acts and system discussed apply to England and Wales only, but Scotland has a similar system and policies under its own legislation. Official government statistics (as in *Social Trends*, OPCS, 1995) are normally produced for the United Kingdom as a whole.

Chapter 2

The organisation of planning and the development process

This chapter looks more closely at the nature of town planning, by first describing the levels of planning and types of plans, and secondly explaining the role of the planner and other land use professionals in the development process. Some planning law will be introduced but this aspect is dealt with in more detail in Chapter 10. In the popular press the word 'planner' is used freely to describe anyone in the world of government or property development who has made the wrong decision! In reality most professional town planners working in the public sector are not the final decision-makers. They are employees of government, their statutory role being that of advisers to their political masters. Although at the local government level it is common for the planners to be blamed for mistakes, it is their political masters – the councillors – as the elected representatives of the general public, who make the final decisions, accepting or rejecting the planners' professional opinions within the local council planning committee. Planners are by no means totally passive in their relationship with their political bosses, and they may have strong views of their own as to how a particular area should be planned. Back in the 1960s, when high-rise blocks were being built, many town planners advised against this form of development, but their views and arguments were ignored by their councillors.

Levels of planning

Central government

The divisions between the planners and their political bosses, and between the private initiators and public controllers of development, run all the way through the different levels of planning described below. In the past the planners had a stronger role (and arguably more power and funding) in carrying out development, as in the case of the post-war New Towns. Nowadays their main role is to develop policy in response to the activities of the private sector, and to seek to control it for the good of society and the environment. The organisation of the planning system is complex (see Fig. 2.1) (Heap, 1995; Healey *et al.*, 1988: 28). There are two main levels of town planning, central and local government. The Department of the Environment (DOE) is the main central government department responsible for town planning. It is headed by the Secretary of State for the Environment, who is a politician (*not* a planner), with Cabinet status, who is supported by three, or sometimes four, junior ministers with specialist responsibilities (Moore, 1995; Chapter 1). The Secretary of State for the Environment has overall respon-sibility for shaping and guiding national planning policy, and has the final say on individual controversial planning decisions. He is advised by professionally qualified staff, including town planners, surveyors, architects and housing managers. The Secretary of State does not have to accept their advice if it is not politically acceptable to the government.

There is no National Plan, as exists in some other countries, but central government has an important role in overseeing policy and the plans produced by local government planning authorities. There is no Ministry of Town Planning as such, although one did exist in the immediate post-war reconstruction period, but there is a minister with special responsibility for town planning matters within the DOE. The names of central government ministries have frequently been subject to change, but town planning itself remains a major central government issue. The DOE is in fact a mega-department within which many other aspects of policy-making for the built environment are carried out, such as aspects of housing, transportation, building and construction, the inner cities, environmental health, conser-vation and historic buildings, and many other matters. It is confusing, as some of these policy areas are also administered in part by other government departments and ministries, such as aspects of nature conservancy, road traffic, and scientific matters related to the environment. There is considerable overlap because the whole central government system grew up 'organi-cally', evolving in a typically English manner rather than being organised as a logical system.

One of the most important roles of the Secretary of State for the Environment has been to give approval to Development Plans. (Following the Planning and Compensation Act, 1991, the local authorities are given delegated powers to approve plans themselves in some cases.) Development plans known as

Figure 2.1   The levels of town and country planning (simplified).

European Commission
Directorates-General

Central Government
Department of the Environment

Secretary of State (politician, MP)   advised by planning, professionals
Approves development plans   (civil servants)
Gives overall policy guidance
Deals with appeals (assisted by the planning inspectorate)

Also Range of other central government departments liaise with DOE on planning
issues, e.g. MOD, Home Office, MAFF, Industry, Transport.

Regional level

Note No significant regional level at present but vestiges of Regional Economic
Planning Boards, committees, plans, e.g. SERPLAN. Growing emphasis on
regional liaison by development plan authorities, and with Europe.

Local government

Decisions are made by the politicians (elected councillors on council planning
committee) as advised by the professionals (planners who are employed as local
government officers). Following recent changes, two types of development plan
system both running:

Two-tier system	Unitary system
Counties Structure Plans Overall policy strategy Minerals and waste disposal	*Metropolitan districts and London Boroughs* Unitary Development Plans (combine contents of structure and local plans) Policy implementation Development control
Districts Local plans Implementation of planning Development control (outline and detailed applications)	New and reconstituted authorities in some shire counties and some provincial cities, from 1996.

Also range of *ad hoc* bodies, initiatives, and plans, including:

Urban Development Corporations, City Challenge initiatives, Single Regeneration
Budget programmes, various nominated, consultative bodies.

Structure Plans are produced by the counties and larger urban areas. These constitute the main planning policy documents, showing the structure of future development. In the London boroughs, and the metropolitan districts (which make up the large conurbations in the north and Midlands), the development plans are called Unitary Development Plans (UDPs). In theory the Secretary of State could put all the plans together like a giant national jigsaw puzzle and end up with a complete national plan! It is important to make sure that there are no sudden or incompatible changes of policy on either side of the boundaries of each county area, and should this arise he has to act as arbitrator between the authorities.

Although the Secretary of State does not produce plans himself, he does produce policy guidelines, upon the advice of his professional staff, as embodied in government White Papers, circulars, consultation papers, guidance notes and directives. Planning Policy Guidance Notes (PPGs) cover a range of strategic issues, for example, PPG 6 deals with policy on major retail development proposals, and PPG 12 with development plans and regional planning guidance, 1992 (see p.276 for list). Such documents are very important as expressions of ministerial policy and are likely to be quoted in planning appeals. (See the *Encyclopaedia of planning law*, a loose-leaf system of four volumes, which is updated every month.) The PPGs are revised from time to time, so they require careful checking for the most up-to-date version. The Secretary of State carries out a considerable amount of consultation with the local authority planners, and with the professional and voluntary bodies concerned with planning (some would say there has not been enough of this in recent years) in order to set policy guidelines. The rules governing planning decisions cannot be reduced to questions of road widths or precise land use zonings, but are embodied in a range of official documents which are subject to interpretation.

Central government has a major role in setting policy guidelines and approving plans, but it is the local authority level of counties and districts which constitutes the main plan-making level and which produces the plans. The present situation represents an uneasy truce, a compromise, for there has always been a considerable amount of tension between central and local government, and between counties and districts at local government level. It is increased when there are, for example, a strong Conservative government at national level and Labour-led councils at local government level. Some would say that the abolition of the Greater London Council (GLC) and the large first-tier strategic Metropolitan County Councils in 1986, and their replacement with second-tier district authorities, was done because the big authorities were predominantly Labour-held, with the GLC carrying out what were seen as left-wing policies right on the doorstep of Parliament.

Much of town planning is concerned with development control, that is, with the granting or refusing of planning permission. The Secretary of State has another important role in dealing with appeals and public inquiries on contentious planning issues and decisions. In practice some of the decision-making is delegated to the planning inspectorate, and many decisions are made in writing rather than coming to a full hearing. Some 500 000 planning applications were received by English planning authorities in 1990, and 80 per cent were allowed. Some 26 000 planning appeals were received, of which 33 per cent were allowed. The Secretary of State has the power to take a more direct interest in any aspect of the planning system with which he is unhappy, and has powers to call in controversial plans and applications (Heap) if it is considered that the local authority has gone against national planning policy in its decision, but there have only been around 100 'call-ins' during the last few years (DOE, 1995). There are other central government ministries and bodies which have a major effect on the nature of land use and development, particularly in the countryside. The Ministry of Agriculture, Fisheries and Food (MAFF) has a major influence on the nature of the countryside, which at times may be at odds with the objectives of the planners in conserving the landscape. There are non-governmental organisations such as the National Farmers' Union (NFU) and the Country Landowners' Association (CLA) which act as strong pressure groups to influence policy. There has been talk of setting up a new 'green' ministry, or a separate ministry of food and consumer affairs, which would provide an alternative to the MAFF and NFU viewpoints (influenced by ideas argued in books such as Shoard, 1980). However, as in many areas of planning, it is generally considered that consumer and community groups are underrepresented in the decision-making process.

The siting of nuclear power stations is an environmental matter, and public inquiries to decide whether more stations should be built are held under the auspices of planning inspectors appointed by the DOE. Recent decisions have hardly pleased environmentalists. The various statutory bodies concerned with the provision of public utilities and services and their privatised successors have considerable separate powers of their own which may contradict DOE policies. The Ministry of Defence (MOD), although not a civilian planning authority, nevertheless has a major effect on the nature of settlement patterns. It has rights over vast areas of land used for training. It is not subject to the normal planning controls in its own activities, and may, for example, build service housing estates in the countryside without planning permission.

Overarching the national central government level of planning, as embodied in the DOE, the pan-European level of planning powers must be added. The European Commission (EC), through its 23 Directorates-General produces policy guidance, and regulations which must be taken on board by all the member states of the European Union (EU). (The European dimension is explained in detail in Volume III; and see Davis, 1992.) The Directorates of relevance to town planning are DG XVI Regional Policy; DG XI Environment, Nuclear Safety and Civil Protection; DG V Employment, Industrial Relations and Social Affairs; and DG VI Agriculture; DG XVII Energy and DG XXIII Tourism. There is a considerable amount of policy guidance emanating from the EC on regional planning, town planning, and environmental matters, but much of this is advisory in status. In contrast, there are certain EC Directives which must be complied with, and which take precedence over UK law. Foremost, EC Directive 85/337 on the Environmental Assessment of certain categories of new dvelopment must be complied with. In this case the regulations, which relate to protecting the environment and to achieving 'sustainability', are stricter than under conventional UK planning law, and definitely much 'greener'. With time more Directives will come into force, and also the influence of European-level strategic planning policy is likely to influence UK town planners' perspective on cities more strongly.

Regional planning

At present there is no significant regional level of planning between the national and the local authority levels, but the intermediate level used to be more important under Labour governments, which sought to co-ordinate both economic and physical land use planning at the regional level. There are signs of it becoming important again, all the main political parties have seriously considered this option. There used to be some very useful regional economic study documents, such as *Region with a future* for the south-west; or *A strategy for the South-East*, produced by the South East Regional Economic Planning Council in 1967 (Ravetz, 1986; Balchin and Bull, 1987). Consultative documents are still produced by government bodies from time to time, but with an analytical rather than policy-making emphasis (such as *Housing, land supply and structure plan provisions in the South-East*, SERPLAN, 1988). There have been various proposals for more regional liaison among county authorities. A series of Regional Planning Guidance notes (RPGs) have been produced for the larger regional urban connurbations, for example *Strategic Guidance for London Planning Authorities* (RPG3, 1995), to ensure co-ordination of planning policies. It should also be remembered that Britain is now a region of Europe and subject to EC-wide planning policy and legislative factors.

Local government

The local government system in England and Wales has been based on a two-tier system for the last 20 years, but currently changes are in progress, as reorganisation moves gradually towards a one-tier or unitary system (Cullingworth and Nadin, 1994: 27–43). Welsh authorities have already been reorganised under the 1994 Local Government (Wales) Act, and major changes have been occurring in Scotland too. Related to this, with the abolition of large administrative counties (such as Avon around Bristol) and their replacement with either previous historical county areas or other smaller, new administrative areas (1992 Local Government Act), many boundaries have been redrawn and town planners are having to adjust their plan-making activities to the new size and level of spatial units created (see 'State of the Shires', *Planning Week*, 9 March 1995, pp.12–13, for list of changes). However, this does not mean that all previous plans are redundant, or that the planners suddenly stop everything and change their policies overnight. Rather, existing statutory plans remain the main guidance documents until they are, in due course, revised. Therefore it is still relevant to discuss the nature of Structure and Local Plans which have provided the basis of planning since the 1971 Town and Country Planning Act and which will still provide policy guidelines for the near future in many areas. Readers should note that the nature of local government change is by no means clear-cut or finalised at the time of going to press, and probably will not be for several years yet. Therefore readers should consult the professional press to establish the current situation nationally (for example read the *Local Government Chronicle*). They should investigate the precise nature of the changes in their own area, as in some parts of the country boundary changes have been phased in already, because the Boundary Commission concentrated on those areas first (such as Cleveland and Avon), whilst nothing much has yet happened in other parts of the country. Also readers should be aware that within individual local authorities, some departments have reorganised their affairs, finances and structures more rapidly than others, as these changes affect not only town planning, but housing, highways, education and social services departments too.

Counties

The shire county planning authorities have been required to produce Structure Plans which were the modern type of Development Plans introduced under the Town and Country Planning Act, 1971, and updated under the Town and Country Planning Act, 1990. As explained in the *Development Plan Manual,* produced in 1971 (DOE, 1972b), as its name suggests, the Structure Plan sets out the overall structure or framework of future development by means of written statements, illustrated by diagrammatic plans. In fact a Structure Plan is essentially a written policy report, running to several volumes, rather than a 'plan' as such. Accompanying the Structure Plan there is also a series of other documents which may be required. For example, a detailed report of survey used to be required to accompany the main Structure Plan document but such is no longer the case. Nowadays, an explanatory memorandum is required, justifying policy, particularly in the case of a revision of an existing Structure Plan (Moore, 1991: 36–7). The plans are deliberately not on an Ordnance Survey base but shown 'squared off' on a diagrammatic grid, so that individual sites cannot be easily recognised. All this may seem rather daunting to the ordinary citizen, but the process of producing a Structure Plan allows an initial stage of public participation when alternative policy options are being considered, and for an examination in public before the final plans are approved. Although there is provision for public participation in the Structure Plan process there has been much criticism of the remoteness and impersonality of the system from community and environmental groups.

The topics which are studied in order to develop the plan are population, employment, resources, housing, industry and commerce, shopping, transport, minerals, education, social services, recreation and leisure, conservation and landscape, and utility services (DOE, 1972b). This list reflects the realisation that for town planning to be effective it is important to understand the human activities which create a demand for the land uses in the first place, to enable needs to be anticipated when seeking to produce plans for the future. Whilst all these things have to be looked at as to potential future demands for land and development, the capacity of the local authority planners actually to influence them directly has been limited, since they are under the control of other local government departments or the private sector. But planners in the past have tried to do so, by seeking to increase their powers and take on the role of corporate city managers and technocrats.

Districts

The shire counties have been further subdivided into, on average, four or five district authorities which carry out the detailed daily work of local government where the counties have tended to concentrate more on overall policy, resource allocation and strategy. Whilst Structure Plans have provided the overall policy at county level, Local Plans have been produced at the district level to show what is going to happen, for example, in a particular village, district or redevelopment area within the next five years. These Local Plans have been produced on an Ordnance Survey map base. Originally there were to be three types: District Plans for larger areas, e.g. a whole village or suburb; Action Area Plans for comprehensive planning of areas expected to be planned in the near future; and Subject Plans dealing with special topics or schemes, such as Country Parks at a county-wide level. Nowadays these are more likely to be all referred to as Local Plans. In spite of the system having been in operation for twenty years, only 20 per cent of all local authority areas have been covered by Local Plans. One of the reasons is that the Local Plans were not meant to be produced until the Structure Plans had been finalised, and some county planning departments took years to produce the latter. The days of the plan set down on paper may be coming to an end as it is replaced by written statements and computerised representations of spatial maps. Increasingly, planning offices store all their information on planning applications, decisions and policies on a computerised map reference system. There is a trend towards local authorities adopting computerised geographical information systems (GIS) (Maguire *et al.*, 1992). There is also a growth in the use of geographical information systems and computer-aided design in the private sector. The Ordnance Survey itself has extended its role beyond merely producing maps to providing computerised spatial information for a wide range of public and private-sector users.

Change and unitary development plans

The government is currently aiming at altering the planning system back to a unitary system in the counties and districts. However, previously in the 1980s the move towards unitarisation had begun in relation to metropolitan areas. Under the Local

Government Act of 1985, the Greater London Council (GLC) and the Metropolitan County Councils (MCCs) had been abolished on 1 April 1986. They were replaced respectively by 32 London Borough Councils and Metropolitan District Councils (Heap, 1995). Each of these 67 smaller authorities has been required to produce its own Unitary Development Plan (UDP). Many of these plans have now come on-line. There are no Metropolitan County councils any more and hence no new Metropolitan Structure Plans are being produced. The new UDPs are meant to combine the best of the structure and local plan approach from the old system. Part I of the new UDPs is devoted to strategic policy statements, like the old Structure Plan, whereas Part II deals with detailed land use issues and planning in specific areas, like the old Local Plans (DOE, 1992). Details of the format were set out in circular 3/88, and further updating of guidance is emanating from the Department of the Environment as an on-going process (PPG 12) (p.277). The legislation setting out the principles is consolidated in the Town and Country Planning Act, 1990. Lessons may be learnt from the experience of the metropolitan authorities which may be of relevance to the new county and provincial authorities.

It could be argued that it is unrealistic to produce strategic-level plans for individual boroughs and districts when many of the issues in the large urban areas can be dealt with only at a conurbation-wide level, for example transportation policy and location policy. Many regret the passing of the GLC and metropolitan county strategic level of plan-making, which proved so necessary when dealing with large metropolitan areas. However, the government made it clear in circular 30/85, on transitional arrangements, and in circular 22/84, on development plans, that many aspects of the Structure and Local Plans should be integrated into the new plans. If a new planning system comes in, it does not mean the existing system stops dead until the new-format plans have been approved; rather, the existing approved plans and related policy statements continue to be used until they are superseded. Just because the format of the plans is changing, it does not necessarily mean that the policies have changed. Existing policies still have the force of law if approved by the Secretary of State for the Environment under the current development plan for the area. Some plans were not finally approved before the abolition of their parent authority. For example, the Greater London Development Plan (GLDP) had been written in draft by 1984 and was ready for full approval by 1986 when the GLC was abolished. The GLDP's policies should still, in law, be seen as binding planning policies because they were passed as the agreed policy of the planning committee of the empowered local government council at the time, the Greater London Council, whose powers passed to the individual London borough planning authorities. There have been problems of implementation (particularly in relation to some of the more radical and socially orientated aspects of the GLDP) because of the different political complexion of some of the boroughs, plus cutbacks in local government finance, and the constraints of other approved policies within the boroughs themselves. As stated earlier, planning is all to do with politics. The GLC and many of the metropolitan county councils were strongly Labour, whereas many of the metropolitan districts and many boroughs are Conservative and therefore likely to approach town planning somewhat differently.

The government has a continuing commitment to speed up and simplify the planning system by increasing the emphasis on the local plan level, and doing away with duplicate tiers of local government. However, there may be problems in the counties, where the strategic land use planning issues are rural rather than urban as in the case of the new London Borough Councils and Metropolitan Districts. The issues which the new rural districts will concentrate on in their strategic policy statements will provide a framework covering new housing, general outlines of the Green Belt, the rural economy, major industrial, business, shopping and other employment areas, strategic highways and transport, mineral working, waste disposal and tourism and leisure.

Planning law

Town planning legislation, and related case law, exist to enable planners to make their plans a reality, and to operate development control on a day-to-day basis. Some of the standard planning law books are Denyer-Green, Heap, Telling, Morgan and Nott, Moore and Grant. Planning law books are frequently reprinted, either with a supplement showing legislative changes or as a completely new edition, because of the changing nature of planning law, and therefore readers should always use the most recent texts. Nearly all development requires planning permission, with some exceptions, such as the extension of a house by less than 15 per cent of its cubic volume (10 per cent for terraced houses), the building of a small porch, or the growing of hedges. This is 'permitted development', i.e. development which does not require planning permission. Such exemptions are set out in the General Development Order. There are so many additional controls in particular areas which may suspend or remove rights under the order that it is wise to check with the local authority whether any proposed development comes under some special policy applicable to the area or type of development. Any building work requires consent under the building regulations, and in some cases approval by the highway authority, which is quite separate from the planning department. There are financial charges for both planning permission and building consent (which are frequently revised upwards).

'Development' is defined in planning law under Section 55 of the Town and Country Planning Act, 1990, as 'the carrying out of building, engineering, mining, or other operations in, on, over or under land, or the making of any material change in the use of any buildings or other land'. Therefore development means two main activities: firstly the development of new buildings and other works, and secondly a change from one land use to another. A planning application form from the local planning office must be completed and submitted in order (hopefully) to get planning permission (or refusal).

Uses are defined for legal purposes in the Use Classes Order (see Chapter 10), which runs from A to D. B1, for example, is mixed business use, which was introduced to allow for high-tech and modern office development, which can include offices, research and development use and general industrial activities combined. At the last count there were around eight B uses, and they may yet again be revised. A change of use counts as development when the activity undertaken in the building changes from one use class to another. For example, if a building changes from being a house to an office, that counts as development, even though no new building has taken place. Not all changes require permission, the general principle being that if the change is from something 'good' to something 'worse' it will require planning permission. As indicated above, certain minor changes count as permitted development and do not need planning permission at all, such as painting the outside of a house. The General Development Order sets out what counts as 'permitted development' (see GDO under 'Government Publications', after the list of town planning acts at end of book). Permitted development rights under the GDO are one of the aspects of national town planning law which have been amended as a result of the operation of pan-European EC environmental requirements (see EC Directive 85/337 listed under government publications at end of book) and the 1995 Environment Act. The GDO is subject to frequent revision.

Ad hoc bodies

In addition to, and often quite separate from, the main central and local government structure of town planning there are many other governmental bodies which administer aspects of town and country planning. There has been a tradition in Britain of setting up a government body to deal with a particular problem or policy as and when necessary, often to be disbanded at a later date, namely the *ad hoc* body (literally 'to this', i.e. for this purpose). Many aspects of town planning are administered through such bodies. The New Towns were collectively administered by the New Towns Commission, and individually planned by a development corporation for each town. These development corporations were intended to be completely separate from the local authority administration of the area in which they were located, in order to concentrate resources and speed up development, without being slowed down by existing bureaucracy. Each development corporation was intended to have a life of thirty years, by which time it was assumed that the New Town would be thoroughly established and could be 'handed back' to the local authority, the staff of the development corporation being disbanded.

Another example is that of the National Parks, introduced under the National Parks and Access to the Countryside Act, 1949. The parks were administered as a whole by the National Parks Commission which became the Countryside Commission in 1968, with a wider remit of conservation management in the countryside as a whole, and is still thriving. A series of National Park boards and authorities were set up to administer each National Park, although because the parks often took up much of the area of existing counties, as in the case of Exmoor in Somerset, there was also a strong emphasis on establishing liaison committees with the county authorities. The National Park boards were seen as relatively permanent, although there have been proposals to transfer their powers back to the counties, or, in contrast, to increase their powers as planning authorities in their own right. National Park administration was subsequently reformed by the 1995 Environment Act, Section 61–79. In recent years there has been considerable discussion from the government as to the possibility of privatising some of these *ad hoc* bodies, a concept which would have seemed foreign to the more 'socialist' creators of some of the schemes.

The government is still creating *ad hoc* bodies, in spite of the commitment to get rid of quangos (arguably another name for *ad hoc* bodies: quasi-autonomous national government organisations), that is, any of the numerous government-sponsored agencies or authorities with independent powers (but, interestingly, an alternative definition substitutes 'non' for 'national' in this acronym). The Conservative government's enthusiasm for generating 'enterprise', and especially for revitalising the inner city, has led to a series of government initiatives aimed at specific urban areas, a range of grants, including the 'City Grant' towards the development of uneconomic sites in inner-city areas, and the proliferation of various funding and controlling bodies, which have been brought together under the SRB (Single Regeneration Budget) as described in Chapter 7, and also in Volume III. Among the best known of these are the Urban Development Corporations (UDCs), such as the Bristol Development Corporation or the London Docklands Development Corporation. This London body was established separately from the existing local authorities in their area (much to their chagrin) and employs its own army of planners, surveyors, architects, etc. However, its main aim was not so much to build new developments itself as to provide the infrastructure, especially roads, and the famous light railway, to encourage private developers to come in and invest in the area. This is a very different approach from the New Town corporations, which always took a much more active role themselves in actually building both housing stock and industrial units to let. There are arguments to support both approaches; town planning is in a sense neutral, as it can be used in the service of both Conservative and Labour solutions to urban problems, the perception of the right way to plan being influenced by the underlying political viewpoint of the planners' masters. Many other types of special planning area have been created in recent years, such as simplified planning zones (PPG 5), and enterprise zones, which will be discussed in later chapters. The main principle of such initiatives is to speed up the planning system or to create an organisational framework tailor-made for the special circumstances of a particular situation without disrupting the existing planning system. Others would argue that a proliferation of *ad hoc* bodies serves only to weaken the planning system and increase the powers of central government.

Other plans

There are a range of other types of plans, including what are known as 'non-statutory' plans. These are not directly part of the development plan system, but are plans produced by local authorities with the approval of their planning committee, which express overall policy direction and which, therefore, in the past have been seen as having some validity as legal sources of policy. However, the government commonly takes the view that such informal 'bottom drawer' plans will have limited weight in planning appeals (Grant, 1990: 138, 299). Commonly, one finds that a private developer proposing a large scheme prepares with the application a 'planning brief' setting out how the scheme meets the planning requirements of the area. Alternatively the planning authority will produce its own developers' brief setting out the planning parameters of what would be acceptable. On such occasions there is likely to be considerable negotiation and joint discussion between developer and planning authority. Many local authorities prepare design guides and planning standards reports which are also taken as the definitive policy of the local authority. The whole subject of non-statutory plans is complicated, but it is important simply to know that they exist and may have a bearing on decision-making in the planning permission process and appeal system.

The development process

The sequence

The purpose of this section is to contextualise the role of the planner alongside that of other development professionals in the process of property development (Grover, 1989; Lavender, 1990). The stages in the development of a scheme by a private-sector development company will be outlined, to draw out the role of the different professional groups in the process (see Fig. 2.2). (Whether the developer is private-sector or government, as in the case of council housing, the principles and stages are very similar.) Note that the diagram is presented as from the viewpoint of the roles of the surveying profession in the process. This is more extensive than that of the town planner and thus enables the whole picture to be presented rather than 'just' the aspects in which the planner is involved. This may be of greater interest to non-town planning students, and will enable town planning students to see their role as others see it. But the planner's role is vital, because if the developer cannot get planning permission there will be no development. As with many dynamic processes, where many people are involved all at once, things happen at the same time or run in parallel and the sequence may vary.

Are the planners the developers?

There is often confusion as to the difference between the planners and the developers. Indeed, some students seem to use the two words interchangeably, or imagine that the planners undertake development themselves. They are broadly two different groups, the developers being mainly the private-sector people who initiate, co-ordinate and implement new building

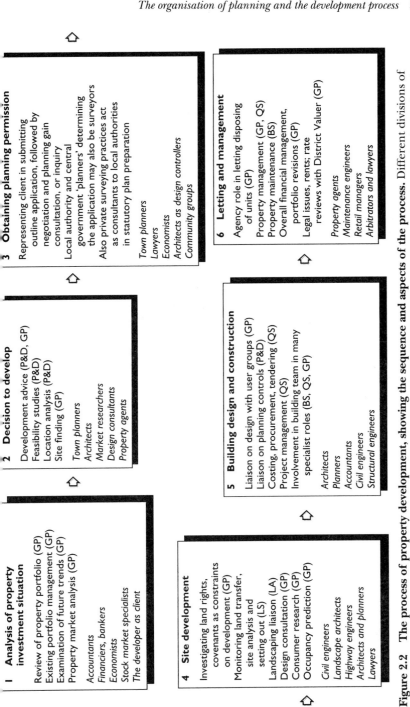

1 Analysis of property investment situation

Review of property portfolio (GP)
Existing portfolio management (GP)
Examination of future trends (GP)
Property market analysis (GP)

Accountants
Financiers, bankers
Economists
Stock market specialists
The developer as client

2 Decision to develop

Development advice (P&D, GP)
Feasibility studies (P&D)
Location analysis (P&D)
Site finding (GP)

Town planners
Architects
Market researchers
Design consultants
Property agents

3 Obtaining planning permission

Representing client in submitting outline application, followed by negotiation and planning gain consultation, or inquiry
Local authority and central government 'planners' determining the application may also be surveyors
Also private surveying practices act as consultants to local authorities in statutory plan preparation

Town planners
Lawyers
Economists
Architects as design controllers
Community groups

4 Site development

Investigating land rights, covenants as constraints on development (GP)
Monitoring land transfer, site analysis and setting out (LS)
Landscaping liaison (LA)
Design consultation (GP)
Consumer research (GP)
Occupancy prediction (GP)

Civil engineers
Landscape architects
Highway engineers
Architects and planners
Lawyers

5 Building design and construction

Liaison on design with user groups (GP)
Liaison on planning controls (P&D)
Costing, procurement, tendering (QS)
Project management (QS)
Involvement in building team in many specialist roles (BS, QS, GP)

Architects
Planners
Accountants
Civil engineers
Structural engineers

6 Letting and management

Agency role in letting disposing of units (GP)
Property management (GP, QS)
Property maintenance (BS)
Overall financial management, portfolio revisions (GP)
Legal issues, rents; rate reviews with District Valuer (GP)

Property agents
Maintenance engineers
Retail managers
Arbitrators and lawyers

Figure 2.2 The process of property development, showing the sequence and aspects of the process. Different divisions of surveyors contribute to an archetypal example of a new scheme for a developer as client. Contributing professions other than surveying are shown in italics. GP General Practice, P&D Planning and Development, LS Land Surveying, LA Land Agency, MS Minerals, QS Quantity Surveying, BS Building and Surveying divisions of the Royal Institute of Chartered Surveyors. *Adapted from Greed* (1992)

schemes, and the planners, *inter alia*, who exercise control over these schemes to ensure they comply with the public interest (Ambrose, 1986). However, this picture is too simplistic, as there are examples of private developers and local authority planners co-operating and entering into a partnership scheme, for example in large shopping developments, so they are not always completely separate in professional practice (Ambrose, 1986).

The term 'developer' is used loosely in the media. Whilst Cadman *et al.* (1983) include the property company which puts the scheme together, the investor financing the scheme and/or the builder within valid definitions of 'developer' in different contexts, Lavender (1990) argues that the word developer is usually reserved for the property development company itself, or the investor on whose behalf it is operating – that is, the individual or organisation which initiates a construction project, and therefore not the builder, designer, user or planner. However, some private-sector developers are only too pleased to keep a low profile and let the planners take the brunt of condemnation from the general public. Prince Charles (1989) has laid much blame on the architects and planners, but some would say that he should be attacking the developers, whom he seldom mentions. The architects in particular are heavily constrained in the designs they put forward by the requirements of their clients and the all-prevailing cost factor. The scheme may be directly financed by pension funds, insurance companies, trusts, etc., which choose a development company to undertake the scheme for them. They will naturally be concerned that their shareholders' and investors' money is being invested wisely. Nowadays many insurance companies have their own in-house property advisers, often surveyors and valuers, who ensure that the portfolio of property investment is well balanced, and that any development project is carefully evaluated. There may be a human need for better facilities in an area, but the extent of need is not the main criterion, developers are interested only if there is a profit to be made from the scheme – that is what it is all about. That is why in Fig. 2.2, the first box is not the decision to develop but rather the analysis of the property investment situation, as property (to the market) is no more than a commodity like racehorses or oil. But if developers do not take into account and respond to human needs they are unlikely to find themselves with a viable scheme.

Feasibility

Before proceeding, the developers might carry out a feasibility study as to the potential catchment area and turnover of the scheme and may bring in the specialist skills of a development surveyor and property researcher to do so, possibly using the in-house expertise of one of the large London companies of chartered surveyors, which produce property market analysis reports. They will also need to consult the local authority planners to find out what the zoning and overall policy are for the area. It is likely that, in large or controversial schemes, planning consultants for the developers will produce a planning brief, setting out the proposals as a basis for negotiation. The local planning authority may have already drawn up its own development brief or policy statement as to what is acceptable in the area – particularly if it is located in an area such as some parts of London where there is already demand to develop and 'site finders' are scouring the territory for development potential. The planning authority and developers are unlikely to see eye-to-eye at their first meeting but by a process of negotiation they can move towards defining a scheme which will be acceptable to both parties. It is quite likely that an element of bargaining will take place to get the best planning gain possible through a 'planning agreement' under Section 106 of the Town and Country Planning Act, 1990 (previously Section 52 of the 1971 Act), and now under Section 106b of the 1991 Planning and Compensation Act, in return for certain concessions on the development control side (Grover, 1989).

Planning gain

'Planning gain' is a non-statutory term which covers additional concessions which the local authority may derive from the developer when entering into an agreement to provide certain amenities in return for a more favourable planning permission. It is not a bribe, as it is for the benefit of the community and has to be directly related to the development in question. Typical examples might be the provision of public conveniences, a creche in a shopping centre, landscaping, seating or street improvements. The stakes get much higher with some London boroughs, which may seek contributions from the developer towards community centres, local schools or sports facilities. In fairness, this is one of the few means left to local authorities nowadays to make the social aspects of planning a reality in view of the cutbacks in local government finance.

Section 12 of the Planning and Compensation Act, 1991, alters Section 106 of the 1990 Act, creating two new subsections, 106A and 106B, which provide for 'planning obligations' (as against 'planning agreements' under the previous legislation) which may be entered into jointly, by agreement, or 'unilaterally' (Heap, 1995) in order to impose restrictions and conditions on the development and use of the land in question, or to require specified operations to be carried out, or to require money to be paid to the local authority in relation to the development (see *The Planner*, 77, 29, 1991, p. 8). From the planning lawyer's viewpoint the changes are intended to overcome common problems connected with planning appeal *impasse* situations in respect to lack of co-operation between planning authorities and developers preventing site development, and to enable the planning requirements laid down within the 'planning obligation' to be enforced against successors in title (obliging them to keep to the planning requirements) as well as against the original developers.

The development process, and the related issue of 'planning gain' are discussed at greater length in Volume II.

Planning applications

In considering whether or not to grant the scheme planning permission (box 3 in Fig. 2.2) the planning authority is concerned not only with the nature of the development itself but with the additional traffic and car parking it is likely to generate, and with the visual townscape impact. Planners do not look at a site in isolation but in relation to its effect on the surrounding area, and the impact of the new development on the existing mix of uses. Are there already too many offices in the area? Would the use of the site for shops preclude its use at a later date for more social uses and the provision of facilities which are lacking? Would the development of a particular site prevent surface mineral extraction at a later date? Planners are therefore concerned with balance and adjusting all the land uses together. The fact that a scheme is profitable to the developer does not necessarily mean that it is right from a town planning viewpoint.

All development has to win planning permission, whether it be private-sector residential development or public-sector council housing. Consent is not a foregone conclusion, although there are special mechanisms for one local authority department to get planning permission from another. Housing is a major land use, and hence a strategic issue in the Structure Plan, which will have implications for the whole nature of the city both physically and socially. New housing has major implications for the transportation policy of the urban area, and means increased demand for basic supporting services such as schools, shops and leisure facilities, as housing generates people. This is over and above the immediate concern of the housing department to meet housing need, or rehouse people on its waiting list.

The planners have not only to look at the detailed nation-wide controls of planning law (as explained in Chapter 10) but also to consider central government policy statements, the implications of Structure Plan policy, as well as any specific Local Plan statements for the area. Any decisions they make must be based on these sources, and not arbitrary. Since the planners are only the professional advisers of their political masters, the councillors, any planning decision must be discussed and approved by the planning committee of the local authority council. Certain matters may also have to be passed up to the county level, and even to central government. Depending on the scale and nature of the scheme, it may also be necessary to advertise it to the general public and invite public participation, and to enter into consultations with statutory undertakers, related government departments and other official groups.

The development process must be contextualised within the political setting of the planning system. In reality the relationship between the planning professionals, their political masters, the 'members' – that is, the councillors on the planning committee – and the community is much more complex, and may be subject to the vagaries of different personalities and interest groups fighting it out to the bitter end. The system is highly political, because land and property are involved, although it is believed that only in a minority of cases do overt bribery and corruption occur. Also on major schemes there may be a great deal of lobbying from community groups, and from pressure groups particularly concerned with the issue in question. There is provision in many cases for public participation and consultation over statutory plans, but the situation is far less amenable in the case of separate planning applications, where only limited advertisement of the proposals may be required (see Chapter 10). The perceived lack of openness, the obscurity and the paucity of communication associated with the planning process is one of the reasons why there has been so much conflict, dissatisfaction and pressure-group activity (Reade, 1987). Every political and legal tactic will be used by different interest groups to promote or prevent a planning decision, and proposals for schemes can drag on for years yet still lead to an outcome that pleases no one.

Delay in gaining planning permission can cost a develop-ment company millions in interest payments, for time is money. A scheme may go to public inquiry to deal with objections from the general public, or, on appeal to the Secretary of State if the application is refused. The planners and the developers are not necessarily adversaries; in some cases the local authority and the developers will enter into a partnership scheme together. The local authority planners have powers which can help the developers, such as land assembly and compulsory purchase, and the developers have expertise in getting a scheme off the ground which is of use to the local authority. It depends, in some degree, on the location, and more particularly on the region, as some areas are keen to attract developers, whereas in south-east England, for example, planners can afford to be more choosy, as there is so much competition for the right to develop different sites. It has even been suggested that the authorities ought to hold auctions and sell the right to the highest bidder, as in California.

Design considerations

When it comes to the design and building of the scheme a whole range of other property professionals come into play (boxes 4 and 5 in Fig. 2.2). First of all, there is the architect who designs the scheme – nowadays it is less likely to be one person than a whole team of skilled people. There are likely to be interior designers, too, particularly if it is a shopping mall type of development, to create the right life-style image for the customers (Fitch and Knobel, 1990; Kunstler, 1993). The planners, both public and private, will be involved in respect of the overall layout, the relationship with surrounding buildings, particularly if the project is in, or adjacent to, a Conservation Area. There is the major question of car parking, delivery vehicle access, public transport if there is going to be any, and the overall circulation, access and general road layout. All this will involve the specialist skills of transportation planners, and also ultimately of highway engineers. The design process is likely to go on for months, because of a thousand and one constraints and the question of the cost factor. Quantity surveyors in particular are responsible for costing the 'price' of the building. It should be remembered that the cost of materials and construction is only a small part of the final value of the property. There is also the cost of the land, the acquisition of the site, which can be a very substantial part of the initial outlay. The value of the development once built is dictated more by market forces than by construction or land costs. There may be statutory requirements for public participation and community consultation on the scheme, and there is usually a level of public opposition to large schemes.

The property lawyer will deal with easements across the site (rights of way), restrictive covenants (private legal controls against certain uses or types of development on the land) and the likely confusing maze of land titles which need to be dealt with. Also separately, people who specialise in building contract law and project management (who may be senior quantity surveyors, general practice surveyors or even architects) will need to sort out the contracts, tenders, and all the legal intricacies of dealing with the large number of people, contractors and suppliers involved in building the scheme. Once the architect has evolved the design, the quantity surveyor must work out the cost, and the project manager or architect in control of the project must put it out to tender and get the contractors in to build it. There are a multitude of detailed design factors and legal matters which have to be taken into account. The construction itself will involve a vast range of professionals such as civil and structural engineers, heating and ventilating engineers, etc., and a host of building trade workers and labourers, all with their foremen, managers and back-up administrators. The land surveyor too has an important role, both at the beginning, in setting out the site, and at the end when the development is completed, at which time it is likely that the Ordnance Survey will send someone along to add the new scheme to its maps ready for the next revision. However, it is equally likely that it will have been sent copies of the new layout beforehand.

Disposal and management

When it is built the development has to be let or sold (box 6 in Fig. 2.2). Subsequently the building and site have to be cared for and managed. Again, this is the job of the surveyor (Cadman *et al.*, 1990; Scarrett, 1983; Stapleton, 1986). There are the maintenance aspects to be considered, but beyond this janitorial role there are all the other financial and legal matters to deal with; bearing in mind that the development is not just bricks and mortar but an on-going investment, so that matters such as rent reviews, dealing with tenants (such as chain stores or commercial office takers) and future letting policy have to be dealt with. In larger schemes specialist facilities management professionals may be utilised. At a later date questions of alterations or redevelopment, or indeed of whether the original owner wishes to sell his interest in the property for something more financially up and coming, have to be considered. The great majority of all office and shopping developments are not owned by the users but let to them, the freehold or head lease belonging to a variety of financial interests, including insurance companies, pension funds and investment consortiums, and sometimes affluent individuals.

Conclusion

Different groups of students will identify with different aspects of this process, and it may be helpful, in order to 'place' one's role, to consult current publications from the CISC (Construction Industry Standing Conferences who are 'mapping' the various contributions of each professional group in 'development' for NVQ (National Vocational Qualification) purposes (CISC, 1994).

Chapter 3

The property professions and the role of the planners

The context

This chapter considers the nature of the town planning profession, comparing it, in particular, with that of surveying, because chartered surveyors are one of the largest professional groups in the property world. The discussion will be set within a wider discussion of the changing nature and context of the property development professions. In the second half of the chapter the various roles of the town planner will be discussed. In the 1980s dynamic economic growth occurred in which property figured as a major commodity. The land use professions were growing and altering out of all recognition, compared with the situation ten or twenty years before. 'Big Bang' (deregulation of financial services) in the mid-1980s altered the financial world, sweeping away restrictions and barriers generations old. It has meant new opportunities for the land use professions in the private sector, but it has also meant that they are now undefended from invasions of their territory, in the areas of property portfolio management and investment analysis, by a range of other professionals, not least accountants, and from world-wide competitors, including Japanese interests, and aggressively run American banking and investment professionals who can make British practitioners appear amateur and old-fashioned in comparison. The 'enterprise culture' faded in the recession of the early 1990s, to be replaced by the 'environment culture', and the property professions are again reconsidering their role and position in society.

Many of the young people entering professional and business areas, including town planning, housing and surveying, are women (Spencer and Podmore, 1987; Levison and Atkins, 1987; Leevers, 1986; Greed, 1991; Greed, 1994). This is having an impact on the nature of professional practice and urban policy. Many women planners question the concept of land use zoning, which separates employment areas from residential areas, that is, work and home. Environmental groups question the 'greenness'

of such separation, which necessitates the use of the motor car. Such zoning is most inconvenient for women who seek to combine children and a career, and an even greater problem for working-class wives without a car who work in decentralised industrial estates far from where their children go to school and from where they live. The challenge this 'alternative' perspective raises will be considered in the final chapter.

Office technology and telecommunications have advanced, and now even the stock market is based on dealing from computer terminals. People communicate instantaneously across vast distances by means of fax machines, portable telephones, computers with modems using e-mail (electronic mail) on the Internet. Some say that modern office blocks will become redundant (like Victorian warehouses and factories), that large-scale commuting will decline, and more people will work from terminals at home telecommuting, with only managerial and professional people maintaining an office at the centre for meetings. In the future it is likely that Britain will become even more part of the international business community, and from a social perspective part of the global village, whilst at the same time cementing its cultural and economic links with the European Community. The old divisions between East and Western Europe have been breaking down, as exemplified by the re-unification of Germany, leading many property entrepreneurs to look at pastures new in the Greater Europe which encompasses the east.

The property professionals

The planners

To summarise, town planners are concerned with all aspects of development, urban and rural; land uses and traffic; and not just with commercial development or housing alone. The profession is concerned with all types of land use, retail, residential, commercial, industrial, open space, etc. Planning is concerned not only with individual land uses but with the whole built environment which they make up, and thus with the overall townscape and design of the areas in which the different urban activities are carried on. Therefore town planning is concerned with developing policies on conservation, improvement, demolition, redevelopment of existing areas as well as, of course, individual new developments on greenfield sites. Also, as has been indicated, there are many different levels and degrees of detail in planning practice, ranging from broad-brush regional guidance to development plans for whole counties, through to designing local areas, and controlling the external appearance of individual buildings. Clearly the planning profession must, of necessity, be made up of a range of people offering a diversity of specialisms to carry this work load.

The main professional body to which most town planners belong is the Royal Town Planning Institute, whose membership consisted of approximately 17 726 in all categories by 1995 (RTPI Records Department; see Table 3.1), of whom around 14 534 are fully qualified corporate members. The RTPI was established in 1913 as a learned association (Ashworth, 1968; Millerson, 1964) of architects, surveyors, public health officers and civil engineers who were interested in town planning, but gradually town planning evolved as a separate profession. Nowadays there are two main ways by which people become town planners. Candidates may take a degree-level course in town planning, or they may take a first degree in some related subject and follow it with a postgraduate course in town planning. In both cases they then have to complete satisfactorily a period of professional experience in practice. Alternatively, graduates who have been working in town planning for a number of years and have substantial related experience may be eligible for membership. In addition all members are expected to undertake continuing professional development.

Town planning is a relatively broad profession, yet numerically it is small compared with the other land use professions, and it incorporates a range of types of people with different areas of expertise. Town planning practice covers a wide variety of different activities and specialisms, and planners tend to gravitate to areas of practice which relate to their particular background and expertise. There are a number of people working in town planning who have dual professional qualifications, combining, for example, architecture, law, civil engineering or surveying. One might find architects involved in those aspects of town planning which relate to conservation policy and design; lawyers involved in development control; economists, statisticians and sociologists involved in the wider policy-making levels of the preparation of Structure Plan policies. Likewise a feature of town planning work is that a wide range of people with different types of expertise work together as a large team, both in the production of the development plans within local government and in the case of large-scale private-sector projects.

This is rather different, relatively speaking, from the situation in surveying practice, where there is still room for the sole practitioner, although in London many surveyors are members of large firms which are subdivided into specialist offices and sections. As a general principle, much of the work which goes on in the land use professions is strongly team-orientated. Although most town planners are employed in central or local government, over 20 per cent are nowadays working in the private sector acting as advisers to a range of public and private and public-sector interests, ranging from property development companies to the smaller local authorities who buy-in expertise when needed rather than maintain a permanent staff. There is a measure of overlap in that some planners are also chartered surveyors who have qualified within the Planning and Development division of the Royal Institution of Chartered Surveyors. In addition to the main professional body, the RTPI, there are other influential town planning organisations. One of the main ones is the Town and Country Planning Association (TCPA), which is not a professionally qualifying body but a respected pressure group founded at the beginning of the twentieth century to promote the concept of Garden Cities and the ideas of Ebenezer Howard (see Chapter 6).

The surveyors

The main professional body for surveying is the Royal Institution of Chartered Surveyors, whose roots go back centuries (Thompson, 1968). The RICS is a much larger body (membership approaching 90 000, including students) than the RTPI. The RICS encompasses a range of specialist groups, including general surveyors, land agents, land surveyors, minerals surveyors, quantity surveyors and building surveyors (Avis and Gibson, 1987). The General Practice division is the largest, in which valuers, estate managers and housing managers are located, containing well over a third of the total membership. Quantity surveyors make up nearly a third of the membership of the RICS and are therefore the second largest group. There is in addition a relatively new Planning and Development division, although many established older members opted to stay in the General Practice division. Some people who are chartered surveyors also count themselves as town planners, either holding the RTPI qualification as well as belonging to the RICS, or simply being RICS in the planning and development profession. A substantial number of people hold joint membership of the RIBA and are architects (Nadin and Jones, 1990). There is undoubtedly an overlap in terms of planning practice between the two professions. However, it would be wrong to imagine that, because relatively few surveyors are employed in town planning authorities, they have little influence on the built environment. They are the main advisers of the private sector; in a sense they are 'the enemy' with whom planning has to contend, because they represent interests which are often in conflict with the objectives of the planning system. The commercial and valuation emphasis throughout the world of surveying colours the word view of all surveyors and is distinct from that of the planners.

Many comparisons between planners and surveyors

Academic or practical?

Around 65 per cent of all town planning courses are run in universities, the rest in polytechnics, a few in colleges of further education. In 1988, by contrast, about 80 per cent of full-time surveying degree courses are to be found in polytechnics, and 20 per cent in universities (Rodriguez-Bachiller, 1988). (However, because of the difference in the size of the professions, at any one time there are likely to be over 10 000 surveying students as against some 3000 planning students going through under-graduate courses.) A number of technical colleges offer surveying courses, and there are many part-time and 'external' routes to qualification. (Prior to the 1960s many more town planners and surveyors used to qualify this way, especially by correspondence through the College of Estate Management at Reading University, and through part-time courses.) Over half of all town planning courses are postgraduate ones, whereas the vast majority of surveying courses are at the undergraduate level. There are a number of town planners, as mentioned above, who took a first degree in geography, economics, sociology or law and went on to a postgraduate conversion degree course in town planning. (For the range of courses see *Planning Week* **76** (12), special issue on 'Planning careers and education', 12 April 1991.)

So the emphasis is somewhat different, with town planning having a rather more 'academic' emphasis than surveying, which has always prided itself on its practicality and common sense. One of the main reasons students give for choosing surveying is that (as would-be students often put it at interview) 'we don't want to be stuck in an office all day' but want to 'get out and about'. There has been continuing growth and diversification of undergraduate and postgraduate education within the land use professions. People tend to choose their profession carefully in relation to future prospects and salary, and at present it is noticeable that surveyors earn more than planners and have a higher, if more precarious, status in the private sector. Such has not always been the case. Indeed, more surveying graduates are now, again, entering central and local government employment, because of the recession which has hit the private sector, where there have been many redundancies as a result of the downturn in the economy in the early 1990s.

Public or private?

Whilst 80 per cent of RTPI members are employed in the public sector and only 20 per cent in the private sector, the situation is almost exactly reversed regarding the RICS, with most surveyors working in the private sector in private partnerships, or for large investment and development concerns. Indeed, the majority of town planning surveyors see their chief role as advising their clients on how to beat the planning system (see the RICS leaflet 'What use is a chartered surveyor in planning and development?' (1989). There are other, quite marked differences between the two land use professions, each of which has its own professional culture (Joseph, 1978; Greed, 1991), the RTPI being somewhat more sociological, political, interventionist and governmental in outlook; the RICS more conservative, private-sector orientated and commercial in outlook – with exceptions on both sides. Also there are a growing number of RTPI planners who work in private planning consultancies, advising private developers or carrying out contract work for local planning authorities, who, therefore, have an influential input into the planning process and policy.

Male or female?

Relatively speaking, most members of the land use professions are stereotyped because they are predominantly male, middle-class and white (Nadin and Jones, 1990). In fact 6 per cent of fully qualified members of the RICS are female. However, 15 per cent of all surveying students, and significantly this figure is now dropping slightly, and 8 per cent of all chartered surveyors under the age of thirty three, are female (RICS, Jan. 1995), although there are relatively few women in the more technological areas of surveying. 20 per cent of the RTPI corporate membership are women (although only 10 per cent are in full-time practice) and, as stated, up to 40 per cent of planning students are female, although the proportion varies considerably among courses. Taking the land use and construction professions together, less than 5 per cent of those in practice are women. In contrast 52 per cent of the population in Britain are female (Morphet, 1983). These factors may be irrelevant to urban policy-making if women's needs are perceived to be the same as those of the men, or if it is believed that the professional man is equally capable of planning for all groups in society. But as research and human experience have shown, women suffer disadvantage in a built environment that is planned chiefly by men primarily for men (Stimpson, *et al.*, 1981: Little *et al.*, 1988; Little, 1994; WGSG, 1984) and so changes need to be made (Howatt, 1987; Greed, 1991).

Even if people enter the profession with alternative views, and believe they can change it by joining in and biding their time until they are in a position to alter the *status quo*, they soon find that they are subjected to powerful professional socialisation processes (Gibbs, 1987; Knox, 1988). Students, especially those from a working-class background, an all-girls school or an ethnic minority, often experience considerable group pressure to accept what they are told by authoritative lecturers and by fellow students, and may be made to feel awkward, untypical, inadequate or ashamed of their own 'different' life experience. Indeed, there is an extensive literature on the problems women encounter, both as students and in practice as property professionals (for example, Brion and Tinker, 1980, and Leevers, 1986, on women in housing; Spencer and Podmore, 1987; Silverstone and Ward, 1980, on women in the professions, including architecture; Greed, 1991, on women surveyors and Greed, forthcoming, on women town planners).

There are relatively few women in the more technological areas of surveying, and greater concentrations in general-practice surveying (especially in the housing option). Although the number of women entering is actually growing at a greater rate than the overall expansion of the profession, even allowing for their small numbers in the past (and the fact that the entry of women to the profession in any number is a relatively recent phenomenon) disproportionately fewer women than men are reaching positions of seniority or full partnership level, and, likewise, relatively few women town planners are reaching the higher positions in local authorities or senior partner level in planning consultancies. This is likely to be one of the main issues of contention for the future. Unless women reach the decision-making levels of the professions they will not be in a position to shape the future structure of the professions or influence the nature of the built environment through their professional activities and decisions. Surveying practice is segmented (Greed, 1991) in that women are more likely still to be found in the public sector and less in the mainstream private sector. Owing to a perceived lack of equal opportunities and employment flexibility in local government, many women town planning graduates in 1989 obtained jobs in the private sector, and this seems to be a continuing trend (Morphet, 1990).

Whilst there is growth, many of the professional bodies are concerned about a future 'manpower' crisis, as there is going to be a substantial drop in the number of school leavers in the future, owing to a falling birth rate over the last twenty years. Of course, once the market starts declining redundancy notices are issued, often on the basis of 'last in, first out'. However, some sectors are still flourishing and there are continuing attempts to attract a wider range of entrants, including women, ethnic minorities and working-class people (not mutually exclusive groups). It was not so long ago that many people from these groups felt they were being actively discouraged from entering the professions. The number of ethnic minority and black members is very low in both professional bodies, although the RTPI has tried to promote a recruitment policy among black school leavers. Interestingly, black women in particular have responded. Black students constitute around 3 per cent of students on built environment courses in some polytechnics, more in London, but overall nationally their numbers are very low, with several colleges having none. Initiatives such as PATH have been introduced in further and higher education specifi-cally to attract black students.

There is considerable concern about the need to recruit more planners from ethnic minorities (Ahmed, 1989). It is estimated that around under 1 per cent of all members of the land use professions are black people (compared with around 5 per cent in the population as a whole) but it is difficult to get exact figures. 'Ethnic issues' should not be seen as separate from so-called mainstream planning topics. For example, although there are perceived links between inner-city planning and ethnic needs, local authorities in the Midlands have specifically developed policies on ethnic minority needs and recreational planning in the countryside, and London boroughs have investigated the likely linkages between urban conservation policy and the specific housing design needs of ethnic groups.

Many observers are commenting that whilst more people are nowadays entering the professions they are not all ending up in the same quality of posts. Indeed, there is clear segmentation of the professions not only on the basis of gender and race but to a lesser extent on the basis of the class of origin of the entrants

(Crompton and Sanderson, 1990). There are very few disabled planners or surveyors around. It should not be assumed that this is entirely because of the nature of these professions, because much of the work is office-based, and not all to do with 'getting out and about' on-site. Some would say that disabled people should be involved in the 'outside' survey and plan-making work because they can more readily point out the barriers to mobility inherent in an urban layout or building design.

Professional or commercial?

In the past the higher professions prided themselves on the fact that they were not 'trade' and in particular that they were not concerned with purely commercial considerations but had a sense of public service and responsibility to the wider community. These principles are enshrined in the code of professional ethics drawn up by each profession, and are usually reiterated in the annual speech of the incoming president's speech of the respective professional body. However, in recent years, especially since the deregulation of financial services, attitudes have had to change, and the professional has become more commercial in ethos.

Other property professionals

Several other major professional bodies are concerned with the environment, such as the Royal Institute of British Architects, the Institution of Civil Engineers (ICE), the Institution of Structural Engineers (ISE), the Incorporated Society of Valuers and Auctioneers (ISVA), the Chartered Institute of Building (CIOB), which has experienced remarkable growth and the smaller Architects' and Surveyors' Institute (ASI). The ISVA is of particular interest because much of the work its members carry out is similar to that of the general-practice surveyor, particularly in relation to valuation, auctioneering and estate management, which touches on the area of town planning from a developer's viewpoint.

The Institute of Housing is a relatively small body, but one with many women in it (Brion and Tinker, 1980) and with some overlap in the nature of its work with the RICS (Power, 1987; Smith, 1989). In the past housing management was predominantly concerned with the management of the local authority housing stock, but the profession has grown in numbers and prestige in recent years in response to the higher political profile of the housing crisis and the proliferation of non-governmental bodies such as housing associations providing housing. The RICS offers a housing option within its General Practice division, albeit with a small take-up but with potential for the future, and many town planning courses offer specialist options in housing issues, reflecting the fact that the professional bodies overlap and link up in respect of their various interests and activities. Nowadays some would say that the local authorities, whilst still managing the bulk of housing, are not the builders, but the enablers, of new social residential development, the development role having passed to the housing associations.

There are a range of other specialist bodies concerned with aspects of property, such as the National Association of Estate Agents, at around 9600 membership, of which 20 per cent are women, and the Institute of Revenues, Rating and Valuation, which has taken on a new lease of life since the controversy about the poll tax and the alternatives. Some solicitors, that is, members of the Law Society, and barristers specialise in town planning law within private practice. Interestingly, this branch of the law is attracting many women. Lawyers employed by local authorities have an important role in the planning process, sorting out the finer points of planning law, and dealing with the details of enforcement, planning agreements and conditions of planning permission. In the wider development process itself there are many other professionals involved, such as accountants, economists and financial analysts concerned with the viability of development. Urban geographers, statisticians, economists and sociologists may be called upon to contribute to the development decision-making process. A growing number of professional ecologists, environmentalists and landscape architects offer expertise in the field of environmental assessment, which is now a planning requirement, brought in by the European Commission. Another trend is for more people to offer their planning skills in an advocacy role on behalf of community groups, to represent the demands of ordinary people as professional community activists and enablers.

The discussion so far has related chiefly to the professions, but they are the tip of the iceberg – the elite few – as many other people are employed in the construction industry. There are vast numbers at technician and trades level in all aspects of the building industry. Many will have little contact with the big high-prestige schemes and will work in the small building firms which exist throughout the country (Ball, 1988) and are so prone to bankruptcy. Many local authorities used to have their own DLO

Table 3.1 Membership of the professional bodies as at January 1995

Body	Full members	Student members	Total members
RTPI	14 534 (20·0%)	3 192 (42·0%)	17 726 (23·0%)
RICS	70 918 (6·1%)	21 267 (15·8%)	92 185 (8·3%)
ICE	52 000 (1·2%)	9 285 (11·0%)	80 250 (3·5%)
ISE	17 131 (1·7%)	6 489 (11·9%)	23 620 (4·5%)
CIOB	25 118 (0·7%)	9 439 (4·3%)	33 557 (1·7%)
CIOH	8 000 (43·0%)	4 116 (56·0%)	12 300 (44·0%)
ASI	4 820 (1·2%)	485 (10·2%)	5 305 (1·9%)
ISVA	5 774 (6·7%)	1 381 (16·5%)	7 155 (8·6%)
RIBA	27 708 (7·2%)	4 102 (28·2%)	31 810 (10·0%)
CIBSE	12 939 (1·2%)	2 225 (38·5%)	15 164 (1·8%)
LI	2 284 (40·5%)	3 653 (42·4%)	3 777 (40·0%)
IRRV	2 361 N/A	1 570 N/A	5 751 (24·0%)
NAEA	(non examining body)		9 657 (21·1%)

Source: The professional bodies as at January 1995. In some cases there are other intermediate or honorary categories which make up the remainder of the total, who are not strictly speaking either fully qualified members or students, such as probationers, technicians, international members, graduate associates.

Key: Female percentages in brackets. RTPI = Royal Town Planning Institute; RICS = Royal Institution of Chartered Surveyors; ICE = Institution of Civil Engineers; ISE = Institution of Structural Engineers; CIOB = Chartered Institute of Building; CIOH = Chartered Institute of Housing; ASI = Architects and Surveyors Institute; ISVA = Incorporated Society of Valuers and Auctioneers; RIBA = Royal Institute of British Architects; CIBSE = Chartered Institution of Building Services Engineers; NAEA = National Association of Estate Agents; LI = Landscape Institute; IRRV = Institute of Revenue, Rating & Valuation.

work force, that is, Direct-Labour Organisation, but are increasingly putting their work out to CCT (Compulsory Competitive Tender), creating efficency but not necessarily more quality for the consumer. Increasingly, as local government structures change, as a result of government pressure to make them less bureaucratic and more cost-effective and entrepreneurial, CCT is being introduced, under which professional staff, such as planners, are hired for specific contracts, rather than being employed permanently. In addition, there are innumerable people working in the office and service sectors involved in all aspects of property, especially agency (including estate agency), investment, financial services, who are not actually qualified within the main land use professions. Large numbers of office workers, mainly women, often carry out fairly skilled quasi-professional work, especially in the realms of estate agency, up and down the land. Anyone can become an estate agent, or for that matter a property developer; all you need is money, or the power to inspire enough confidence in others for them to take you seriously and invest in you.

The European Community

Since 1992 the EC has been going through a further phase of harmonisation and trade barriers have been progressively reduced. The Channel Tunnel opened in 1994, and the British Isles became physically, and possibly more culturally, linked to the Continental mainland. Already plans are afoot to create powerful trans-European property professional groups in which the British bodies are seeking a prominent position, for example the FIABCI (a prominent European group representing the interests of property professionals). British bodies have to compete or harmonise with such bodies as the French *Confédération Nationale des Administrateurs de Biens* (*biens*, 'goods'). *Biens immobiliers* are 'real property' in the sense of land and buildings (as in *agence immobilière*, an estate agency; as against *biens mobiliers*, personal property, such as chattels, anything which is movable and not fixed to the ground, e.g. furniture, ornaments).

There is now open trade, in theory at least, in a market of over 300 million people, larger than the United States. This situation is greatly welcomed by chartered surveyors involved in the more commercial side of property development, but other property professionals have reservations. Harmonisation of standards and procedures will affect the building industry, especially in the areas of public procurement (that is, public works contracts); building standards, construction product standards; and mutual recognition of professional qualifications and education. Germany is particularly concerned, as it has such a flourishing and efficient building industry, and has therefore had a major input into the proceedings. Some erstwhile Socialist, East European states now offer great potential for the activities of property developers moving in from the West, and for indigenous entrepreneurs, whilst others remain politically and economically unstable.

There are already links between British and other European planners, but there are often considerable differences of opinion and culture as regards the ideal urban form, because of the greater emphasis on higher density and less suburban residential development on the European mainland. British planners were particularly concerned about the assumptions of the European Commission in a consultative document, *Green Paper on the urban environment* (EC, 1990), which was based on the characteristics of a typical Continental European city where uses are normally much more concentrated than in Britain and the suburbs are often seen as a low-status 'cultural desert'. The Commission has been criticised for assuming that it was possible to define an ideal city which was applicable right across Europe regardless of national differences and climatic factors. Nevertheless, as stated in the last chapter, EC law now takes precedence over UK planning law (a matter of much controversy).

There is no exact equivalent of the British chartered town planner (or surveyor, for that matter) in European countries. The professional cake is divided in different ways, with architects, civil engineers, economists and geographers taking the role of 'the planner' in different situations (see Davies, 1992, which refers to the RTPI *Planning in Europe* study pack). More fundamentally, there is something essentially English, even quaint, about being a 'professional' and belonging to a chartered body, as against holding higher degrees and demonstrating competence in a particular specialism, both of which are more commonly criteria of being accepted as a 'planner' in Europe (and North America, for that matter). There is a great deal of mystique associated with the English idea of a professional elite (and the ideal of the professional gentleman) which does not fit well the realities of the modern international competitive business world, or with demands of a more educated population for greater involvement in the decision-making process in town planning (Knox, 1988). Indeed, the very role of the planner is under question (Howe, 1980).

The role of the planner

Umpire

Traditionally the role of the town planner was seen as similar to that of the referee, or umpire, who set out the pitch, resolved conflict between opposing teams and enforced the ground rules, the framework of fair play, within which the 'game' of property development was played out. The planner's brief was to ensure that towns and cities developed logically and conveniently, with an emphasis on zoning. This provided a framework for the design of the road network and the provision of other infrastructural services, and gave the market confidence in the future security of the area. Planning control ensured that space was available for the non-profit-making social uses which were essential to the urban population but which were not attractive to the private sector as an investment, such as recreational space and facilities, schools, health and community buildings, sewers and drains, all of which were provided by other local government departments and statutory undertakers.

This accommodating and non-controversial role of planning has been criticised by the 'left' (broadly, socialists) as reinforcing the *status quo*. Proponents of this viewpoint have seen the planner as 'oiling the wheels of capitalism', that is, enabling business to function more efficiently by organising the urban physical framework within which it operates (Simmie, 1974). On the other hand some on the 'right' (broadly, conservatives) have welcomed the role of the planner as the referee or umpire when it has been to their advantage but have also criticised the planners when their decisions have gone against them. It is an interesting question whether planning leads the market or the market leads planning. The private sector has tended to see planners as over-concerned with social issues at the expense of economic progress. The planning process has often been seen as too slow and bureaucratic, and there have been endless attempts to speed it up. But this slowness is often due to the fact that planners have to take into account the views of a wide range of affected parties and the city-wide implications of developing a particular site, and to consider wider social and environmental factors as well as the immediate exigencies of the market, in coming to their decisions. Whether or not one considers the planning system fair depends on whether one accepts as reasonable, or biased, the criteria or rules by which the game is played (Goldsmith, 1980; Montgomery and Thornley, 1990). Many urban groups have criticised planners for being hopelessly partisan as white male middle-class, middle-aged car drivers. This is particularly so in the case of their role as neutral decision-makers whose job involves the allocation of scarce resources within the urban situation, namely land, facilities, amenities, roads and parking. It is often felt that those with cars seem to get many more resources allocated to them than those who use public transport.

The majority of the politicians, that is, members of Parliament at central government level and councillors at the local government level, like the planners, are men. Women's low representation in planning committees at the local council level must affect the nature of urban decision-making (Barron *et al.*, 1988). There are still relatively few women in Parliament (Vallance, 1979), and very few chief planning officers are female (Nadin and Jones, 1990). Very few of the senior officers in local government as a whole are female, and many are of the view that this inevitably affects the nature of decision-making – indeed, it affects what gets on to the agenda in the first place. In contrast, women, as compared with men, are often the leaders and

instigators of community action related to the built environment
– for play areas, road crossings, green issues, housing. There is a
strong gender dimension to the whole public participation and
community involvement debate in planning, 'community' often
being defined, by default, as meaning in effect women and
children, ethnic minorities and inner-city working-class people.
These are the very people who are unlikely to be in on the
decision-making process in the first place, dominated as it is by
members of that middle-class group from which planners derive.

Technocrat

It is difficult to pre-judge whether the planners 'get it right' or
not, because planning is all to do with making decisions about
the future, about deciding whether or not there is a need for a
particular development or scheme in a certain area. It is easy to
criticise them after the event, much less easy to predict what the
future is going to be like in the light of changing economic and
technological conditions. As will be seen in Chapter 7, back in
the 1960s, under the influence of North American planners, town
planning became obsessed with prediction of future trends in
employment, population and car ownership – and generally got it
wrong. Planners saw themselves as powerful technocrats who
could offer society answers to all its problems on the basis of what
they saw as their advanced knowledge of the science of town
planning. With their newly developed computers they would
supplant the need for democratically elected politicians, the
private sector or the general public, who, it was believed, never
know what was best for them. The 'white heat of technology',
squeaky-clean, uncomplicated approach to planning ignored the
variety and untidiness of existence. Planning, by its very nature, is
concerned with the future as it is seeks to control what is going to
be built, and therefore a preoccupation with the future
is legitimate in moderation. The problem is how to predict
change, and how to shape the future in a manner which is fair
to all.

Economic planner?

Whilst social issues are of great importance, some would argue
they are determined by underlying economic factors (Pickvance,
1977). People may live in an area in the first place only because
there is work there. Over-concentrations of people in a particular

region, such as the south-east, can lead to the problems of urban sprawl, traffic snarl-ups and high land prices, whilst other areas are underpopulated and in decline. The regional aspect of planning has come to a head in recent years because of the congestion of the south-east. Many would argue than in order to shift the emphasis of settlement away from the south-east there must be a movement of jobs, and therefore of investment, industry and commerce, into less populated regions. Economic planning (Balchin and Bull, 1987; the main book on economic regional planning) has always been seen, particularly by Labour governments, which favour a high level of state intervention, as an essential companion to realistic town planning, and this is reflected in many textbooks (Hall, 1994). Town planning involves the allocation of scarce resources, that is, urban land, goods and services; and is therefore seen as an aspect of economic planning. But there are many other factors, divisions and changes within society which can affect the nature of land use, over and above the employment aspects stressed in traditional regional economic planning. Many rural or coastal areas with limited employment opportunities are experiencing population growth due to retired people moving in, people buying second homes and people commuting considerable distances to work in the nearest town.

The economic planner has taken on a new lease of life as market analyst in the private sector. In the past it was accepted that the town planner and the related organisations of state control offered a viable alternative to *laissez-faire* and the vagaries of the market. The traditional skills of the planner in the analysis and prediction of social trends can be used to look for new opportunities in the market rather than to find and provide for human need through the public sector. There are advantages and disadvantages to each system, and it is up to each student to weigh their relative merits. Many are concerned that regional economic planning and controls on the location of industry have not been prominent enough features of modern town planning since the mid-1970s (Balchin and Bull, 1987).

Economic planning issues are dealt with in detail in Volume II, both in relation to the regulatory role of the state in the urban economy, and from the private property market perspective. The role of economic planning in regenerating the inner city, through programmes such as the Single Regeneration Budget, is covered at an introductory level at the end of Chapter 7. The relationship between town planning and the urban economic context, which arguably generates the demand for land use and development in the first place, is discussed fully in the following texts: Rydin, 1994; Stoker and Young, 1995, and Atkinson and Moon, 1993.

Environmental watchdog?

There are many pressure groups concerned with the environment, rural and urban. The 'green' movement is much publicised, with its concern about the natural environment, depletion of the planet's resources and the greenhouse effect. There is also concern about civic design and the appearance of the built environment, accompanied by much criticism of modern architecture, as exemplified by Prince Charles. Town and country planning, arguably, has always been concerned with such issues, but planners take a broader view, not looking only at the end product, the environment. They have to look at the factors which create certain types of environment in the first place. (Few environments, even in the countryside, are entirely 'natural'; see Chapter 9.) In drawing up statutory plans the planners have to analyse the physical, economic and social factors which create and shape the demand for the different types of land use and development, taking into account such issues as population, employment, industry, transport and housing demand. Many would suggest that town planning needs to go beyond its traditional concern with the built environment and extend its powers over such matters as pollution, agriculture and ecological issues. Industry, for example, is not just a land use, it is a polluter of the atmosphere and the whole ecosphere too. This trend is reflected in the European Community, with planners being given increased powers to assess the environmental impact of new development as discussed in Part III. The Environmental Protection Act, 1990, seen as a ragbag without a central strategy by many environmentalists, was also a step towards greater control of the pollution and contamination of land. Subsequently, the 1995 Environment Act consolidated previous changes and established a more comprehensive green agenda for planning law and policy making (Ball and Ball, 1995; Lane and Peto, 1995).

Likewise, in respect of urban conservation, many consider that concern with the visual and aesthetic aspects of architecture and civic design, unless linked to awareness of the practical, functional and financial constraints of building and construction (e.g. what grants are available under what legislation), constitutes only a partial view. One of the professional skills of the town planner is the ability to look at the whole situation: both cause and effect. Some would say that there is over-emphasis among the environmental movements on dealing with immediate crises, or journalistically attractive issues, however important, rather than on developing long-term strategies and looking at the social, economic and political factors which shape the environment. Some shoppers think they are 'green' if they use unleaded petrol to drive to their out-of-town hypermarket and recycle the carrier bags they have used: many planners would ask, would they be doing better by campaigning for a return to smaller local shopping centres within walking distance to cut down traffic congestion and pollution in the first place? Developers might see this solution as uneconomic in market terms, but environmentalists would see it as highly economic in global ecological terms – and shoppers without cars would welcome it.

Social engineer?

Although town planning is, by definition, concerned with planning land use and development, it has a major effect on people's lives, and may be seen as a branch of social policy. This impact has sometimes been unintentional, because the planners did not realise all the consequences, but at other times it has been quite intentional. Yet planners have not a good track record of anticipating and planning for people's needs in existing cities, especially in the inner city. Paradoxically they may nevertheless see themselves as social engineers when constructing new communities. There has been much criticism, particularly from the left, of the social effects and pretensions of town planning. In the post-war New Towns of the late 1940s planners sought to influence people's behaviour by means of the way they designed the environment. They rehoused people at high densities to engender a sense of community. More recently some have carried these ideas of environmental determinism (that is, seeking to influence and determine people's behaviour through the design and planning of the environment) to the inner city in seeking to reduce crime and vandalism by detailed design measures. Planners have often been criticised by those on the left for seeming naïvely to offer 'salvation by bricks', seeking to solve deep social problems through physical land use planning. It was argued that this would achieve only superficial change, typified as 'tinkering with the superstructure' (Bailey, 1975), as will be seen in Chapter 11. Many planners had no such delusions about the nature of town planning, knew its limitations, and never intended their plans to be seen in this light. They simply believed they had a valid contribution to make in organising the built environment, without having any aspirations to social engineering.

Critics of the efforts of town planners to improve society argue that the physical land use pattern of our cities is only the physical manifestation of deeper structural social and economic forces and inequalities, and that one must therefore change the system before one can change the city. Of course, this argument diminishes the importance of the built environment as a fact of life. People are not disembodied entities in a social and economic vacuum (Harvey, 1975: 24) but physical beings who live and work in buildings, and walk and/or drive to and from them, and who also need drains, sewers and water, and all the other services. Nor can one stop everything and plan for the millennium or 'wait until after the revolution' if the traffic is piling up, the city is grinding to a halt, local people urgently need local shops and better facilities, and others are homeless or living in sub-standard property meanwhile. Indeed, the built environment is not fixed but perpetually changing in response to social and economic forces (Hamnett *et al.*, 1989). Perhaps the ideal planning system is one which can solve urgent problems here and now whilst setting policies and goals for long-term change, in co-operation with other policy-making bodies responsible for the wider social and economic aspects of urban life.

Corporate manager?

The view of the planner as a co-ordinator with a generalised overview of a complex urban system emerged in the late 1960s (McLoughlin, 1969; Eversley, 1973). Local government reorganisation in 1974 provided the opportunity for planners to take on a new role within the corporate affairs of the local authority, but this role was not sustained in all cases, as a result of subsequent political, financial and organisational changes. More recently, in the private sector, planners have emerged as team leaders co-ordinating specialist experts such as ecologists, highway engineers and landscape architects. Moreover several leading housebuilders have given planners a high profile in their corporate structure. This overarching role, which transcends the conventional view of the town planner, may also be seen in countries where a great deal of new development is occurring, such as Australia, where there are stronger links between the town planning and landscape architecture professions, and where there is greater concern in general with the environmental and ecological aspects of development. In Eastern Europe the planner has had a traditional socialist role as decision-maker and city manager (albeit within a cumbersome political committee structure), particularly in countries where there was no private property market to speak of. This role may now be transformed in the reconstruction period to something more aligned with the corporate manager role, in view of the massive projects likely to be undertaken which will require the co-ordination of inputs from a range of specialists, and detailed local knowledge spanning the social, economic, physical and environmental realms.

Conclusion

Although planners may in the past have had high ambitions, delusions of grandeur even, of running the whole world, the reality is that much modern planning is a frustrating business of seeking to make a change here, an improvement there, as and when the opportunity arises, i.e. when developers apply for planning permission, or when government money is available for new schemes. The planners cannot just 'knock it down and start again': they have to work within the constraints of the existing urban structure and private land ownership. Their power to control and direct development is limited by the issue of whether their policies will stand up at a planning appeal: the fact that one scheme is ecologically better than another is not necessarily relevant. Most land and property is privately owned, and the planners' powers are limited to controlling rather than replacing the private sector by their professional activities. Money is no longer forthcoming for major government-led projects as was the case with the New Towns programme in the post-war period, when the planners had a more positive role in creating and designing development.

The role of the planner is seen as increasingly negative, as controlling the development of others, or as caretaker of existing urban areas rather than creator of new cities. The planner has some opportunities for a more direct role in the development process, in schemes undertaken jointly between the private sector and the local authority, in certain inner-city programmes, and increasingly in working directly in partnership with developers in the private sector. Nevertheless many planners still cherish a belief that one day they will be able to put their ideas into practice. In some local authorities still, especially those which see themselves as progressive, there is continuing emphasis on creative, proactive town planning, using all the legislative, political and managerial means available. There are also examples of ambitious town planning schemes being promoted by the private sector, both in Britain and overseas, for example for complete new towns, business complexes or leisure facilities, some of which undoubtedly incorporate a dimension of social awareness within the overall commercial framework.

PART II

The evolution of modern town planning

Chapter 4

Urbanisation and the industrial revolution

This section traces the development of town planning from the industrial revolution to the present day. It looks at the changes which occurred in the nineteenth century, which called forth the demand for town planning, concentrating on the overall themes. (For more detailed information see Ashworth, 1968; Burke, 1977; Mumford, 1965; Morris, 1972; Cherry, 1981, 1988; Ravetz, 1986; Hall, 1994.) It is important to study the roots of town planning in order to understand the factors which contributed to the form it takes today, and in order to place town planning in the wider context of the rise of state intervention. Many of the theories, ideas and even some of the legislation from these early days of British town planning are still influential today.

Whilst much of this section consists of an historical account, where appropriate, background material and basic concepts are incorporated on the social aspects of planning which also have a direct bearing on the subject at the present day. (Chapter 11 deals with the development of urban social theory.) Environmental factors are highlighted, but attitudes towards these issues at the time of the industrial revolution were somewhat different from what they are today. One could argue that industrialisation would have never happened had environmentalists had more influence then (although a few visionaries such as William Morris were already warning of the ecological effects). It is curious that those on the left in the nineteenth century, such as Marx, were quick to condemn capitalism and the oppression of the working class, but apparently had no argument with industrialisation, seeming unaware of the implications for the natural environment.

Physical change

At the beginning of the nineteenth century Britain was undergoing major economic and social change (Ashworth, 1968;

Briggs, 1968). There was already a long historical tradition of town planning (Burke, 1977; Mumford, 1965) dating back to the world of ancient Greece and Rome which had provided Western civilisation with the classical style of architecture and urban design (Chapter 8). Its influence is evidenced, for example, in the classical plan and architecture of such cities as Bath, which developed in the eighteenth century, and in the grand master plans of major capital cities of Europe, such as Rome, Paris and Berlin, with their magnificently laid out squares and ornate buildings. Town planning prior to the industrial revolution, compared with the modern day, was based in the main on quite narrow objectives, such as the creation of beautiful architectural set pieces. Nineteenth-century town planning was more down-to-earth in its concern with public health, sanitation and with meeting the functional requirements of industry and transport. Georgian town planning catered for different groups, mainly the upper and middle classes, as against nineteenth-century planning, which sought to meet the needs of the industrial working class, especially in respect of housing. The demand for town planning was called forth by a combination of the effects of three main factors, industrialisation, urbanisation and population growth, and the related problems of overcrowding and disease. The industrial revolution, as the term suggests, transformed Britain from a predominantly rural agricultural society to a modern industrial urban society (Ryder and Silver, 1990). Earlier changes in agricultural methods in the eighteenth century had led to greater yields with fewer farm labourers. In some areas the result was a surplus of workers, leading to migration to the towns, providing the necessary work force for the industrial revolution.

Industrialisation

Development of new forms of technology, in particular the invention of machinery which could produce manufactured goods more quickly than the human hand, led to major changes in the nature of work and the duties of the work force. Originally, for example, textiles had been produced by hand, by individual people sitting at their loom or spinning wheel in their own cottages. The introduction of mechanical forms of power which drove several machines at once required the assembly of many workers (called 'factors') and machines, such as the spinning jenny, all together in one building, which became known as a factory. At first industrial development occurred on a fairly small scale, fitting in among its surroundings with little disturbance, because the early woollen mills and factories were powered by water. The early industrial settlements were relatively rural, being alongside fast-flowing streams in hilly countryside.

Later coal was used to fuel steam engines which could power many more machines at once by means of drive belts running throughout the factory. New industrial settlements grew up alongside the coal mines, particularly in the north, the Midlands and South Wales. The emphasis shifted from the production of textiles in rural areas, to iron and steel, and then manufactured goods, in highly urbanised areas as a result of technological developments. These were aimed at the home market and at the expanding overseas markets which resulted from the growth of the British Empire in the nineteenth century. People flocked to the newly industrialising areas, resulting in rural depopulation and regional redistribution of the population, broadly from the south towards the north (the opposite of today) and across from the West Country to South Wales.

In the later stages of industrialisation other forms of power were developed which could be transmitted greater distances, such as gas and electricity. In theory anything could be developed anywhere, provided the financial backing was available (leading to the phenomenon of 'footloose' industry which went wherever was most economic). However, development was inevitably attracted to areas which had already established themselves as industrial centres, because they offered concentrations of skilled workers, the necessary infrastructure, the commercial expertise to help run the businesses and the markets needed to sell them. Nowadays access to transport routes for distribution purposes, especially the need to be near motorway junctions, or within prestigious motorway corridors such as the M4, is likely to be more important than being near sources of power because of the ubiquity of the national grid. Modern high-technology industries are so different in their education and skill requirements from those of the past that industrialists may find suitable personnel more likely to be drawn from the traditional office and 'quaternary' workers (see below) of the south and south-east (who, incidentally, are less unionised), than among the skilled and unskilled manual workers of the north and Midlands (Massey *et al.*, 1992).

The work force may be classified as follows. Primary workers are those engaged in basic industries such as agriculture, mining, heavy industry. Secondary workers are those involved in manu-facturing. Tertiary workers are those involved in office work and service industry. Increasingly nowadays a further category is recognised, namely quaternary workers, those involved in research and development, higher professional work and the creation of knowledge (basically the thinkers and innovators). One can see a gradual progression over the last two centuries from an emphasis on primary workers as the key sector, across the other categories, until today quaternary workers are regarded as the prime sector for the future. Nowadays one also comes across the phrase (from America) 'blue-collar workers' (factory and manual) as against 'white-collar' non-manual office and managerial workers (and even 'pink-collar workers' for women office workers). The industrial revolution occurred over 150 years ago, and the class and occupation definitions developed at that time are barely appropriate to today's situation, although they are fossilised in traditional sociological theory.

The transport revolution

Not only had the goods to be produced, they had to be transported to their markets within Britain or overseas. In the late eighteenth century the turnpike road system developed, serving the early years of the industrial revolution around the turn of the century, but it proved an expensive and bumpy way of transporting manufactured goods, and bulky or heavy freight called forth the development of the canal system, which was backed especially by the Staffordshire pottery manufacturers. Although at their height waterways provided an extensive network connecting the main industrial centres, markets and ports, they were soon overshadowed by the development of the railway system. Nowadays the canals provide a valuable environmental asset which is painstakingly being restored in many parts of the country, only latterly with any government support. The railways developed as a result of the invention of the high-pressure locomotive (mobile) steam engine. (Horse-drawn rail transport had been used only to a very limited extent in coal-mining areas.) The first main passenger railway was the Liverpool & Manchester, opened in 1830. Growth continued, until in the 1870s there were nearly 16 000 miles of railway.

In the nineteenth century Britain was a major maritime and trading power, and this inevitably affected the settlement pattern and nature of urbanisation at home. The technological changes did not occur in a vacuum. Raw materials and ready markets were provided by the territories comprising the empire. New docks became an important form of development, as can be seen today in London, Liverpool or Bristol. Britain had always been a maritime nation and there was already a vast amount of trade in exotic goods, including the infamous triangle of trade in sugar and slaves between Africa, the West Indies and Europe, involving ports such as Bristol long before the industrial revolution. Nowadays it is hard to remember that the London dockland with its marinas and up-market housing was once a warehousing area with extensive working-class housing alongside the docks.

Urbanisation

The growth of industrialisation was accompanied by the growth of towns and cities, and also by population growth (Table 4.1). Table 4.2 shows the tremendous rate of urban growth which was occurring in the new industrial towns and cities, which were doubling and tripling in size. Whilst there was overall growth, there were also, as mentioned, large movements of population from one part of the country to another, both on a regional basis and as migration to the towns from the countryside. This may be summed up briefly: in 1801 80 per cent of the population was rural; by 1991 80 per cent of the population is urban. In 1811 the population of London was 1 million, in 1910 it was 7 million and by 1991 it had declined by over a million.

Not only were there changes in the number of people in the towns and cities but, inevitably, there was a decline in the quality of their lives due to disease and overcrowding (Ravetz, 1986). Conditions were not very different from those in rural areas at the time, but people could get away with fairly

Table 4.1 Population of England and Wales, 1801–1901 (million)

Year	Total population
1801	8·9
1851	17·9
1901	32·5

See Ashworth (1968: 7) for fuller details.

Table 4.2 Urban growth, 1801–1901

	Population		
Year	Birmingham	Manchester	Leeds
1801	71 000	75 000	53 000
1851	265 000	336 000	172 000
1901	765 000	645 000	429 000

See Ashworth (1968) for fuller details of many towns.

elementary methods of sewage disposal in villages, whereas the sheer concentration of numbers in the new cities increased the likelihood of disease developing in the crowded alleyways and tenements. Such problems could not be solved by individual personal efforts but required civic initiatives and national solutions.

How bad was it?

Not everyone was suffering and living in poor conditions as a result of the industrial revolution. Sometimes it seems as if the evils of the past are overstressed to legitimate the increased (and questionable) powers of the planners today, or to give a misleading impression of continuous progress. It is false to suggest that the entire population worked in factories, lived in the north and suffered from poor housing. Some of the literature creates images of everyone wearing cloth caps, clogs and shawls and scurrying off to the mill in the morning from small terraced houses. It may have been true in parts of the north of England, but in fact conditions varied considerably according to people's social class and the region in which they lived.

Relatively speaking, there was an increase in overall national prosperity. There was a tremendous amount of building of commercial premises, of town halls, libraries and the beginnings of modern high-street development, with rows of individual shops and early department stores, all these buildings together creating the foundations of the modern Central Business District. The Victorians also invested heavily under the streets in the form of sewers and drains as a result of public health reforms. As will be seen, by the end of the century the city fathers (Bell and Bell, 1972), having made their pile, could sit back and distribute their bounty in the form of public works. Civic pride and public buildings went hand-in-hand with reform, which often took the form of 'gas and water socialism', that is, investment in public works to build the urban infrastructure. Whilst there is still much criticism of this period it must be remembered that many towns are still dependent on Victorian sewers, and that the Victorians left an immeasurable heritage of public investment which has not been continued into the present day despite increased state intervention and national wealth. There was also emphasis on the building of town parks and playing fields, nowadays often seen as a luxury by developers and local authorities alike. Many are in danger from redevelopment, located as they often are in what are today central sites with high land values.

Likewise not all residential development consisted of sub-standard working-class housing and slum properties. The nineteenth century saw a massive amount of house building, and it included the middle-class villas, town houses and substantial terraces which still occupy large tracts of our cities. There were also large areas of good-quality skilled artisan and respectable working-class housing consisting of miles of little terraced houses built on a grid layout. Much of it remains ideal housing stock even today. The problems of the time arose chiefly where large numbers of working-class people were concentrated in poorly built housing around the new factories and mills. They were located there because at the beginning of the industrial revolution there was very little money or time for commuting and the transport systems had not yet developed, so people were huddled together in proximity to their workplace. At first it was a matter of converting existing housing. For example, larger inner-city town houses were subdivided; in some cases whole families were living in one room, and some even in cellars (Ashworth, 1968). Some factory owners provided cheap housing for the workers, although they might deduct the cost from their wages: the philanthropic (literally 'lovers of mankind') reforming factory owners were the exception to the rule.

Many local builders cashed in, building sub-standard tenements and terraces which were 'jerry-built' (the phrase apparently deriving from the reputation of a particularly bad builder of that name). Houses were often 'half a brick thick' (i.e. with thin, sub-standard walls) and back-to-back: a terrace would contain twice as many dwellings because the houses were divided at the ridge of the roof, creating two rows, one facing the street, the other the back alley.

Suburbanisation and transport

For centuries, cities had been relatively close-knit because their extent and the distance between different land uses or amenities was governed by the distance which people could comfortably walk. With the introduction of mechanical means of transport, people could travel further and more quickly, and cities began to spread out horizontally. With the development of the railway system, those who were more affluent moved further out and commuted in, starting the trend to suburbanisation and decentralisation which has been such a feature of urban development in Britain over the last 150 years. Many small towns owed their prosperity to the railways. Some were more directly involved as major interchange points on the network, e.g. Crewe, or as the site of railway works, e.g. Swindon. The railways were not nationalised and unified until the mid-twentieth century, and so considerable variety of architecture developed, each company having its own style, as in the case of the well-conserved railway village at Swindon.

Tramway systems contributed even more to decentralisation, especially after electrification near the end of the century. (In Britain they were gone by the middle of the twentieth century, but many European cities still have them.) The bicycle became popular in the late nineteenth century and is enjoying a come-back today. With the invention of the internal combustion engine, public transport was augmented by omnibuses, which were not limited to a fixed track like trains or trams and could go anywhere. Buses, and of course the subsequent development of the private motor car, led to a veritable explosion of suburbanisation, for, provided there were roads, people could for the first time in history travel anywhere they wanted at considerable speed. These changes in transport technology further encouraged cities to grow and to segment into distinct land use zonings, with a tendency in particular for the industrial and residential (the work and the home) areas to separate out. At the same time the traditional Central Business District, that is, the centre with all the offices, shops and civic buildings, remained pivotal, expanding and acquiring increased importance in servicing the needs of trade and finance which had expanded as a result of the industrial revolution.

The logical conclusion in order to create maximum efficiency was to abandon the traditional radial concentric form of cities and build linear developments along the main routes, with concentrations of housing preferably located at relatively high density, clustering around each railway station or tramway route. It was important to have enough people living close by, within walking distance. This led to various theories developing in Europe. For example, Arturo Soria y Mata suggested the concept of the linear city. He visualised it stretching right across Europe from Cadiz in the south of Spain to St Petersburg in the north-west of Russia (Hall, 1994)! The linear form could be joined up to form a circular 'ring' city, or turned in on itself as a figure-of-eight, as in Runcorn New Town plan in the 1960s. Soria y Mata succeeded in building only a few kilometres outside Madrid (Hall, 1994).

The motor car gave much greater flexibility anywhere there were roads. As car ownership grew, public transport receded. Nowadays people without cars in some districts are probably worse-off in terms of transport than their forebears were in the nineteenth century. The motor car caught on early in the United States, even among people of relatively low income, thanks to the mass production methods of Henry Ford. Frank Lloyd Wright (1869–1959), an American architect, developed the idea of a city planned entirely for the motor car, 'Autopia', as proposed for Broadacre City in the 1930s. It was to be based on a very low-density grid, every house being like a homestead with a one-acre plot on which the residents would grow their own food. The settlement would have had no centre in the traditional sense, but districts would focus on the petrol station. His vision is what some American cities actually became like, such as Los Angeles, where everybody drives rather than walks. Those who have no car, e.g. the poor, or are unable to drive, such as the young and the old, are at a severe disadvantage, and have to depend on limited public transport or the goodwill of others.

Rural and regional perspectives

As a result of the development of the railways Britain 'shrank'. It was now much easier to travel, and few areas were remote from a railway station. Indeed, the urban–rural division was rapidly breaking down. Moreover some of the industrial settlements, whilst appearing very urbanised and concentrated around the mill or mine, were in fact near the countryside. In the Welsh valleys or parts of Derbyshire a short walk takes one out of the industrial environment and into the open country. The effects of industrial activity, especially mining, encroached to some extent, spewing out slag heaps and pollution, leaving an extensive burden of industrial dereliction. Such land is still being reclaimed, for example by the Welsh Development Agency in South Wales, and as part of projects such as the Garden Festival at Ebbw Vale in 1992. The situation was very different in the south of England, where a good deal of manufacturing industry developed within inner-city areas, often as back-street businesses in erstwhile residential districts. Many houses on main roads were converted into shops or business premises. One can from the top of a double-decker bus see clearly that the shop fronts have been added. Urban development seemed to spread out, on and on, in all directions, with hardly a break, for mile after mile in London. In fact some of the most industrialised, urbanised, as well as commercialised, areas were in the south, in the inner London boroughs with large working-class populations to match. In the south the office and commercial revolution followed hard on the heels of the industrial revolution, creating a new 'proletariat' made up of clerks, typists, service industry workers and shop-keepers who were often mistakenly perceived as middle-class (or 'petty-bourgeois') and unworthy of special attention, in spite of their low incomes and poor working conditions. Many would argue that the emphasis in regional economic planning policy of the 1960s, which favoured the 'depressed' northern areas, was actually at the expense of these other groups of working people in inner urban areas in southern towns. Some would argue that this was a contributory factor to the decline of the inner city today, in which high levels of unemployment and poverty persist (as will be seen in later chapters).

Social change and land use patterns

The parameters

Not only were the settlement pattern and the nature of cities changed as a result of the industrial revolution, there were also major changes taking place in the nature of urban society itself and in the patterns of daily life. The changes which occurred in the nature of social class divisions, the family, and community, and the relationship between home and work in people's daily lives will now be examined: all were to be manifested in the layout and zoning of towns and cities. The aim in this chapter is simply to introduce some of the basic concepts and definitions; the theoretical development of urban social studies will be dealt with in Chapter 11, but relevant reading includes Ryder and Silver (1990), Joseph (1988), Haralambos (1990) and Hurd (1990).

Particular emphasis will be put upon the dimensions of class and gender, because these are two of the main divisions in society running through the last 200 years of urbanisation. The former has long been an integral consideration in urban studies, whereas the latter has been given increasing emphasis in recent years, probably because so many more women are now going into the urban professions, and it has become highly topical. For clarification, 'gender' is normally taken to mean the social role of women in different cultures – for example, in our society it is normally expected that women are the ones who care for children and do the housework (although women have other gender roles in other societies). This is in contrast to 'sex', which is taken to mean the biological characteristics of women; for example, in all societies only women give birth to children but the gender role of caring for them may differ somewhat between societies, and indeed between social classes. 'Class' is also a complex word to define. A typical twentieth-century definition of a social class is 'a number of persons sharing a common social position in the economic order' (Chinoy, 1967). Strictly speaking, therefore, it refers to people's occupation, and thus their socio-economic standing. However, it has all sorts of other meanings, especially social ones as to an individual's worth, accent and life style. For the purposes of this chapter 'class' should be taken in the common sense of meaning people's social position in terms of their work and way of life.

Class, past and present

As a result of the industrial revolution the structure of society changed. New class divisions and occupations emerged as a result of new technological inventions and changes in the wider economy. In the traditional rural society of the past, a relatively static feudal system existed, the inhabitants of a typical village consisting of the landowner and the peasants, with possibly a vicar and just a few skilled tradespeople in the middle, but without an intermediate middle class or large numbers of working-class people employed in factories rather than on the land. People had no social class as such but, rather, were born to a certain status which governed all human relationships. The static and deferential nature of pre-industrial social attitudes is summed up in the anonymous ditty:

> God bless the squire and his relations,
> And keep us in our proper stations

With the coming of the industrial revolution the whole social structure was transformed as large numbers of people moved from the villages and set up home in the new industrial cities, swelling the ranks of the new working classes. It now became acceptable to classify people in terms of their work rather than what they were born as, i.e. class definition was based on what they did, especially their occupation, rather than on status, which would relate to who their father was or which end of the village they came from. Most noticeable was the development of a new industrial working class, or rather we should say classes, as they were many and varied. However, it should be remembered that, in spite of all these social changes, a small minority continued to own the bulk of the wealth and the land (Norton-Taylor, 1982).

There are many theories about the nature of classes (Chapter 11). If you ask a sociologist, 'What is class and how is it defined?' you will get as many different answers as there are sociologists! In fact there are major problems as to the question of what factors should be taken into account. Therefore a short digression is in order at this point, to explain modern classifications. If the sociologists cannot decide, the statisticians, planners and market researchers have to, in order to survey people. The following scale of social classes corresponds to many people's 'common sense' idea of class and is quite widely used, although strictly speaking the categories are measures of occupational category rather than class as such. The Registrar General (the official responsible for the census) divides the population into six socio-economic groupings which broadly correspond to the sociological idea of social classes. The question of who exactly goes into each category, i.e. how different jobs are defined, is established by the *Standard Occupational Classification* published by the Registrar General (OPCS, 1995), which contains lists of hundreds of commonplace and obscure occupations, and makes fascinating reading.

Table 4.3 Socio economic groupings

I	Higher professional and managerial
II	Lower professional and managerial
IIIN	Supervisory and lower/routine non-manual
IIIM	Skilled manual
IV	Semi-skilled manual
V	Unskilled manual

N means non-manual, M manual.

Market researchers use the same occupational classification as the Registrar General, but mix them in slightly different ways into order to produce different socio-economic groups. In particular they want groupings which suggest a certain level of income (and therefore purchasing power) rather than just occupation. One of the most commonly used scales is the Social Grading Scale. This classification is frequently used by property market researchers, for example in establishing the likely demand for and turnover of a new shopping development. The scale was devised by National Opinion Polls. It runs from A to E. A, B and CI and CII correspond to I, II, IIIN and IIIM above, with class D covering IV and V. A sixth class, E, is used for the unemployed, pensioners, housewives not in paid employment and the permanently sick or disabled. This scale is therefore more concerned with spending power than with social class. NOP Market Research Ltd define the classes as follows in Table 4.4, opposite.

From a feminist viewpoint (that is, from a viewpoint which stresses women's perspective) there has been much criticism of the fact that in many of these official scales it is often assumed that the occupation of the head of the household, i.e. the

Table 4.4 Social Grading Scale

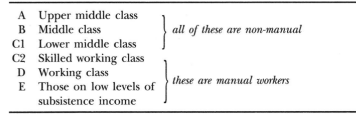

A	Upper middle class	
B	Middle class	*all of these are non-manual*
C1	Lower middle class	
C2	Skilled working class	
D	Working class	*these are manual workers*
E	Those on low levels of subsistence income	

husband, is representative of the whole family, when many women have their own jobs, and will have different needs, interests and levels of personal spending power from their husband's. Also, many grown-up children are upwardly mobile and have a higher social class than their parents. It is interesting that, at last, the 1991 census form actually asked the occupation of all the adult members of each household and not just of the 'head' of the household. This approach to defining class has created some strange anomolies, particularly in respect of so-called cross-class families where, typically, the husband is in a skilled manual job and the wife is in an apparently middle-class office job. Some traditional sociologists and market researchers continue to use the inaccurate 'head of household' type classification. When using statistical sources it is important to ascertain first of all what particular classification the data are based upon (Goldthorpe, 1980; Crompton and Sanderson, 1990). Even if women are graded separately, the main occupational classifications given above are based primarily on men's jobs. The *Surrey Occupational Class Scale* was developed to allow for women's occupations as well as those of men (Arber *et al.*, 1986; Abbott and Wallace, 1990). It goes as follows. Note that categories IV and VI contain the bulk of women's occupations.

Table 4.5 Surrey occupational class scale

I	Higher professional
II	Employers and managers
III	Lower professional
IV	Secretarial and clerical
V	Foremen and self-employed manual workers
VI	Shop and personal service workers
VII	Skilled manual workers
VIII	Semi-skilled manual workers
IX	Unskilled manual workers
X	Unemployed and non-employed.

Class and gender

Whilst male factory employment was the largest growing sector in the nineteenth century, in the late twentieth professional, office and service industry employment has been the largest growing sector, with large numbers of women entering the office sector in particular (Greed, 1994). Unfortunately many planners seem unaware of the implications of the change and are still developing their economic strategy and development plans on the basis of male employment and male land use and activity patterns only (Grieco *et al.*, 1989). Indeed, class definitions did not 'work' for women even in the nineteenth century. As Tannahill (1989: 346–7) has pointed out, of the 16 million male and female inhabitants of England and Wales recorded by the 1841 census a little under a million were in domestic service. Ten years later, of the 3 million women and girls aged ten or over who worked for a living, 751 641 (one in four) were domestic servants. By 1871 the figure had risen to 1 204 477, showing a rate of increase double that of the population as a whole. Throughout the nineteenth century, and indeed until 1914, domestic service was the largest single source of employment for English women, and the second largest overall.

Relationship between work and home

As a result of the industrial revolution, changes occurred not only in the range of occupations, and related class structure, but in the nature of work itself, with more people working outside the home. Rather than staying in their own workshop or home, as in the traditional craft industries – e.g. weavers living and working in cottages with large windows up in the weaving loft to let in maximum light on to the loom (as can be seen in the buildings even today) – workers were concentrated with the machines in one place, the factory, which people had to attend for set hours every day. In contrast the traditional agricultural worker's life was governed by the seasons, and by the length of daylight. Women's activities had not been divided rigidly between household tasks and going out to work, indeed many forms of employment which were eventually industrialised, such as weaving, were originally carried on at home along with everything else, such as cooking and child care. The factories, dependent on the same sources of power to drive the machines, were often clustered together, creating distinct factory zones, with the housing huddled around them. In time the early planners sought to segregate the land uses, creating separate industrial and residential areas, which, as we noted, tended more and more to be located further and further away from the workplace.

As increasing numbers of women took up work in factories and went out to work like the men, and domestic service declined, they too were affected by these land use trends. All this tended to segregate women's lives, for the zoning, whilst hygienic and efficient, made it difficult to combine work and home, and was scarcely ideal for men, either. Indeed, the approach to early town planning reinforced the fact that society itself was defined and structured in relation to work, creating a mono-dimensional existence, compared with the traditional rural community, where work had been constrained by the seasons, by religious festivals, or by the individual's ability to control its pace.

Family structure

Changes occurred in family structure, which indeed is still evolving to the present day. The traditional pre-industrial rural family was fairly large by modern standards. Most British people nowadays are brought up in a 'nuclear' family, consisting of the basic nucleus of the wife, husband and their immediate offspring, classically 2·4 children on average. This concept may be based as much on myth as on statistical reality, since the situation has changed rapidly in recent years (Hamnett *et al.*, 1989). In pre-industrial societies, as in Third World agricultural societies today, families were more likely to be extended families, consisting of the nucleus of parents and children but, vertically, also including grandparents and grandchildren, and, horizontally, perhaps also uncles and aunts, nephews and cousins, all sharing the same dwelling. Indeed, the borderline between the extended family and the concept of the tribe, and of the village in which everyone is related to everyone else, is only a matter of degree.

During the industrial revolution it was generally younger couples who moved to the new industrial towns and cities, leaving the older people behind, although sometimes sending money back to support them. Birth rates were suprisingly high in the new industrial towns, despite the restricted size of the housing, which consisted typically of two-up-and-two-down terraced houses, and high infant mortality levels, for many families of six or more (Whitelegg *et al.*, 1982; Lewis, 1984). As time went on families became smaller, and paradoxically housing for the working classes became somewhat larger. Nowadays it would seem that there is a trend towards more flexible forms of accommodation for the increasing number of single-person households, which may consist of the widowed elderly, the divorced, single-parent families or young people leaving home to set up on their own. Size, structure and rate of household formation all have implications for the nature of housing design, and ultimately affect the layout of towns and cities.

Conclusion

Nowadays the local planning authority needs to be aware of such demographic changes in deciding how much land is going to be needed for new residential development. Of course, other factors such as class, and ability to pay, come into it as well, as does the fact that, although we do not have the same rate of population growth as in the past, nevertheless many people require more privacy and higher standards of housing, which also create a demand for more. Also regional movements of population, especially to the south-east, are going to increase the demand for housing in some areas, even while property may be left unsold and vacant in less prosperous parts of the country. Of the 18 million dwellings in Britain, it is estimated, about a million will be vacant at any one time because of the above factors, not forgetting, of course, that substantially more may be between owners in the process of conveyancing.

Chapter 5

Reaction and reform

The purpose of this chapter is to look at the beginnings of modern town planning. First, the reforming legislation will be described. The early reforms simply sought to deal with the worst effects of disease, overcrowding and slum development, and had much in common with the 'sites and services' approach adopted in Third World cities today: dealing with the absolute basics of sewerage and drainage. Later the emphasis moved from this, albeit necessarily, negative controlling approach to seeking to create, more positively, whole new ways of living. In the second part of the chapter examples will be discussed of the model communities which were put forward by visionaries and philanthropists, including the concept of the Garden City which was to have such a major influence on twentieth-century town planning. This theme, of the visionary founding fathers of town planning, is developed further in the next chapter, in which the ideas of the architect Le Corbusier will be discussed, because he is seen as an integral part of the twentieth-century modern movement.

Why did the town planning movement first arise? Some would argue that the growth of state intervention in the urban environment, and model settlement building were obviously the result of an altruistic concern for social welfare, aimed at reducing the worst effects of highly competitive private enterprise and 'Victorian values'. Others would see the aim as more utilitarian: 'to oil the wheels of capitalism', that is, to provide an efficient, well-ordered urban infrastructure for business, and to quell discontent and the possibility of revolution. A significant number of the reformers were from a Quaker or Nonconformist background and were motivated by social conscience and religious vocation (Tawney, 1969). They depended on their personal wealth rather than public position to get their schemes built, some nearly bankrupting themselves in the process.

Whatever the motives of the reformers and model community builders, it was generally accepted in society that something had to be done. The spread of cholera and other waterborne diseases made intervention necessary, there being two major outbreaks in 1832 and 1849. Because cholera was a waterborne disease, which was no respecter of persons, although it might originate in working-class districts it could spread anywhere along the insanitary water systems of the city. As Peter Hall points out (1994: 18), in 1854 a Dr Snow showed the relationship between a major cholera outbreak and a single polluted pump in the Soho district of London. Increased state intervention to provide sewerage and drainage systems was needed (Briggs, 1968: Cherry, 1988).

Legislative reforms

Local government reform

To implement these reforms there was a need for an effective administrative structure. The Municipal Corporations Act, 1835, laid the foundations for this, enabling the creation of locally elected urban councils, i.e. local authorities, which had the power to levy rates on householders and businesses, and to use the money to employ professional and administrative staff in order to carry out improvements and building programmes (Macey and Baker, 1983; Smith, 1989). All this seems exemplary on paper, but there have been many criticisms of the growth of bureaucracy and the insensitivity of the local government fraternity, which from its inception has fostered a top-down paternalist form of government, rather than more co-operative, grass-roots approaches, with greater participation by those on the receiving end, the consumers of urban goods and services. The residents may feel the services are not run as they would like and they have very little control over what the benevolent state has decided is good for them. But, as will be seen in this book, this governmental approach was only one means of dealing with the problems, as there were also many individuals and voluntary bodies seeking to tackle the problems, carrying out improvements, and even building modern communities themselves. Others would argue that the community needs professional services and that they should be valued at the going rate.

Public health

State intervention and provision became more acceptable (especially because of the need to establish a city-wide drainage programme to stamp out diseases such as cholera, as mentioned above). In 1840 a select committee, headed by Edwin Chadwick, on conditions in the towns had been established, leading to the *Report on the sanitary conditions of the labouring population* and *the means of its improvement* in 1842. In 1843 this was followed by the establishment of a Royal Commission on the Health of Towns, and the Health of Towns Association was founded. The Sanitary Act, 1847, required sewers and drains to be provided in all new residential areas. The Public Health Act, 1848, went further, being one of the first Acts intervening in *how* houses were constructed, and therefore potentially added to the cost for the developers. This Act required that all ceilings must be at least 8 ft high (nowadays ceilings need to be slightly less than this, about 7 ft 6 in., or 2·3 m). At that time some ceilings were scarcely 6 ft high. Low ceilings had health implications, as they reduced the likelihood of light penetrating the building, and reduced the circulation of air, leading, it was thought, to germs and diseases lurking in the dark corners of badly ventilated rooms. It was in the interests of industrialists to go along with these reforms, for if too many people fell ill there would not be enough workers for their factories.

Many owners of property (especially the landlords of sub-standard property) resented the general trend of such legislation, as it went against the centuries-old principle enshrined in private real property law that a man had a right to do what he wanted with his own land, and that an Englishman's home was his castle. The growth of the public health movement, and the mixed reaction it received, reflect another fundamental unresolved dualism in the development of the town planning movement itself, namely the inevitable tension in trying to solve what are essentially social problems, especially those of poverty, by imposing physical standards on the built environment. No doubt if people had had adequate wages in the first place they would have not had to live in sub-standard housing. In fact town planning itself has frequently been condemned for seeking to deal with the effect rather than the cause of urban problems, and on emphasising control rather than the solution to problems, whether it be public health problems in the last century or traffic problems at the present day.

Whilst the public health movement may be seen as providing a valuable input to the development of the modern town planning movement, it may be argued that the division of powers which evolved in the nineteenth century, and further developed within the structure of local government in the twentieth century, between the functions of town planning and public health departments (generally renamed 'environmental health' department) has not been helpful. For example, town planners retain considerable control over the 'outside' in controlling the design and layout of the built environment, but have little control over the design of the 'inside' of the built environment. This issue has been of particular concern to those seeking to obtain better access, and amenity provision within buildings, for groups such as the disabled, the elderly, and those reponsible for baby and childcare (Greed, 1994). The nature of the division of powers among and between the various professional and regulatory bodies responsible for the control of the built environment is still a key factor in determining whether a modern planning authority has the legal right to impose some design requirement upon a developer (as discussed in Volume II within the context of achieving policy implementation). Ironically the ground rules were established by nineteenth century public health legislation, at a time when both society and cities were very different from today.

A digression into housing

The government was concerned with conditions inside existing houses, as well as with the construction of new dwellings. Prior to the First World War, around 90 per cent of people rented the house they lived in (Merrett, 1979). Many of the newcomers to the industrial towns scarcely even achieved this, and would live in lodging houses, and other forms of temporary accommodation, until they had established themselves and were able to rent a terraced house. In 1851 the Common Lodging Houses Act and the Labouring Classes Lodging Houses Act were passed, under the sponsorship of Lord Shaftesbury, enabling the inspection and better provision of lodging houses. From the beginning the development of town planning and housing management go hand-in-hand. The Artisans' and Labourers' Dwellings Improvements Act, 1868 (the Torrens Act), increased further government controls, being followed by other Acts of the same name in 1875 and 1879, which increased powers in dealing with insanitary buildings (Ashworth, 1968).

Note that all this was done in the name of public health, and was chiefly aimed at the working classes (Smith, 1989). It was considered politically unacceptable to control the design of middle-class housing – indeed, it was not necessary, with high ceilings and large rooms, although the sanitation often left much to be desired (Rubenstein, 1974). Nevertheless these early Acts paved the way for later, wider controls over all classes of housing and types of land use by means of town planning. There were some limited controls on middle-class housing, and commercial buildings already in London that had existed ever since the Great Fire in 1666. Also private restrictive covenants were widespread in 'good' residential areas, being intended to preserve the tone of the neighbourhood by, for example, preventing the conversion of houses into shops, the redevelopment of gardens (which would increase the density), or the keeping of pigs or poultry. By the end of the century many of the larger northern cities such as Manchester, Liverpool and Newcastle had also increased their controls on urban development, by means of private Acts of Parliament, before the main national town planning Acts of the early twentieth century had come into being. The importance of well-laid-out cities and town planning was widely accepted as a boost to commerce and a benefit to the citizens.

Government initiatives were augmented by a wide range of private reforming endeavours. There were already a number of early housing societies concerned with improving the conditions of the working classes. One of the best known and most productive was the Peabody Trust, set up in 1862 by George Peabody, an American philanthropist. Many of his buildings can still be seen today in areas of London such as Islington, Whitechapel, Vauxhall and Bethnal Green, and most of these are in the style of walk-up tenements. There were other schemes, many of which were based on sound commercial principles, in that subscribers received what was then a reasonable rate of interest on their investment: '5 per cent philanthropy'. Many of these structures look grim by today's standards, but they were better than existing alternatives.

Attitudes towards the nature of housing provision for the working classes had come a long way from the poor-law philosophy of the beginning of the century, which actively discouraged and punished people for seeking help. Official attitudes were strongly influenced by the theories of Malthus (1798), who took the rather unenlightened view that overpopulation was caused by the poor themselves. He suggested that nothing should be done to ease the conditions of the poor, as this would only cause them to 'breed' faster and thus make the problem worse. (The fact that poverty was more often caused by low wages or unemployment, or that rich men often had many children in Victorian times and did not become poor as a result, was not considered.) Ever since the 1662 Law of Settlement and Removal Act ('an Act for the better relief of the poor of this kingdom') homeless 'sturdy beggars' had been seen as a burden on the parish. The problem became greater with the movement of people generated by the industrial revolution, and also with more people being pushed off the land as a result of modern farming methods, this being reinforced by the various enclosure Acts such as that of 1801. In 1832 the Royal Commission on the Poor Law investigated the whole situation, resulting in the Poor Law Amendment Act, 1834, which actually reduced the level of help in spite of growing demand. In order to reduce the numbers looking to the parish for relief (help) the view was taken that conditions should be so harsh in the workhouses that people would see admission as only a last resort. This attitude still pervades certain aspects of council housing provision, and the housing benefit system, even today, and is a million miles away from the value systems underpinning the creation of the garden cities and the development of the modern town planning system, in which people were more likely to be seen as having a right to good housing.

Later developments

The year 1875 was a landmark in the development of state intervention into the built environment. Several important Acts were passed. The Artisans' and Labourers' Dwellings Improvement Act increased local authority powers to deal with whole areas, as against individual buildings, giving them compulsory purchase powers, and the power to build schemes which provided accommodation for the working classes – this being a major step towards the modern-day powers of local authorities to carry out compulsory purchase and to take control of the building of an area themselves. The Public Health Act, 1875, was also a major landmark and set minimum standards for the design of houses and also for the layout of streets, so it was in a sense one of the first true town planning Acts. This was achieved by giving local authorities the power to introduce by-laws themselves, controlling the layout of new streets and housing schemes. It required that every house should have rear access, which was meant to solve the problem of back-to-back houses, which shared a common party wall. To summarise, in these Acts the three functions of local authorities were to clear existing areas, to build themselves, and to control the development of others.

Normally, under the by-law regulations, the width of the street had to be at least the same dimension as the height of the buildings' front wall up to the eaves. Surprisingly this created, incidentally, a rather enclosed, reassuringly human scale in such areas. This sense of human scale in residential areas was lost with the introduction of much wider streets to make way for the motor car and more generous front gardens in housing estates in the early twentieth century. In 1890 the Housing of the Working Classes Act increased local authorities' power to build new houses themselves, thus creating an early form of council housing. By this time developers were losing interest in building cheap housing for the working classes to rent, and turning their attention to the more affluent emerging owner-occupied middle-class suburban housing developments. Council housing was to go on to become a major feature of our towns and cities in the twentieth century. It is only since the 1980s that this sector has been in decline, following various negative housing Acts, and a push towards owner occupation, which has now reached around 70 per cent (Malpass and Murie, 1990). Up to 1909 only 10 per cent of people owned their own house, and most of these were upper middle-class people. Many perfectly respectable middle-class people rented their housing, as is still the case to a greater degree in other European countries today.

Model communities

Private initiatives

Legislation was one major response to the problems of the nineteenth century, but there was also a strong emphasis on individuals seeking to carry out their own reforms, in particular various factory owners, often of a Quaker, Nonconformist or socialist persuasion, who tried out experiments to change society at their own expense. Whilst some critics would accuse them of being paternalistic in their approach (like the welfare state today?), others would argue that they did not have to do it – there was actually a surplus of workers and high unemployment during much of the nineteenth century – and that they were operating on the best of intentions and a sense of public duty. However, some may have been motivated by more businesslike, 'utilitarian' principles, which may be summed up in the principle that happy workers are good workers and loyal to the firm. There are parallels with the situation in Japanese firms today, many of which provide accommodation and lifelong provision for their workers.

Whatever the motives behind them, such initiatives were brave experiments which contributed to the development of town planning. Unlike some modern town planners, many of the ideas of such reformers were not limited to space alone but comprised social, economic and political plans for the whole of society. It is interesting that, whilst some of their physical land use planning ideas were carried through as the basis of twentieth-century town planning, other aspects were completely forgotten or dismissed as cranky, too political or too religious, as will be seen in due course. In this chapter the earlier examples are to be discussed, and in the next those which were built at the turn of the century under the influence of the Garden City movement (Cherry, 1981, 1988; RTPI, 1986).

New Lanark

Robert Owen (1771–1858) was one of the earliest 'town planners' and an early socialist who had many new ideas, and tried them out, in respect of just about every aspect of human society, including education, housing, health, trade unionism and even birth control. Like many of the reformers, Owen came from humble origins. From working in a draper's he rose to be manager of a Lancashire cotton mill, and then married the daughter of David Dale, the owner of the New Lanark Mills in Scotland. New Lanark was already a self-contained and planned industrial village when Owen arrived, the first buildings having been completed in 1786, and by 1790 the population had reached 2000. In 1800 the mills were taken over by Robert Owen from David Dale, who had set up the original scheme. During the next twenty-five years Owen developed his schemes for community living and education. The Institution for the Formation of Character was established, which significantly included nursery schooling, and adult education, as well as training for children. The town also included Britain's first co-operative store. However, the housing was provided in the form of tenements, with minimal plumbing, shared kitchens and communal lavatories. It was all rather grim by today's standards, and somewhat regimented, with regular inspections of the dwellings being undertaken by Owen himself, to look for bedbugs. New Lanark was set in a narrow valley along a fast-flowing stream which provided water power to run the machinery. New Lanark is not really very industrial to look at. Owen wanted to spread his ideas by setting up 'villages of co-operation'. In fact there were several Owenite communities set up by his followers, both in Britain and in North America, such as New Harmony in Indiana. Also he wrote *New view of society* in 1813 and *Report to the county of Lanark* in 1821, and his ideas spread widely. Indeed, when Ebenezer Howard visited the United States he was influenced by the Owenite communities, as also by the wide range of religious communities such as Salt Lake City and the various Mennonite communities founded in the land of freedom which sought to create heaven on earth (Hayden, 1976).

The Bradford–Halifax school

A second flowering of the model towns movement occurred in this era of rapid industrialisation. Colonel Akroyd, a rich mill owner, built two model communties, the first at Copley in 1849, the second at Akroydon in 1859. George Gilbert Scott, the great Victorian architect, was employed to design Akroydon, which consisted of modest terraced and town houses for the workers, with the family hall of the Akroyds set on a hillside above, so that Akroyd could look down and see his experiment at work (a common Victorian predilection). This model community is now surrounded by subsequent suburban development, and does not look particularly special, but at the time the layout and design were seen as quite innovative.

Akroyd did not want his workers to remain tied to him, and, along with other fellow philanthropic factory owners in the Halifax area, pioneered the concept of home ownership for his workers, establishing the Halifax Building Society in 1845; at the same time many workers who were renting their properties from the factory owners were given preferential agreements. At the time this was seen as quite radical, if not socialist, whereas later both building societies and owner occupation became associated more with capitalism, as housing provision for the working classes moved towards direct state provision and renting rather than encouragement for workers to meet their housing needs through subsidised owner occupation. Whilst some still condemn what they see as tax subsidies to owner occupiers, in fact state-subsidised owner occupation has been seen as a perfectly acceptable form of housing policy in other countries, especially the United States. Indeed, many working-class owner occupiers on low incomes today want more tax allowances and financial help, not less, for mortgage payers and simply cannot understand the attitude of those who want them abolished.

Another key figure in the Halifax school was Titus Salt (1803–76) who founded the village of Saltaire in 1851, on the river Aire. His business was based on producing cloth from the wool of alpaca goats, the wool being imported as a raw material from overseas. Saltaire is nowadays protected by conservation area policy, but in recent years it has been under threat, because of proposals to build a motorway through the Aire valley which would involve the demolition of some of the factory buildings. Salt himself is famous in the history of industrial relations for being the first factory owner to introduce an official tea break for his workers. Salt was generally seen as a benevolent employer but he organised housing allocation strictly according to the seniority of the workers' jobs, with overseers receiving substantial double-fronted houses and factory hands getting only small terraces. However, no expense was spared in terms of architectural detail, a classical Italianate style being used for all the buildings, including the factory, all built in a soft, golden stone similar to Bath stone.

Salt did not always understand the difficulty people had in carrying out their essential domestic tasks, for example he banned housewives from hanging out their washing across the backs and apparently would gallop down the back lanes on his horse, sword drawn, to cut the washing lines if they did. However, paradoxically, he did provide communal wash houses, and many social amenities such as libraries, canteens, allotments, schools and almshouses. Saltaire was a relatively small scheme, with only 800 houses but many public buildings and amenities. However, it had a strong influence, disproportionate to its size, on many subsequent model towns in North America and Europe, especially the Krupps' model town at Essen in Germany and on George M. Pullman's company town on the outskirts of Chicago.

The garden city movement

The ideas

There is a marked change of style from the relatively high-density utilitarian developments of the early nineteenth century to the lower-density, more luxuriant Garden City schemes of the latter part of the century in which the housing consists of traditional cottages with gable ends and front gardens rather than tenements or plain terraces (Cherry, 1981; Hall, 1989). As time went on designing ideal housing for the working classes became a popular branch of architecture, although some of the schemes were so expensive that they contributed more to the development of fashionable middle-class domestic architecture than to providing a model for cheap mass-produced housing, for example Bedford Park (Bolsterli, 1977). There had always been a tradition on the large country estates of designing quaint little cottages for agricultural workers, often in the picturesque style, which in themselves would provide an interesting feature of the landscape when viewed from the windows of the stately home (Dresser, 1978; Darley, 1978).

The services of famous architects such as Unwin, Parker and Lutyens were employed in the design of the various Garden Cities and garden suburbs developed towards the end of the nineteenth century (Service, 1977; Dixon and Muthesius, 1978). Raymond Unwin, in particular, was in favour of low-density housing with gardens; with Parker he coined the phrase 'nothing gained by overcrowding' and sought to demonstrate in his plans that a high-density grid layout of terraces were not necessarily the best ways to save space (Hall, 1994). Notable literary figures and members of the upper class were involved in campaigning for better conditions, such as Beatrice Webb, John Ruskin, William Morris, Charles Dickens, Charles Booth, Cardinal Manning, Charles Kingsley, Arnold Toynbee and the American Henry George, all of whom were connected with the Garden City movement and the early town planning cause. Many women were active in the early housing movement, the best known being Octavia Hill, who in 1875 wrote a book, *Homes of the London poor*; she went on to set up many housing initiatives and arguably influenced the nature of the whole modern housing management profession (Smith, 1989; Macey and Baker, 1983).

Ebenezer Howard's book *Tomorrow: a peaceful path to reform of 1898* (renamed *Garden cities of tomorrow* in 1902) put forward his main town planning ideas for the creation of an ideal community (Howard, 1960; and see Fig. 5.1–3). Howard believed that although the industrial revolution had been accompanied by overcrowding, bad housing and environmental problems, it had brought many benefits. Therefore he sought to combine the best of the modern town and the new industrial society with the best of the countryside and the traditional way of rural village life in the town-country, or garden city, as he called his ideal community. This idea is shown graphically in Fig. 5.1, where the Garden City is seen as a powerful 'counter-magnet' which would attract people away from the overcrowded industrial cities and the backwardness of the countryside alike.

Howard did not appear out of nowhere but was part of a group of men and women concerned with social reform and the quality of the built environment in the wake of the industrial revolution. Howard envisaged the creation of Garden Cities of a population of approximately 30 000 each, divided into smaller neighbourhoods of 5000, acting as counter-magnets to existing conurbations, and together forming larger 'social cities' linked in a complex regional network across the country (Fig. 5.2). He envisaged this network being joined together by the most modern public transport (his was the age of the train), new settlements being formed as and when the population expanded.

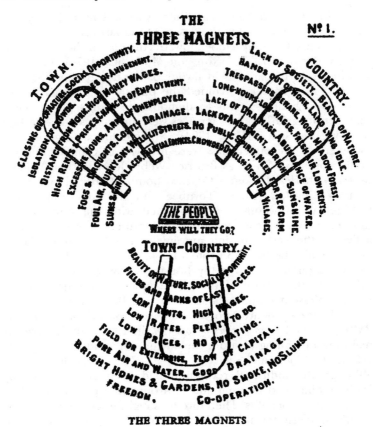

Figure 5.1 Ebenezer Howard's 'three magnets'. *From Howard (1898)*

This would result in planning on a national scale as eventually a complete network of interconnecting cities would be created, covering the whole country, whilst existing cities would return to a more normal size and a more pleasant environment. There is much debate about what Howard really said and what would happen to existing conurbations, as can be seen by reading the on-going saga, even today, in the Town and Country Planning Association journal (just about every month there are discussions of Howard's ideas). Howard is often misrepresented as favouring an escapist, folksy way of life based on 'green' principles. In fact he was advocating a realistic way of restructuring the economy and community of Britain, by means of a complete network of Garden Cities which would act as counter-magnets to the existing conurbations, and which would re-establish the urban–rural balance which had been shaken by the industrial revolution.

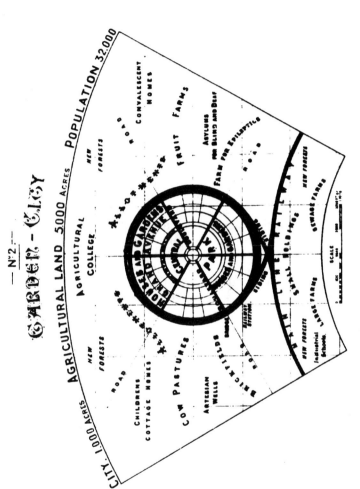

Figure 5.2 Howard's conception of the Garden City and its rural belt. *From Howard (1898)*

Howard, therefore, was not only planning cities at the macro level but had a complete regional and national land use strategy, and had thought through how the cities would be subdivided at the micro, neighbourhood level. The idea of dividing cities into neighbourhoods of 5000 population each was to be carried forward and put into effect in the neighbourhood units which formed the basic structural component of the post-war new towns; the magic figure of 5000 being seen as the ideal size if a group of citizens was to retain a sense of community, a questionable concept going back to the days of the Greek *polis*, or city state, of antiquity. He also had many innovative ideas on zoning the different land uses and activities within the Garden City, as can be seen from Fig. 5.3 – for example, he put all the industry on the outer ring, on the periphery of the city, another feature which was followed in much post-war town planning. He envisaged relatively low densities within the residential areas, with plenty of trees, open space and public parks, as well as generous private gardens around each house, all essential features of creating the Garden City layout. But he was not just playing at creating beautiful stage sets, as some of his critics imagined, since everything had a scientific purpose: to reduce disease, encourage people to grow vegetables in their generous gardens, and create a general sense of well-being, harmony and community spirit.

He proposed that there should be a Green Belt around the city, which he saw as being used by the Garden Citizens for agriculture: it was not a mere buffer zone between town and country in the modern sense of the phrase. He sought to reunite town and country in the economy of the Garden City and in the division of labour and the nature of the work options which people had. Indeed, he wanted to create what would nowadays be called a complete lifestyle package. In order to unite town and country in everyday life, as well as in the plan, he saw the town's citizens working in and controlling the agricultural land around the city as well as engaging in modern industrial activities (Howard, 1960).

Clearly, Howard was not just concerned with physical town planning but had ideas about every aspect of the social and economic characteristics of the community, from city-wide level down through the local neighbourhoods to the family level, ideas that related to how people lived, and how land and property were owned. He did not see himself as a socialist but came from a more liberal tradition which advocated communitarianism rather than communism *per se*. He envisaged much of the land being owned co-operatively when that was considered to be the best solution, but he also allowed for private ownership of shops and

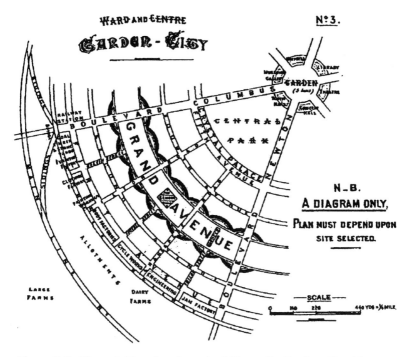

Figure 5.3 The neighbourhood ward of Howard's Garden City. *From Howard (1898)*

businesses – very much what today would be called a mixed economy approach. Likewise the idea of dividing the city into distinct neighbourhood communities was not only a practical solution to the phasing and development of the town, and the provision of essential amenities and facilities in a logical manner. He also wanted to engender a sense of community among the residents, and believed that by dividing his Garden City into identifiable neighbourhood sectors, each with its own school and shops, this aim would be best achieved; a theme which was to re-emerge in the post-war new towns. His interest in 'community' also reflected the influence of the sociologists of the day, who were concerned with the problem of the decline of traditional communities and the potential breakdown of society in the large impersonal cities, as will be discussed in Chapter 11 in relation to the concept of the neighbourhood unit in modern New Towns.

Unlike that of many modern town planners, his vision was not limited to the big issues in the public realm of life, for he did not despise the domestic, private realm of the family – indeed, the whole concept of the Garden City was a celebration of domestic petty bourgeois virtues. He was aware of the problems of the burden of domestic work and family care, which had been publicised by the feminists of the time. Therefore he sought to incorporate attempts at co-operative housekeeping (as mentioned in Chapter 3) into the layout and running of the Garden City (Pearson, 1988). At the time many men and women were looking at ways of rationalising domestic work in the same way as production outside the home had been industrialised, and apparently rationalised. The issue had become pressing in many households as women sought greater emancipation.

It was becoming more difficult to find servants, because of competition from higher wages in the factories, an issue which was to become acute after the First World War. The 'servant problem' was a middle-class one, but co-operative housekeeping would also alleviate the toil of working-class women, both in their own households and in those where they worked as servants. There were all sorts of other ideas around, especially in North America, for reducing the problems of housework, including the idea of a conveyor belt running round the town from which individual households would collect their meals, replacing the dirty dishes to be washed-up in the communal kitchen in the centre of the town (Hayden, 1981)! The Garden City concept was originally intended as an alternative chiefly aimed at the working classes who formed the bulk of the overcrowded population of existing cities, although it also reflected many middle-class attitudes on how to solve the servant problem, which is a paradox. As will be seen, Garden Cities later came to be seen as being more for middle-class people, with disparaging images of Fabian intellectuals and liberated women on bicycles regarded in the popular press as the main inhabitants of these rarified communities.

Howard was not only a theorist but a man of action. In his day there was no adequate state system of town planning, so whatever was to be done had to be achieved through private investment and development. He attempted to start the process by setting up the first Garden City Company before the First World War, starting developments in Letchworth in 1903, and later in Welwyn Garden City in 1920, both on the edges of London (now well and truly in the commuter belt). These enterprises ran into business difficulties. However, the sites he had recommended for the rest of the ring of Garden City counter-magnets which he proposed were later adopted by the planners under the New Towns Act, 1946, as the location of the first phase of British New Towns.

Howard's greater influence was in what he wrote than in what he built. Various aspects of his work continued to be influential in the development of modern town planning, such as the subdivision of settlements into neighbourhoods, the creation of local and centralised hierarchies of amenities and facilities, Green Belts, land use zoning, approaches to public transport and, interestingly, an enthusiasm for bicycles which were (at that time) a recent innovation, hence the provision of cycle paths in many post-war new towns. Possibly most influential of all in the Garden City movement itself was the emphasis on traditional small cottage-style housing, with gardens, at medium to low density as the main form of residential development. It contrasts with the emphasis on model tenements for the labouring classes as found in much early charitable development and some model communities in Britain, e.g. the Peabody buildings in London, but particularly in Europe.

Many other aspects of Howard's ideas have been lost with time or have proved politically and ideologically unacceptable to later generations. In particular modern-day feminists point out that all the ideas of co-operative housekeeping were soon abandoned by later planners. Also the variety of ideas about creating a new economic order based on co-operation and reconciling the town and the country were reflected but weakly in the state planning system with its emphasis on control and sterile land use zoning. Howard's ideas were copied in the building of many garden suburbs, most of which favoured the mock Tudor (half-timbered, with gabled ends) Garden City architectural styles. Indeed, this style of housing became even more popular in the 1930s and came to represent the epitome of home ownership for the new middle classes, popularised by speculative house builders and estate agents' advertisements of the time. So much so that nowadays mock Tudor semis and detached suburban houses are seen by many as the normal and natural form of development. It is noticeable that in the 1990s there has been a considerable revival of the pseudo-Tudor style. Many highbrow architects look on it as artificial and generally in bad taste, but it has endured the test of time better than the so-called modern movement with its impersonal glass and concrete, a style which has never been popular with the people who, after all, are the ones who live in the houses.

We now look at some of the main developments which were based on variations of Garden City principles, bearing in mind that some of them were started before Howard actually put his ideas down on paper, but he was nevertheless highly influential within the intellectual circle to which he and their creators belonged.

The communities

Howard was not working in isolation; he drew encouragement from a range of like-minded people, and in turn influenced the work of many of the later model community builders, who built in the Garden City style. For example, George Cadbury (1839–1922) moved his chocolate factory out of Birmingham to Bournville in 1879, and built the main settlement around it from 1895. W. Alexander Harvey, who was employed as the architect, believed in designing the layout in sympathy with the topography, stating, 'it is nearly always better to use the contour of the land, taking a gentle sweep in preference to a straight line'. This contrasted with the gridiron type of layout characteristic of many of the earlier settlements, and was a precursor of the trade mark of much, especially English town planning with meandering roads and a generally 'natural' appearance. The houses were built to a very low density of seven or eight houses to the acre, with large private gardens for horticulture, lots of trees and open space, and wide roads, and with adequate provision of schools and shops. Some of the houses were for sale from the beginning, but the whole settlement was strongly linked to providing for the work force of the factory. The style was the mock Tudor cottage style so favoured by the reformers. Cadbury was a strong supporter of Ebenezer Howard's ideas and was on the board of directors of the first Garden City at Letchworth (Gardiner, 1923).

Port Sunlight was built by Lever Brothers, the soap manufacturers, across the Mersey from Liverpool. William Lever (1851–1925) with his brothers started off as a grocer, making soap and candles in the back room of his shop. He bought fifty-two acres on Merseyside, and started building a factory there in 1888, then began his model village in 1889, though it was not completed until 1934. Again the scheme is low-density, with houses at five to eight houses per acre. However, the houses are mainly grouped in blocks around allotment gardens, without any private back gardens, much to the annoyance of generations of residents. Lever employed a number of architects but was himself the main influence on both the architecture and the town planning. He endowed the first Chair of town planning at Liverpool University (Cherry, 1981; Ashworth, 1968).

Joseph Rowntree (1836–1925) is the third most notable of the philanthropic factory owners of the late nineteenth century who built a model community, in this case at New Earswick, near York. He employed Unwin and Parker as architects, again developing Garden City-style houses, which in this settlement were grouped around culs-de-sac. The style and space standards of the houses were to act as a model for the council houses introduced under the Housing and Town Planning Acts, 1909 and 1919, and in particular the Tudor Walters standards for council housing design (superseded by the Parker Morris standards in more recent times). The architectural style at New Earswick was also to be influential in the developments of Hampstead Garden Suburb, Wythenshawe in Manchester, and the first Garden City at Letchworth, albeit in a slightly more attractive, up-market way. Also, there were a variety of smaller garden suburb-type schemes throughout the country, but by the early twentieth century these had often become nothing more than an architectural shell used by developers to sell houses to the new middle classes, and many of the original communitarian ideals had long since been forgotten.

Model communities do not have to be built for philan-thropic or utopian reasons, and there is no reason why private developers should not use the style, if not the spirit, of the Garden City movement. There were several purely commercial Garden City-type experiments in North America, and in the 1980s in Britain there were proposals for a ring of entirely private up-market new towns within the London Green Belt, put forward by Consortium, the development group which is strongly influenced by the heritage of the Garden City concept, but its proposals met with such opposition from both central and local government, and from such pressure groups as the Council for the Protection of Rural England, that they were abandoned. Indeed, the influence of the Garden City movement reverberates right through the twentieth century, influencing the style and layout of inter-war 'semi-detached suburbia', albeit in debased form, contributing to the post-war New Towns programme, and more recently informing the views of private developers in their approach to the design of residential estates. Garden City ideas also spread world-wide, and schemes can be found in Japan, Australia, North America, Germany and many other countries.

Traditional styles

The desire of the Garden City architects (and subsequently the speculative builders of semi-detached, half-timbered suburbia) to recreate the English village led to the revival of many of the traditional styles of domestic architecture (vernacular architec-ture, see Munro, 1979; Prizeman, 1975). The Garden City movement's ideas and architecture were not limited to the realms of town planning, rather they reflected a wider popular interest in getting back to traditional country life and architecture, no doubt as a reaction to the experience of rapid industrialisation and urbanisation. Half-timbering became particularly popular at the turn of the century on the new suburban housing estates. Interestingly, some of these styles have made a come-back in recent years on executive housing estates. However, many of these styles were not genuine, either in the nineteenth or in the twentieth century, and employed substitute, mass-produced materials. A summary of traditional vernacular building styles is given in Appendix II.

The development of state intervention in the first half of the twentieth century

The new century

This chapter traces the development of town planning to its culmination in the post-war reconstruction period of the late 1940s during which the foundations of the present planning system were laid. Emphasis is given to the development of the ideas of Le Corbusier and the modern movement in architecture, and to other social, economic, political and technological changes which helped shape the built environment, not least the gradual spread of the motor car.

By the beginning of the twentieth century the various aspects of built environment policy such as public health, housing management, building control and town planning were separating out into different functions of local government, as represented by different professions. The town planning movement had been developing throughout the latter part of the nineteenth century, increasingly occupying itself not just in dealing with the immediate crises of disease and overcrowding in respect of working-class housing, but formulating ideas on how to replan whole cities to accommodate the demands of modern industrialised, urbanised society. The interests of town planners were not limited to housing or to working-class areas but, by now, were concerned with planning for all land uses and all social classes. However, relatively speaking, a fairly straightforward spatial (physical) emphasis in town planning predominated until well into the 1960s, when planning became more concerned with the 'aspatial' (social) results of the physical land use policies which it had introduced but less self-confident and more critical of its own role.

By the early twentieth century it was realised that urban problems could not be solved once and for all by producing 'the plan', but that planning was an endless process of policy-making, control and implementation. Patrick Geddes, a Scottish town planner, had written a book stressing the importance of a methodological scientific approach summarised in the schema 'survey–analysis–plan' (Geddes, 1915; Boardman, 1978). Planning was becoming a recognised higher profession in its own right, separate from surveying and engineering. The Royal Town Planning Institute was established in 1913 (Ashworth, 1968: 193). The Town and Country Planning Association had been founded as a major pressure group which grew out of the Garden Cities movement. However, there were, as yet, few legislative powers to make planning a reality, and it was not necessarily seen as an appropriate local government function.

Visionaries

The new technology

A major constraint on the development and nature of cities is the level of construction and transport technology available. Cities can grow upwards and/or outwards, or they can be close-knit and compactly built, with everything based on walking distances. The Garden City approach used fairly traditional forms of low-rise construction in the shape of mock Tudor cottage-style houses, but it nevertheless adopted the latest developments in transport to enable the city to spread outwards, horizontally, utilising trams, trains and bicycles. Whilst the Garden City movement may be seen as going back to the past to reclaim traditional values, and re-establish harmony with nature and the countryside, the other main school of thought, the European high-rise approach to town planning, as epitomised by the ideas of Le Corbusier, saw the ideas of the past as outdated and sought to create a new age of progress based on the conquest of nature by means of science and technology. Le Corbusier sought to use modern building technology to enable his cities to spread vertically, even suggesting the idea of mile-high skyscrapers. Rather than being thought to embody worthwhile homely values and a well-ordered sense of domesticity, the urban masses were seen as ignorant, backward and therefore uneconomic, in need of re-education and reorganisation to serve the needs of the new industrial society, with its harsher, no-frills, streamlined view of life.

The European high-rise movement with its emphasis on clean, uncluttered lines and the use of pristine white concrete, glass and steel, represented a reaction against what was seen as the chaos and illogicality of traditional cities (Pevsner, 1970). In Victorian times real architecture, as against industrial engineering and factory building, had to be highly respectable, covered in carved stonework and incorporating features from historical architectural styles to show how learned the owner was. Victorian architecture was essentially eclectic, that is, it copied bits and pieces of other architectural styles, particularly the Gothic and the classical. The architects of the new century rebelled against this approach, which they saw as fussy, over-decorative and non-functional in style, and for many years, right up to the late 1960s, the modern movement held sway. It has now been followed by a period of reaction in which traditional values, conservation and appreciation of classical and historical vernacular styles have come back into favour.

Why was the vertical extension of cities as expressed in the high-rise movement essentially a European rather than English trend? In Europe there had been a need, right up to the last century, to provide defensive measures, particularly city walls around individual city states, because the political situation was far less unified than in Britain. It was not until the beginnings of aerial warfare that walls became redundant. The Garden City movement reflected a trend throughout English history to have undefended open cities fringed by low-density urban sprawl and suburban villages around the main urban centre. In Europe the need for defence had led to a greater acceptance of living at higher densities, with buildings packed closer together, often consisting of apartment blocks of several storeys (Sutcliffe, 1974).

In the past it was generally accepted that the natural limit of upward growth was about six storeys, the maximum practical height the average person was willing to climb in what were effectively walk-up tenements. With the development of new forms of power, e.g. gas, electricity, and new technological inventions and machinery, it became possible to build higher still. Steel-framed structures enabled high-rise buildings to be built; previously most buildings had been held up by load-bearing walls which stood by their own weight. In a steel-framed structure the walls and windows are effectively curtains hung from the steel skeleton. The invention of the mechanical lift, particularly the electric elevator in North America, meant that people could live higher without walking up all the stairs; in fact the sky was the limit. The social results when applied to cheap council housing where the lifts do not work and people have to walk up the stairs is another matter altogether from the situation in a carefully maintained block of expensive private flats (apartments).

New movements such as functionalism, futurism and modernism began to arise at the beginning of the new century

(Pevsner, 1970). 'Form follows function', 'beauty is function, function is beauty' became the battle cries of a new generation of architects, who tried to create a new non-decorative, honest, 'styleless' style known as functionalism, promulgated by Walter Gropius in Germany. He was an internationally famous architect and principal of the Bauhaus, a highly influential experimental school of architecture, art and design active in the inter-war period. After the Second World War some of the European functionalist architects came to Britain and worked in the London County Council (LCC), contributing their designs to the post-war reconstruction planning and housing programme (Hatje, 1965). The influence of the functionalist style and the Bauhaus on interior design is to be found in a faint echo in Heal's and Habitat furniture today.

Futurism was concerned with creating a new space-age society, using the new technology and materials to the full. For example, Sant' Elia's multi-level city of 1914 looked like something out of science fiction or a Star Wars film, consisting of huge apartment blocks more suitable for androids than humans. With time much of this architecture proved not to function well at all and was in need of maintenance within a short period of being built: it was certainly unlikely to last into the future. The concrete discoloured, reinforcements deteriorated, window frames rusted, lifts broke down and flat roofs leaked. Traditional vernacular styles of building proved in the long run to be more functional; having been dismissed as sentimental, old-fashioned and bourgeois by the *avant-garde*, it has now come back into fashion. Building styles that utilised local materials such as stone and slate took account of local weather conditions by using different pitches of the roof, etc., which had often been developed by trial and error over the centuries by local builders and carpenters. For example, even details like window sills projecting from the wall to prevent rainwater dripping off and running straight down the wall, causing discoloration, were observed by all traditional master builders, but were ignored in the streamlined buildings of the modern movement.

Le Corbusier

Le Corbusier (1877–1965) is probably the best known architect associated with the modern movement (Pardo, 1965). A Swiss, working mainly in France, he popularised the ideas of the international style. He was influenced by his visits to New York. In Europe there was initial resistance to what was seen as a non-traditional, colonial and commercialised American form of architecture of questionable pedigree. In fact he did not actually invent a new building style; rather, he made the North American style acceptable in Europe as the newborn international style. Le Corbusier had been impressed by Henry Ford's approach to the mass production of motor cars, and believed dwellings could also be mass-produced on an assembly line, the components being slotted together on-site.

Living in France, his concept of housing tended to centre on the apartment or flat. He envisaged multi-storey living, high-rise blocks of flats in which each individual dwelling unit was to be based on scientifically worked out dimensions – a modular unit to meet the needs of the average person (man?). He said, 'a house is a machine for living in', *une machine à habiter* (Ravetz, 1980). This is a limited view of a house and presumes that the architect can produce a standardised unit for the needs of the standardised human being. He had very little understanding of the everyday lives of ordinary people, mixing only with architects like himself.

His solution to the congestion and problems of modern industrialised urbanisation was to knock it all down and start again, that is to say, 'comprehensive redevelopment', a philosophy which has been popular with certain groups of architects and planners throughout the twentieth century. He wanted to demolish and rebuild Paris, but the city authorities fortunately did not go along with his ideas. Housing and other land uses were to be piled one on top of the other, to create a vertical city of high-rise blocks with vertical neighbourhoods in each. The blocks were to stand on pillars, freeing the space at ground level for landscaped public expanses of grass and trees. Indeed, Le Corbusier even suggested that 90 per cent of the ground could be left free by piling people up in such blocks. (See Le Corbusier, *The city of tomorrow* (1929) and *The radiant city*, of which there are several later editions; there are innumerable books on Le Corbusier.) There are similarities to the Garden City approach in the emphasis on open space, but this was to be provided communally and not in the form of individual gardens. (Le Corbusier did allow for low-rise housing in some of his schemes, but not for all.) Le Corbusier is often accused of being totalitarian in his views. He had great faith in the concepts of progress and rationalisation through industrialisation. He said, 'We must create the mass-production spirit,' by creating mass-produced housing. This is a far cry from participatory planning, with the architect one of the priestly caste of experts who believe, because of their superior intellect, that they know what is best for people.

Architects such as Le Corbusier tended to pour scorn on individualism (except their own, of course) as they sought to impose their ego on the rest of humanity. Modern architecture in general is often accused of creating impressively massive buildings from a visual and townscape aspect but lacking sensitivity and awareness as to how individuals and families actually live, leading to the classic problems of where to put the washing, where to let the children play, where to spread out the bits whilst repairing the motor bike without them being stolen, to name but three normal aspects of modern family life. But Le Corbusier's followers would say that the high-rise buildings we see today are mere imitations and not a bit like he would have done it ... Le Corbusier had a flourishing architectural practice and is well known internationally for a range of individual building commissions. It may be argued that Le Corbusier was originally influenced by American ideas, and not vice versa, and it is only in North America that one sees high-rise development undertaken on an immense scale, with no expense spared. Whilst in Britain at the height of the 'high-rise movement' the average tower block would reach around 12 storeys at the most, and everyone thought these buildings were enormous, at the same time in the 1960s Marina Towers in Chicago was constructed, containing 60 floors, twenty of which are dedicated to car parking. Most North American cities nowadays contain enormous high-rise office complexes, some of which include a residential apartments component, as commonly found in Dallas, Chicago and New York. The Sears Tower in Chicago, at 1454 feet, is arguably the tallest building in the world, but the Seagram Tower in Toronto is held by Canadians to be the tallest building in North America, reaching a third of a mile high, although the top section consists of an elongated radio mast structure. Elsewhere in the world, Hong Kong boasts the tallest buildings in Asia, if not the world, and definitely some of the most artistically designed prestige high-rise office blocks, and also some of the highest density and highest rise residential buildings.

The high-rise element was only one aspect of a whole range of other town planning ideas. Like Howard he believed in the importance of land use zoning (vertical as well as horizontal in his case), and the centrality of transport, even suggesting an early form of urban motorway weaving between his blocks for the newly invented motor car. Most of his plans remained ideas in books, but nevertheless he greatly influenced succeeding generations. He never had the opportunity to build one of his cities in Europe. However, he was responsible for designing the new state capital of the Punjab at Chandigargh: a fairly conventional medium-rise scheme. The Western architecture, the emphasis on scientific land use zoning, and the ample provision of wide roads for motor cars may have been ideal solutions to the problems which existed in Europe, but the city seems out of context and out of place in India, with its limited motorised traffic and more rural way of life. Le Corbusier is probably better remembered for a much smaller scheme in the south of France, the Unité d'Habitation block of flats, built in 1947 near Marseilles, a medium-rise development with the main building combining social and commercial uses alongside the dwelling units, including a nursery, shops, common rooms and a rooftop sports area.

Social change

Increased prosperity

Totalitarian schemes, and egotistical ideas, from people such as Le Corbusier, in a sense belong to the last century, and run contrary to the democratisation and increased wealth of the twentieth, even when they have embodied 'modern' ideas. More recently people have had the wherewithal to make their own choice as to what they wanted, and many opted, as we shall see, for the individual house with a garden rather than a flat in a high-rise block. Whilst the problems of the nineteenth century may be seen as associated with poverty, i.e. most people having too little, in the twentieth century new problems, such as suburban sprawl and traffic congestion, emerged which were the result of increased affluence among large groups of the population (not all). This growth was mainly concentrated in the south and Midlands, whereas parts of the north, and the older industrial areas in general, were experiencing high levels of unemployment and far less house-building activity. Indeed, cheap labour from these depressed areas moving down to work in the south in the construction industry was a contributory factor in the building boom of the inter-war years.

Another economic revolution was taking place, as far-reaching in its effects on society as the industrial revolution, namely the development of commerce and offices, which has gone on to the present day. It created a new middle class of office workers, administrators and managers in the 1920s and 1930s. These were the new commuters from houses in the sprawling suburbs. Thus town planning became as concerned with protecting the countryside from the spread of the town as with controlling the quality of urban development within it. This was accentuated by the rise of the internal combustion engine and the motor bus, and later by the spread of mass ownership of the motor car. But private car ownership never topped 2 million before the war and then actually went down after the war until economic recovery in the mid-1950s, increasing ever since, with over 20 million vehicles on the roads today.

In 1909 the Housing and Town Planning Act was passed. It was to set the agenda for the future scope and nature of town planning in Britain. The Act, introduced under a reforming Liberal government, enabled the creation of a much extended mass council housing system, which coincided with the decline of much private-sector rented housing. Also under this Act local authorities were expected to produce 'schemes', as town plans were called in those days, showing the location and layout of the new developments, but in the process of planning these individual schemes they were inevitably moving towards considering questions as to the layout and design of whole towns and their likely future growth. In fact they often put the housing estates out on the edges of cities where land was cheapest and where they were less likely to cause conflict or reduce property values than in middle-class suburbs.

The First World War

The First World War, 1914–18, was a social and economic watershed. Following the war, partly from fear of social unrest, there was a demand for better housing and improved social conditions for the working classes. Society was still divided on class lines. Many women had been drawn into factory employment, especially in the munitions factories, during the war. Although many had to hand their jobs back to the returning men, new factory and office jobs gradually opened up for them. The Sex Disqualification (Removal) Act, 1919, enabled women to enter the professions officially for the first time, because of the manpower shortage (Lewis, 1984). Women had previously been involved in voluntary work, dealing with the issues of housing, public health reform and even town planning. However, although they dealt with matters of land and property, it must be remembered that most women had had little right to own property themselves until the reforms of the late nineteenth century (Hoggett and Pearl, 1983).

The Housing and Town Planning Act, 1919, introduced a massive council house building programme specifically aimed at providing 'homes fit for heroes', that is, for the soldiers returning from the Great War. Under the 1919 Act 213 000 houses were built, then the first Labour government introduced the 1924

Housing Act (the Wheatley Act), giving greater emphasis to the state provision of housing (Macey and Baker, 1983; Smith, 1989). Standards were set, based on the Tudor Walters report of 1918, the first of the big housing reports and influenced by Garden City ideas. It was superseded by the Parker Morris Report (1961), which has subsequently been replaced by a range of other measures related more to cost cutting than design. The early standards were based on the principles adopted in the model communities, particularly Rowntree's model factory town at New Earswick. The occupiers of the early council houses were chiefly respectable skilled working men and their families. Early council housing was not specifically concerned with homelessness, or housing the poor, functions which various charitable housing trusts and the Octavia Hill approach to housing management had been more concerned with. Then, as now, provision for single people, single-parent families, widows, the disabled and the elderly was always secondary to, rather than balanced with, provision for families.

The 1919 Act also required local authorities to produce schemes, i.e. town plans, for settlements over 20 000, showing the overall land use zonings and the location of the new housing estates in particular. This part of the Act, like most of the planning Acts until after the Second World War (1939–45), was difficult to administer and enforce, owing to lack of resources and skilled personnel. In many respects the town plan was only advisory, or illustrative, in that it was often no more than a land use map showing what had been already developed rather than what was proposed for the future, but it was a beginning. The standard of planning varied widely in different areas, with some local authorities taking the lead, others virtually ignoring planning altogether. Although it was weak from a town planning viewpoint, the Act laid the foundations for a series of subsequent inter-war housing Acts which extended the state's role in the provision of housing.

The inter-war period

The 1920s and 1930s, although characterised by periods of depression and high unemployment in the older industrial areas of the country, especially in the north with its declining heavy industry, were also, paradoxically, times of extensive private house building in the more prosperous south and Midlands. Labour and materials were relatively cheap, and farmland was readily available to buy up for suburban housing schemes owing to a decline in agricultural prices and imports of cheap food. As mentioned earlier, there was a growth in the south-east and Midlands of the relatively affluent middle class and white-collar workers as the business and office sector of the economy continued to grow.

Vast areas of private speculative housing estates were built around towns and cities, and people escaped out of the urban congestion into the fresh air and sunshine of the Home Counties, a movement which had already started with the growth of the railways in the nineteenth century and which grew apace with the extension of the Metropolitan Railway into the countryside around London at the turn of the century, spawning 'Metro-land' (Jackson, 1992; Betjeman, 1974). In 1910 90 per cent of all housing was rented, owner occupation being limited to the more affluent classes (Swenarton, 1981). Even in the inter-war period the vast majority of people rented their housing either from the local council or from private landlords; owner occupation accounted for a quarter to a third of housing tenure, depending on the locality, whereas nowadays it is approaching 70 per cent. The building society movement was growing among the new middle classes, the 'mortgagariat' who were able to buy their house with a building society mortgage.

Between 1930 and 1940 alone 2 700 000 houses were built (cf. Legrand, 1988), and much of this development was occurring as urban sprawl. The Town and Country Planning Act, 1932, in an attempt to control the flood, required local authorities to produce zoning maps designating restricted areas for housing development, and requiring developers to get a rudimentary form of planning permission. In fact many developers virtually ignored the legislation, as the penalties were minimal and difficult to enforce. Also the local authorities were required to pay compensation if permission was refused, which naturally discouraged them from doing so. If there was no plan available when developers wanted to build they were granted what was known as 'interim development control' permission. In practical terms all this meant was that the planners often drew up the land use zoning plan after the developers had built – hardly positive town planning!

Developers often chose to build along existing roads to save money, creating long ribbons of development cutting into the countryside on the outskirts of towns. Visually this housing blocked the view of the landscape, although there might be fields behind the houses. Socially long spread-out rows of houses made the provision of schools, shops and social amenities difficult. From the traffic aspect, as car ownership grew, a whole series of garages and driveways opening straight on to the main road caused major traffic problems. The Restriction of Ribbon Development Act, 1935, attempted to control this linear development, and required developers to build in more compact units with integral estate roads off the main road. The Act also covered many other aspects of land use and development and was in a sense another early town and country planning Act in all but name. It must be pointed out that ribbon development is in no way part of, or comparable to, the concept of linear cities in which whole neighbourhoods and all the land uses are strung out like beads on a necklace. The pre-war Acts were difficult to enforce and there was growing public pressure, from some quarters, for greater control. Amenity and rural preservation groups were springing up who feared the spread of suburbia and the loss of agricultural land. The erection of electricity pylons across fields for the national grid and extensive road building also meant that there were fewer and fewer unspoilt beauty spots. Property owners resisted the loss of the right to develop, and state interference in general. On the broader economic front there was also a demand for better government policy to counteract the effects of unemployment. There was a need to create a more balanced distribution of jobs, people and housing in the country as a whole, and thus to help break down the 'two nations' division between north and south which became more noticeable as the depression of the 1930s deepened.

Post-war reconstruction

The Second World War

Unemployment and many other social and economic problems were temporarily 'solved' overnight with the declaration of war in 1939 which required the call-up of the majority of the male work force, leaving the women to 'man' the factories and armament works. Back in the 1930s the government had introduced a minimal level of state intervention and regional planning in the form of the Special Areas Act, 1934, which set the principle which was to be developed further in the post-war reconstruction period of designating specific areas of unemployment and economic decline for special treatment, namely the north-east, South Wales, Cumberland and Glasgow districts, all areas which had experienced decline in heavy industry. The policy was to attempt to take work to the workers rather than the opposite of taking workers to the work (the 'on your bike' philosophy). The latter was discouraged because of the massive level of population migration to the south, which was putting great pressure on housing, services and the infrastructure (as it still is today). It was considered bad economics, as some areas in the north were taking on the form of ghost towns as everyone moved out, leaving empty houses, disused factories and neglected roads and public facilities, i.e. wasting existing facilities. These problems have continued to haunt the government over the ensuing fifty years to the present day. In spite of decades of intervention, particularly by the Labour government after the war, the situation has not yet balanced out. Following the 1934 Act, in 1937 the government set up a Royal Commission on the Distribution of the Industrial Population, which produced the Barlow report (Ravetz, 1986). The relationship between town planning and regional planning in the wider context of the well-being of the economy is a theme which will be addressed in the next chapter. There was increasing enthusiasm for state planning solutions to urban and regional problems in the inter-war period, particularly among leading intellectuals.

The Second World War was another watershed in the development of British town planning. Relatively speaking, modern town planning really became a force to reckon with only from 1945 onwards. The war effort required a greater level of state intervention and state planning than was previously acceptable, in controlling industrial and agricultural production, and in setting up regional and national government agencies to co-ordinate the effort, *laissez-faire* being temporarily suspended during the state of wartime emergency. People began to become more used to planning and control. Following the war there was general acceptance that in order to re-establish the economy and reconstruct society there was a need for as much overall government control and planning as there had been during the war effort. A series of shortages, cold winters and political reaction in the late 1940s meant that the Labour government which had been elected after the war lasted only until the early 1950s, partly because people reacted against the continued imposition of rationing and state controls. The new Tory government repealed only the more extreme aspects of the Labour government's planning legislation and continued the town planning and state housing policies of the day, although it lifted many of the restrictions on private businesses and property development. The wartime bombing of large areas of housing and industry, and the flattening of many historic town centres and inner housing areas, had made comprehensive redevelopment and planning a necessity. So planners were given extensive powers of compulsory purchase, land assembly and decision-making – often against the wishes of the remaining residents, who sometimes considered they suffered more at the hands of the planners than of the Germans. Many areas that the planners would have never been able to get demolished had been removed for them by the bombing, and the opportunity had at last arisen to put planning theory into practice.

Reconstruction planning, 1945–52

After the war there was again a need for 'homes fit for heroes'. As after the First World War, there was considerable unrest, and demands were strong for a better society to compensate the workers for their contribution to the war effort. The Labour Party, elected after the war, was in a strong enough position to carry out extensive reform, to implement a programme of nationalising basic industries, and to build the welfare state. However, there was also a general consensus amongst all political parties that there was a need for more rationalisation and planning in general, as was evidenced by the wartime coalition government in setting up various committees to consider the future nature of Britain. This was optimistic, considering that at the time they did not know when the war was going to end, or who was going to win. The Scott Committee reported in 1942 on land utilisation in rural areas and, linked to this, the Dower report on National Parks was produced in 1945, followed by the Hobhouse Committee on National Park administration in 1947. The Uthwatt Committee produced a report on the vexed question of compensation and betterment in 1942. The Reith report on New Towns was produced in 1946, being preceded by the Dudley report in 1944 on the design of dwellings, which had a particular bearing on the New Towns (Cullingworth, 1988). The 1944 White Paper *The control of land use* set out the agenda for future planning control. Also during the war, in 1943, the Ministry of Town and Country Planning was set up (to be replaced in 1951 by the Ministry of Housing and Local Government, and in 1970 by the (still existing) Department of the Environment).

Other notable events were the production in 1944 of the Greater London Development Plan by the prominent planner Patrick Abercrombie, which was to form the basis of much post-war town planning in the capital, which already had a more advanced planning system than other provincial cities because its problems were so much greater. Prior to the war London had already designated its own Green Belt under the Green Belt (London and Home Counties) Act, 1938. Abercrombie's plan also made proposals for a series of inner and outer ring roads around London to cope with future levels of traffic; one of the descendants of these original ideas coming to birth forty years later in the form of the M25. It had already been envisaged that new expansion would occur in a series of satellite New Towns outside the Green Belt, in locations comparable to Howard's original ideas and as part of the overall strategy for the London conurbation and the south-east.

Town planning was one component of a much broader social and economic programme of post-war reconstruction aimed at creating a better, more rationally organised welfare state. There was a strong emphasis on greater equality but the aim was not to create a socialist state, rather the goals reflected the typically British compromise of settling for a 'mixed economy', and reform rather than revolution, in which both private enterprise and state intervention could play a part. Overall there was an emphasis on trying to create greater efficiency, order and progress by providing modern facilities, planning having an important role in co-ordinating all this. Indeed, planning became the philosophy of the post-war period, the spirit of the age, being seen as the solution to all problems such as economic overproduction, overpopulation and, of course, unruly urban growth into the countryside, and civic chaos. The aim was to 'Build a better Britain' literally. Britain had industrialised earlier than any other European countries in the nineteenth century, and was now at a disadvantage in possessing much out-of-date capital equipment, plant and machinery, and had in a sense rested on its laurels, depending on the support of the wealth of the empire, much of which it was losing in the post-war period. Other European countries were also producing a solid state-funded physical and social infrastructure to provide the basic requirements for the development of their economy.

The development plan system

The main plank of post-war reconstruction planning was the Town and Country Planning Act, 1947. Under this Act all development had to receive planning permission (Cullingworth, 1988). Local authorities had to prepare development plans showing the main land uses by means of coloured zonings. The system was based on a master plan, or blueprint, approach. The plans were to be prepared on the basis of the survey–analysis–plan approach originally promoted by Geddes (1915). There was a shortage of suitably qualified planners, so many 'planners' were likely to be from a surveying, civil engineering, architecture or public health background, all professions in which there was a minimal social dimension, and which were predominantly male.

The planners may have been unaware of the wider economic, political and social complexities of town planning, but in any case the new system was firmly weighted towards a physical land use approach. The main types of plans to be prepared under the 1947 Act were the county map, which was produced on an Ordnance Survey base at 1 in. to the mile, the county borough maps, which covered the main urban areas at 6 in. to the mile, and supplementary town maps showing details of smaller towns and specific urban areas. Also there were the comprehensive development areas (CDAs), which dealt with town centre redevelopment in detail. The plans were meant to be reviewed every five years but the amendment system proved lengthy to implement, and generally the plans were seen as slow and inflexible in response to change.

To make the new planning system work there had to be strong powers of control. In certain circumstances compensation was paid if a planning refusal deprived a developer of his inherent right to develop. More political was the decision to impose betterment levy (tax) on developers who benefited from an increase in land value because of a planning decision or land use zoning. For example, agricultural land zoned as residential land would vastly increase in value. Originally the betterment levy was 100 per cent, but this was later reduced and eventually virtually abolished under the Conservative government of the 1950s. The 1947 system represented a half-way house between nationalisation and a free market. It effectively nationalised development value, rather than nationalising the land itself. There has been a continuing saga over the last forty years over the question of compensation and betterment, Labour governments generally advocating taxation of development rights, if not land nationalisation itself (for example, the last Labour government introduced the Community Land Act in 1975), with Conservative governments reversing such policies. Nowadays any gains made as a result of the planning system are treated as capital gains through the normal taxation system. But many would argue that the present proliferation of planning gain at local authority level constitutes an unofficial form of betterment levy or land tax to get the developer to pay more towards the infrastructure of his scheme in these days of local government cut-backs when the local authority cannot afford the bill for all the roads, community facilities and public services a new scheme generates.

Many consider, in retrospect, that town planning of the post-war reconstruction variety was unrealistic, as there is no ideal single once-and-for-all solution or perfect plan for everyone. Also planners were unprepared for the rapid changes which occurred in the post-war period, in particular the growth of the private motor car, and the increase in private house-building and owner occupation in the 1950s when the building licence controls and 'rationing' were removed. The Conservative Prime Minister Harold Macmillan summed up this new prosperity in the remark 'You've never had it so good' but there were hidden and enduring pockets of poverty both in the inner city and in the depressed regions where people had never had it at all!

The new towns programme

Much of the post-war housing and new development were located in the New Towns. The New Towns Act, 1946, in many respects fulfilled the dreams of the late Ebenezer Howard. The New Towns were developed in three main phases, the first (Mark I), built immediately after the war, consisting mainly of satellite settlements around London on sites which were very similar to Howard's proposed ones. This stage was followed by a much reduced second phase of Mark II New Towns under the Conservatives in the 1950s, and then by an extensive third phase, known as Mark III New Towns, built under the Labour government of Harold Wilson in the 1960s (Aldridge, 1979).

The majority of Mark I New Towns were built around London, but there were a few others in the immediate post-war period built in the depressed regions, such as Cwmbran in South Wales, whose function was to act as a growth point for revitalisation of that side of the Welsh valleys (Fig. 6.1). One could argue that concentrating investment in one New Town at the expense of existing settlement was not the best way to regenerate a region, and might in fact lead to the further decline of some of the poorer settlements. New Towns were seen by politicians as a tangible mark of progress, which they could point to and say they had achieved something. Piecemeal small-scale development in and around existing urban areas was far less politically attractive although, arguably, socially more worthwhile.

Regional planning

The issue of the location of the New Towns was tied up with another cornerstone of post-war planning – regional planning. Major differences had developed in the economic situation of different regions, as explained earlier, with unemployment and depopulation in the north-east and overpopulation and congestion in the south-east. In a sense the war had solved the

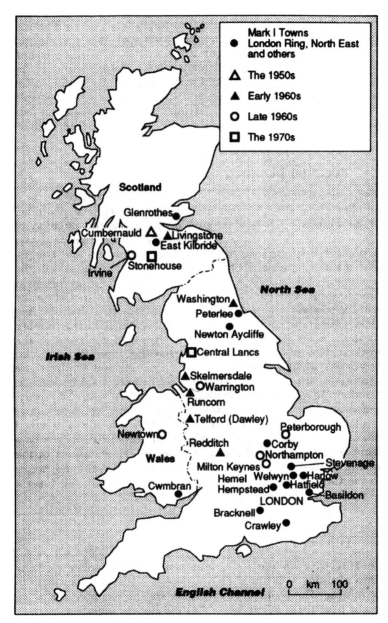

Figure 6.1 **The New Towns of Britain.** *From RTPI (1986)*

unemployment problems overnight and given the government time to think. Indeed, wartime munition factories were often the basis of post-war trading estates. The Distribution of Industry Act, 1945, gave grants and incentives which encouraged firms to move to these areas, following the principle of taking work to the workers. However, some would say that this approach penalised businesses which wanted to develop and expand in the more prosperous areas. And even in the most prosperous cities, such as London, there were distinct areas of unemployment and poverty which needed jobs but could not compete with the more favoured areas. Balchin and Bull (1987) provide a detailed discussion of regional planning and an account of its development is continued in the next chapter. A related aspect of the post-war planning programme was the National Parks and Access to the Countryside Act, 1949 (see Chapter 9) within the context of a national land use strategy (Hall, 1994).

Did they get it right?

Looking back on the scope and nature of immediate post-war town planning, it is interesting to note that certain issues seem to be missing. The problem of the motor car, for example, was not a major issue then, as car ownership did not rise significantly until the 1960s. Most people depended on public transport, and the 1950s were still very much the age of the bicycle as well as the train, bus, motor cycle, moped and scooter. In 1951 86 per cent of households had no car (Mawhinney, 1995). Many of the early post-war town centre redevelopment plans were based on a complete underestimate of the future needs and effects of the motor car and parking. Many housing estates had narrow roads, impractical for parking, and no garages or car spaces. Indeed, in planning council estates it was considered that a family which could afford a car did not need a council house, and so provision for the motor car was minimal (even when bus services were inadequate and the estate was miles from anywhere). However, as stated earlier, there were problems associated with ribbon development and a generally higher level of car ownership in the south-east, particularly in London, where there had always been traffic problems.

There seemed to be little enthusiasm for the retention of the historic heritage of cities, from either the architectural or the social viewpoint. Indeed, there was a tendency to despise Victorian architecture and to categorise many older residential properties as slums, or as awkward buildings in the way of the clean sweep of progress. It is now accepted that many valuable historic buildings were demolished just because they were old. Concern for the past expressed itself more in the preservation of archaeological remains and historic monuments than in urban conservation.

One of the aims of post-war planning was to solve the housing crisis. In fact several commentators argue that Britain ended up with more homeless, not fewer, as a result of the net effects of clearance policies (Ravetz, 1980; Donnison and Ungerson, 1982). In some areas there was so much slum clearance, and inadequate new housing development (because local authorities ran out of money), that the end result was a net loss of housing stock! All this activity was motivated by a desire to clear the slums and put people in pristine, out-of-town council estates, but often the sense of community in working-class areas was demolished along with the housing. Some even go further and claim there was a definite policy of destroying working-class communities for political reasons, whilst others would say that many old housing areas were in the way of 'progress' and had to be demolished for expansion of the Central Business Area to take place (Cockburn, 1977).

Planners were accused of having a naive view of the nature of social problems and their causes. If the government does not try to tackle the underlying problems of poverty and disadvantage in society it is inevitable that certain areas of cities will become poor and run-down and slums will develop; simply because the people cannot afford to renovate the properties. Indeed, it may be argued that we need areas like this in our cities and that they provide an essential safety net. Consider how since the gentrification of so much of the centre of London many people have nowhere to go who would previously have eked out an existence in the run-down areas, and in the now much reduced private rented sector. Many, like Billy Fury, thought that in the Britain of the 1950s we were 'only half-way to Paradise' (Wilson, 1980).

Chapter 7

Reaction and rethink: the development of town planning in the second half of the twentieth century

The 1950s

In the euphoria of immediate post-war socialism many imagined that in the future the bulk of new development would be carried out by the state, and indeed until the lifting of the restrictive building licences in the early 1950s most new development was built by the government, including council houses, public buildings, factories and public works (Hall, 1994). There was a major need to rebuild public buildings and the infrastructure, and priority was given to industrial building. In the early 1950s the pent-up demand of the private sector was given free play and vast numbers of new houses were constructed, testing the new restrictive planning system to the full. However, local authorities had no qualms about entering into partnership schemes with the developers to build town centres. In the early stages the emphasis was on building shopping centres in the form of modern precincts on the American model to meet rising consumer demand. Many monotonous concrete shopping centres date from this time. Although such schemes were intended to be up to date they totally underestimated the need for related car parking which was to emerge in the 1960s. When the bombed centre of Coventry was redeveloped it was assumed that cars could park on the small reinforced roof covering part of the new shopping centre (Tetlow and Goss, 1968). Shoppers complained about the unfriendliness of the architecture and design of many of these new centres, the unnecessary steps, escalators which seldom worked, lack of public conveniences, and a paucity of sitting areas and meeting places. When the Conservatives came into power in the early 1950s they continued the national commitment to building houses, and to town planning itself, only revising the compensation and betterment tax aspects of the 1947 Act, but keeping the rest substantially unchanged.

The 1960s

High-rise development

Town planning took on a new impetus in the 1960s with an emphasis on new building, increased state control and large-scale projects, in particular high-rise developments (Sutcliffe, 1974). The ideas of Le Corbusier and the functionalists increased in influence (see Chapter 6). For example, the development of a large complex of council housing at Roehampton, near Richmond Park, in London, owed much to the ideas of Le Corbusier, consisting of white blocks of flats on a green landscaped slope with the buildings raised up on pillars. The high-rise movement went on to become widespread throughout the country but the standard of the blocks varied considerably. Less than 5 per cent of the population live in blocks of flats of six storeys or more. It was imagined that by building high it would be possible to house the same number of people in the modern blocks as had lived in the cramped terraced housing of the inner city before the site was cleared. However, this was not feasible because strict Sunlight and Daylight Regulations were applied which required the buildings to be spaced out to ensure that they received adequate light and did not overshadow each other or existing development (DOE, 1971). By the time provision (even inadequate provision) had been made for play space, landscaping and increasingly for car parking around the base of the blocks, there was not much in it as against building high-density low-rise development (see Chapter 10 for an explanation of density).

It was argued that it was cheaper to build high, but it depends on what is included in the cost. All the services had to be carried up into the building vertically, water, gas, electricity, waste disposal and sewerage. The need for higher technical standards to send all this up the building considerably increased the cost. Various studies showed that it might be marginally cheaper to build up to a certain point, but beyond that the cost increased considerably. Usually floor six, and certainly floor ten, was when the 'threshold' was reached and costs climbed rapidly (see 1960s DOE design bulletins, for example *'Schemes at medium and high densities'*, 1963, now out of print). The Labour government of the day encouraged high-rise as the solution to the nation's housing problems by giving local authorities subsidies to build blocks of flats, thus distorting the argument as to whether they were cheaper than conventional housing. Harold Wilson, the Prime Minister, was a great believer in the 'white heat of technology' and favoured the fast prefabricated techniques of system building. The schemes were never popular with the residents, and the collapse of Ronan Point, an inner London residential tower block, in the late 1960s confirmed their fears. A woman on one of the top floors got up in the morning and switched her gas oven on, there was an enormous explosion, and the side of the building collapsed like a pack of cards. The public outcry helped swing the pendulum back towards traditional construction (Ravetz, 1986).

There were the practical problems to young families with children living in small flats without the 'overflow' space of a back garden for play, storage and somewhere to hang the washing. There were structural problems of faulty construction, condensation, noise between flats with thin party walls, smelly, inefficient waste disposal chutes, and communal heating which was often too expensive for the residents to use. There were psychological problems of the effects of height. Socially, people felt isolated because there was no longer any street life to walk out into, people were filed away in their little boxes along each corridor. They felt unsafe, and unable to achieve adequate 'surveillance' of the area around their dwelling. They could not see from inside their flats who was going along the corridor, and many of the lifts, communal areas and entrances were heavily vandalised, with strangers wandering in and out (Coleman, 1985). Most of the flats were built by local authorities, that is, they were council housing and therefore built 'on the cheap'. However, high-rise can work for some people in some areas. There are several high-rise blocks in the up-market district of Mayfair in central London (often occupied by wealthy foreigners); and in seaside resorts, especially along the south coast between Bognor Regis and Brighton, in which the retired elderly predominate. Flats can work for some people at some income levels; just look at America or the Continent. It is all a matter of quality of construction, level of back-up services, life style and income of the residents.

Ironically, many blocks of council flats built as an alternative to nineteenth-century slums have now become slums themselves. Paradoxically those that have been taken over by private developers and upgraded have been greatly improved, but then, of course, are no longer part of the social housing sector. Some local authorities have adopted drastic measures, 'beheading' tower blocks, that is, turning them back into lower-rise housing or maisonettes, at considerable expense. Some blocks have simply been blown up, having become uninhabitable. One of the key social questions here is whether it is the people who make the buildings 'bad', or is it the buildings that make the people 'bad'? Even allowing for poor construction and design faults, some estates are also very heavily vandalised. Some would argue that it is the level of housing management and estate supervision (Roberts, 1991) which is at fault on high-rise estates which consist predominantly of rented property where nobody has a sense of ownership or belonging. These questions, and the whole issue of 'environmental determinism', are discussed further in Chapter 11.

Property boom

There was growing demand for office space, and high-rise office blocks were seen as a valuable asset to pension funds and insurance companies, sometimes being worth more for investment purposes empty than occupied (as rates were not payable on empty buildings) (Marriot, 1989). Centre Point in London at the junction of Tottenham Court Road and Oxford Street, built in the 1960s, was an infamous example of this situation, and was occupied in a sit-in by housing activists at one point in its chequered history. In fact the 1960s were a period of growing community discontent and urban pressure group activity against the activities of the planners and developers (Aldous, 1972). The activists included early housing pressure groups such as Shelter (Wilson, 1970), people protesting against what was happening in what was to become known as the inner city (Donnison and Eversley, 1974), and a multiplicity of local groups fighting the developers and planners against the demolition of their local area, as in Tolmers Square in London. More broadly, as a reaction to the market-led development of the 'Surging 1960s', the beginnings of other movements which were to become central twenty years later could be discerned on the horizon, such as the environmental movement (Arvill, 1969) and the 'women and planning' movement (Cockburn, 1977).

Although the planners had immense powers they did not generally use them on behalf of the local community. On the contrary, the local authority often went into partnership with the developers, doing its bit by using compulsory purchase orders to assemble the site, prepare the infrastructure and generally smooth the way for the property bonanza. Many saw this unholy alliance, and tangled web of relationships between planners and developers, as the opposite of what town planning was meant to be about, that is, facilitating a more social and environmentally concerned approach to urban development. The property boom benefited the land use professions, creating a demand for a greater range of property professional specialisms and levels of expertise, and in particular revitalising the quantity surveying profession (Marriot, 1989) because the cost factor was everything, and sophisticated project management was required.

As time went on developments became more sophisticated. By the 1970s enclosed shopping centres were appearing, an improvement on the windswept facilities of the 1950s. From the outside these often looked like medium-rise office blocks. Inside they consisted of multi-level shopping malls, the ultimate development of precinct shopping. The problem was that many of them were closed at night and patrolled on the perimeters by security guards, thus taking away the citizen's right to stroll around the town centre in the evenings. There was no point in visiting some of these centres after the shops had closed, as the whole complex would be locked, and many lacked any of the cultural or entertainment facilities usually associated with town centres. Shopping precincts and pedestrianised centres were regarded as dangerous because they had no through traffic and were completely devoid of people at night, except for muggers loitering in the shadows. Ordinary people, particularly local residents who had seen their communities and houses demolished to make way for these central area developments, demanded more accountability from the planners, more planning for the benefit of the local people and less for big business interests.

New towns

In the 1950s, under the Conservative government, Cumbernauld in Scotland was the only Mark II New Town commissioned, because the Conservatives favoured a policy of expanding existing provincial towns such as Swindon and Andover to take 'overspill' from the large conurbations under the Town Development Act, 1952, rather than building complete new towns. Neither Labour nor Conservative thinkers paid much attention to what planners would today call the revitalisation of the inner city, rather the emphasis was on decentralisation and the removal of 'non-conforming uses' to greenfield sites. The Slum Clearance Act, 1957, had given local authorities even greater powers of demolition, and led to much criticism from working-class communities in the areas affected: the very people it was meant to be for had very little opportunity to decide for themselves what they really wanted.

In the 1960s there was a return to the emphasis on New Towns. The Mark III New Towns created under the Labour government consisted of regional centres in depressed areas which were meant to act as economic growth poles and also of a second phase of overspill New Towns in prosperous areas in the Midlands where they were intended to take the pressure off existing cities and provide new opportunities for investment and growth. Cynics would say that they were located mainly in Labour constituencies in the Midlands and north. They are generally larger than the earlier New Towns and are not intended to act as counter-magnets but rather to act as centres in their own right. Some would subdivide the Mark III New Towns further and call Milton Keynes Mark IV. Milton Keynes is virtually a city rather than a town, and had a target population of a quarter of a million. In Mark III New Towns neighbourhood design and overall planning structure became more sophisticated. For example, one finds arrangements based on New Towns being divided into intermediate districts of say 15 000, these being subdivided into smaller neighbourhoods and local areas. The assumption that people would walk to the shops and use mainly public transport was now a thing of the past. For example, the design of Milton Keynes was conceptualised primarily as a transport grid (with some similarity to Broad Acre City, Autopia) and ample provision of motorway-standard roads was provided, with pedestrians taking second place. This was a reflection of the central fixation of 1960s planning on the motor car.

No New Towns have been designated since the early 1970s. When recession hit these artifically created settlements economic and social problems were amplified in the more vulnerable New Towns located in the north and Midlands. Many of their industries were multinational and had no real local ties, so they simply moved out to catch the next government grant elsewhere. Whilst some of the New Towns, especially those in the south, including Milton Keynes, have gone from strength to strength, others are looking the worse for wear nowadays. Many are now coming to the end of their period as officially New Towns. Under the New Towns Act, 1946, the New Towns were overseen by the New Towns Commission, individual towns being run by development corporations which existed quite separately from the local authority in whose area they were located. The New Towns were intended to be de-designated after thirty years, and most have now passed that stage (Potter, 1989), so officially there are now no more than about two New Towns. Although the government New Town policy has been wound up, there has been interest in recent years in the development of private New Towns. In particular, Consortium Developments, as has been mentioned, pressed in the 1980s for a ring of New Towns around London, predominantly in the Green Belt. Proposals for New Towns at

Tillingham Hall in Essex and Foxley Wood in north-east Hampshire were both rejected by the Secretary of State for the Environment. Consortium, which was made up of the main housing building companies, has been disbanded.

New Towns were financed initially by Exchequer grants, but they were also intended to be entrepreneurial and financially self-sufficient once they became established. They also had a strong social role, for example most of the housing in the Mark I New Towns was rented. However, this gradually changed and by the time Milton Keynes was built over 70 per cent of the housing was owner occupied, with the large developers coming in and building virtually the same sort of houses as they would elsewhere, the only difference being that they had to build in conformity with the neighbourhood unit principles and overall master plan of the development. Nowadays the bulk of New Town housing, nationally, is owner occupied, tenants having had the opportunity to buy their houses from the erstwhile development corporations. Buying your own home on the cheap is no bargain if the building stock is in need of repair and modernisation (having been built under the 1947 Act) and there is no employment locally.

Transportation planning

In the 1960s planners responded to the increase in car ownership by looking to North American transportation planning. It seemed to be taken as read that the car was a good thing and that everyone would soon have one. In fact less than 40 per cent of households had a car (see *Social Trends* or the AA or RAC for the current figures). In those days it may not have been such a problem, as there were fewer out-of-town shopping developments and one could still go about one's daily life without the use of a car. However, there had always been a problem of lack of adequate transport for people stuck out on housing estates, private or council. The whole 1960s strategy of planning put great emphasis on the commuter's journey to work and mathematical models were developed to show trip generation, origin and destination, and trip allocation (Roberts, 1973). In contrast with today, town planning appeared very pro motor car, and few seemed to consider the consequences. In parallel, land uses and developments were beginning to decentralise and disperse, although it was not until the extension of the motorway system that developers became attracted to out of town sites alongside motorway junctions (as discussed in Walker, 1996, in Volume III, in relation to retail decentralisation).

There has been much criticism of transportation planning, especially the emphasis on and definition of the 'journey to work', from a range of interest groups, especially from non-car owners. It has been pointed out that women workers often make intermittent broken journeys and trans-radial rather than radial journeys, often outside the rush hour if they work part-time. For example, a woman's daily journeys might be home → school → work → shops → school → home, and not necessarily by car. Women who work full-time and have a car are also likely to break their journeys in a similar manner, and have to contend more with the pressures of achieving it all within the rush hour. Transportation-based mathematical models were also applied to retail development, such as retail gravity models. Again, it is wrong to assume that most shoppers' trips will necessarily begin and terminate at home, as, for example, women may shop on the way to or from work, and therefore new retail development may be better located nearer to employment areas than residential areas.

Meanwhile cycling campaigners were suggesting better ways of planning junctions and main roads (Hudson, 1978), and the emerging environmental and community planning groups were challenging the whole basis of town planning and demanding 'Homes, not roads' (Aldous, 1972). Pedestrians were seen as people who got in the way, slowed the traffic down and were best diverted through uninviting underpasses or time-consuming footbridges (Myerscough, 1975). It took years for these attitudes to change. Although cyclists' needs are again being considered, policies are weak. Sometimes cyclists are allocated half a footpath or underpass route alongside the pedestrians, which is dangerous for pedestrians, halving their space and unsatisfactory for cyclists too, whilst the motor car continues to take the lion's share. In the 1960s town planning became for all practical purposes car planning as the urban motorways, car parks and multi-level intersections were built to meet the needs of progress, and in the process the whole structure of cities was being altered (Bruton, 1975). In many respects this emphasis on the motor car left many people who were not car users in a worse position than they had been in the 1950s. An added factor was the Beeching cuts in the rail network in the early 1960s which closed many branch lines (just when suburban areas were growing which needed them). The number of railway stations was reduced from 5000 in 1958 to 2500 in 1968, subsequently reached an all-time low of 2358, but has now increased again to 2472 (Planning Bulletin, 5, 14 February 1992, p. 18).

Professor Colin Buchanan, a Scottish traffic engineer and planner, produced a report for the government entitled *Traffic in towns* (1963) in which he suggested ways of planning for the motor car whilst creating the minimum disturbance for residents living in inner-city areas. He suggested that 'environmental areas' should be identified in each town, identifiable neighbourhoods or districts which environmentally and socially formed a unit. Road widening and new urban motorways should be restricted to the edges of these areas to avoid traffic going through them and causing conflict. He suggested that, within the environmental area, roads should be mainly culs-de-sac, thus preventing traffic from taking short cuts and causing problems for local residents. His ideas were in many ways similar to the concept of the Radburn superblock upon which many new town neighbourhoods were based (see Chapter 10). They were also foreshadowed by a traffic engineer with the unlikely name of Alker Tripp, a London police commissioner who in the 1930s had suggested planning London's traffic on the basis of traffic precincts (areas) (Hall, 1994).

Scientific planning

In the 1960s computers were introduced to the planning process for the first time in Britain. Consequently, much use was made of mathematical models and scientific prediction methods for developing and justifying policy, especially transportation planning, which lent itself well to computerisation, with all those quantifiable trips and cars! Every respectable planning office got its own expert to cope with the computer (in those days one computer could fill a whole building). Retail gravity models were very popular – and still live on in parts of the private property sector. They are used to predict the likely demand for new floor space in shopping centres in relation to the size of the surrounding catchment area population and the distance they have to travel to reach the centre, relative to the attraction that other existing centres offer. Such approaches have been much criticised, not least by women, who constitute the majority of shoppers. Not all retail space is of the same quality, nor of the same use value to a particular individual. Secondly, the calculations were usually based on assumptions of people travelling chiefly by car, when many women have no access to a car during the daytime. The frequency of public transport, and the availability of facilities such as creches and child-friendly environments, public conveniences, reasonably priced goods and tea places are far more likely to act as inducements to use the centre.

Mathematical and scientific facts are not neutral, non-political or self-evident. Social and aesthetic factors cannot be measured in financial and numerical terms, although the social disruption of an area may be as important a factor as the cost of traffic congestion. It is not true that 'if you can't count it, it doesn't count', as some planners of the time opined, but in spite of scepticism and criticism from community interests, and transport user groups, there was also a proliferation of mathematical methodologies for predicting urban change, and aiding decision-making, e.g. cost–benefit analysis, threshold analysis, network analysis, etc. (Mishan, 1973; Lichfield, 1975; Roberts, 1973). The mathematical techniques of this period were good at quantitative measurement of factors which could be easily measured, but weak on evaluating qualitative social factors. Nowadays the use of qualitative methods is coming in more, which enable the evaluation of the immeasurables that make one scheme more successful or profitable than another.

This trend to 'scientific methods' was demonstrated *par excellence* by the enthusiasm planners developed for what was known as systems planning in the 1960s (McLoughlin, 1969). Basically the city was seen as an integrated human activity system, in which it was possible to measure and track changes, so that the planner could control the future state of the city. The ideas derived from the science of cybernetics (in the Greek, *kybernetes*, literally 'helmsman', 'steersman' – note the gender). There was a move, therefore, in the approach to plan making, from the traditional survey–analysis–plan approach to first setting goals and objectives and then looking at ways in which the city might be controlled to achieve those ends. Nowadays town planners are long since disillusioned with such ideas, although one still finds aspects of these 1960s approaches perpetuated in some branches of urban economics and regional planning. There was a danger in treating society as a gigantic scientific tidy system, which apparently operated according to neutral scientific laws, rather than as a disorganised, somewhat chaotic result of competing interest groups and political factions all trying to get their own way (Foley,1964).

The new development plan system

The traditional approach to plan making, based principally on simplistic land use zoning, was inadequate to deal with rapid change. The planners wished to incorporate advances in planning theory, and more public participation into the plan-making process. Therefore a new development plan system was introduced in the late 1960s, first on an experimental basis in just a few authorities (known as PAG authorities, that is, those selected by the Planning Advisory Group), but later extended to all local authorities. The result was the Town and Country Planning Act, 1968, later consolidated into the Town and Country Planning Act, 1971, which was intended to introduce a more flexible and accessible type of development plan, known as the Structure Plan. (Paradoxically, by nature the new plans and the jargon they were written in were even more confusing to the general public than the 1947 version).

Under the new system the plan consisted of both a written policy statement and diagrammatic plans of the policy directives (Chapter 2). The system was meant to be based on planners continuously monitoring change in the urban environment (using their new computers) to see how, for example, economic change would affect the demand for new industrial sites, or how changes in family structure were likely to affect housing demand. The planners sought to identify goals and objectives which they wanted to achieve as the basis of the plan, rather than drawing up a rigid once-and-for-all master plan. These goals, relating, for example, to the expansion of a particular area, or the provision of a certain level of facilities, could be reached in a variety of ways. The new Structure Plans were meant to be able to accommodate change rather than restrict it, provided it tied in with the urban goals that had been set, allowing a more flexible approach based on negotiation and agreement rather than preconceived land use plans. So a more incremental, that is, step-by-step, approach was adopted in order to achieve the long-term objectives. Ironically the new system proved even more long-winded and inflexible than the previous one and many local authorities had great difficulty producing the new Local and Structure Plans, let alone carrying out continuous monitoring. In these cases planning continued regardless, on the basis of existing plans and non-statutory plan updates as approved 'adopted plans' of the planning committee and therefore, in the interim, having the force of law. As stated earlier, the system is currently in transition again.

Disillusionment

There was considerable opposition to all these changes in the built environment, in architecture and in the planning system itself. Many people objected to the development of the new Manhattan-style skyline in British cities, where the high-rise movement dominated. Conservation groups became increasingly concerned at the visual impact (until then the highest buildings had been the church towers) and at the wanton demolition which was occurring (Esher, 1983). Many Victorian town halls narrowly missed destruction, and many a Georgian terrace was sacrificed. The government also introduced subsidies for hotel building in the late 1960s, leading to a spate of high-rise American-type 'plastic' hotels to encourage tourism. Quite what the tourists who had come to see the quaint old England thought can be imagined. Towns throughout the country were becoming more and more alike, with the same shops, the same shopping centres, high-rise blocks and traffic problems. People felt the new planning system had made the planners more remote, not more accountable.

A desire to return to more traditional values, and disillusionment with the Brave New World of the planners and property developers led to emphasis on improvement and conservation policies. The Civic Amenities Act, 1967, gave powers for the creation of Conservation Areas, and the listing of buildings of historical and architectural importance became a major issue. Developers adapted to these changes, such as Haslemere Estates, which made its fortune by specialising in the refurbishment of historic town squares and prestige buildings for offices (being the first in the field). This form of accommodation soon became more up-market and fashionable than an office suite in an impersonal concrete block.

There was considerable pressure for greater public participation in the planning process. Many ordinary people's houses had been cleared in the name of progress. Householders found their properties were being condemned without consultation as 'unfit for human habitation', i.e. slums (as Ravetz, 1980, graphically describes in relation to an actual example in Leeds). People wanted more emphasis on housing improvement and modernisation and less on clearance. The Denington Report (1966) reflected public concern, and proposed a change of direction away from clearance towards comprehensive improvement of both older housing and the surrounding environment. All this culminated in the Housing Act, 1969, which introduced 'general improvement areas' (GIAs) and increased the grants available for individuals to do up older property in inner areas. It marked a turning point in government policy and the beginning of serious recognition of and concern about what came to be known as the problems of the inner city. Whilst this legislation did benefit many inner-city residents or working-class people, it had unexpected results. Young middle-class couples were beginning to move back into the city centres and do up the houses.

Some were former students who had lived in such areas for financial reasons but on graduation, with a good salary, they were able to do the houses up. Thus began what became known as gentrification (trendification), that is, the colonisation of working-class areas by affluent middle-class people, the forerunners of the yuppies twenty years later. In the process property values went up and remaining working-class residents were gradually pushed out.

The 1970s

Recession and reaction

By the mid-1970s the bottom had begun to drop out of the property boom as oil prices increased, owing to wars in the Middle East, and the economy became generally more depressed. However, in spite of increased oil prices, there was still a growing demand for planners to take into account the needs of the motor car. This, in many respects, conflicted with the desire to plan in a way which took account of the need for conservation and the importance of local communities. Planning for the working classes had taken a back seat, with many of the needs of the poorer members of society still unmet, although there was a Labour government during the mid-1970s which was meant to be more aware of such issues. (It also drew its support from strong motor manufacturing unions and so suffered a conflict of interest regarding environmental issues.) In the early 1970s the economy took a dive into recession and unemployment because of the oil crisis. Traditional manufacturing industry in the depressed regions such as steel manufacturing and shipbuilding declined even further, and traditional secondary industry in other areas was affected. Paradoxically there was growth in other sectors of employment, particularly in the service sectors and in the new micro-chip industries, where it was noticeable that many of the jobs were taken by women who had the requisite skills and were cheaper and less unionised than the men.

The promise of the new leisure age prophesied in the 1960s where everyone would work three hours a day and play football the rest of the time (as some planners put it) was beginning to wane as unemployment reappeared. However, there were other groups, particularly the middle classes in the growing quaternary sector of management, the professions and technological research, who were experiencing higher levels of affluence and seemed to have more money for goods, e.g. boats to moor in the new marinas created out of derelict docks (only 3 per cent of households own a boat; only 5 per cent own a caravan). It would seem that two classes were developing, those with work and those without, and that a radical distribution of work opportunities would be required for everyone to benefit from the new age of leisure and technology: a suggestion which was politically unacceptable in terms of regional planning. Structure planning originated in a period of economic growth and prosperity. It is a very different matter to produce a strategy for decline. The quantitative mathematical emphasis in plan making was not the most appropriate way of dealing with these sensitive qualitative social and community issues.

Regional planning

An important digression will now be made to explain the development of regional planning in the post-war years, before continuing the discussion of planning for the inner city, because this branch of what is effectively *economic* planning was so closely linked with town planning for many years in the post-war period. The main landmarks of legislation over the years will be highlighted, but only some of the detail of percentage rates of grants and incentives will be given, because much of it has been repealed, and it only confuses; the aim is just to give a general idea of what sort of things were eligible for grants and how the system worked. It is more important to understand the reasons for the policies than the details.

One of the main reasons for regional planning was to reduce congestion in the south-east and to stimulate investment in depressed regions, and thus to create greater balance between regions. There have always been two sides to regional legislation. On the one hand restrictions have been imposed on where industry can locate. Secondly, grants were given (usually 20–40 per cent on average, but sometimes sinking to 15 per cent under Conservative governments or rising to 75 per cent under Labour in special cases) for such things as buildings, machinery, plant, infrastructure, training, etc. Also incentives and perks were given for the relocation of key workers and management from the south-east to the depressed areas. The government constructed trading estates, factory units, recreational facilities and housing, and even decentralised government departments from London to places such as Swansea in Wales (DVLC and the Royal Mint) or

Strathclyde in Scotland (some say, so that they get fewer callers dropping in with their problems).

The pre-war situation was discussed in the last chapter. The post-war Barlow Commission, and the related Distribution of Industry Act, 1945, had extended intervention so that wider 'development areas' covering 20 per cent of the population (as the depressed areas identified were called), still focused on these localities, were covered by the legislation on the basis of their levels of unemployment. Related to this, under the Town and Country Planning Act, 1947, industrial development certificates were first introduced (their use becoming more extensive under subsequent Acts) which restricted new development of over 5000 ft^2 in prosperous areas, thus encouraging industrialists to relocate – note, without distinguishing between inner and other urban areas therein, and no doubt causing unemployment in the area of origin. Advance factories were also established in the depressed areas in the immediate post-war years which happened, too conveniently, to tie in with the location of the disused wartime munition factories, e.g. on the Treforest estate in South Wales.

In 1958 there was another Distribution of Industry Act which extended powers to non-development areas where unemployment was high. Then in 1960 the Local Employment Act replaced the existing system with development districts which covered 10 per cent of the country (much smaller areas) but targeted aid more in giving 20 per cent grants on plant and machinery in these areas, and extended the system of development certificates. The Local Employment Act, 1963, gave building grants of 25 per cent on new industrial development in development districts, and also tax allowances and 10 per cent grants for plant and machinery. A range of grants were introduced for the improvement of derelict land of up to 85 per cent of the cost, and special grants for the provision of infrastructure and the attraction of key workers to development areas.

Economic and physical planning took on central importance under the Labour government of the 1960s. In 1965 regional economic planning boards and related advisory councils were established in order to create an intermediate regional planning level. They formed the institutional framework for the intended development of a much more carefully organised regional strategy, although their executive powers were fairly limited. Attempts were also made at a National Plan (an economic one, short-lived) and a whole series of national economic planning bodies were created to oversee economic development in the different industrial sectors (Little Neddies, as

they were called). A particular problem as perceived by the
Labour government, was the concentration of office development
in London. The Control of Offices and Industrial Development
Act, 1965, introduced office development permits (ODPs) for all
new office development in the south-east and Midlands over
3000 sq. ft, and the industrial development certificate system was
also made stricter for these areas. The Industrial Development
Act, 1966, tidied up what had by now become an unwieldy system,
creating five large development areas which covered 40 per cent
of Britain, introducing a range of grants and incentives.

The Special Development Areas Act, 1967, introduced
another level of area. However, wherever the boundaries are
drawn, and whether the areas are large or small, there will always
be resentment that some are in and others are out. Following the
Hunt report in 1969, the Local Employment Act, 1970, was
introduced, which designated a further series of intermediate
areas with their own grade of grants and incentives. The Industry
Act, 1972, was the last of the Labour government's big regional
planning Acts, the like of which has never been seen since. It
further developed a complex hierarchy of aid and control based
on several categories of area, consisting of development areas.
special areas, intermediate areas and derelict land (Hall, 1994;
Heap, 1995). In addition in 1975 the Labour government
introduced the Community Land Act, yet another attempt to
cream off the profits of property development for the benefit of
the community.

All these years of regional planning had not solved the
country's economic problems but would things have been worse
without it? The Conservative government which took over in the
late 1970s believed much of regional economic planning was only
supporting 'lame ducks' and actually penalising growth in other
areas. In particular it was felt that the government's policy should
more realistically reflect the changes in the economy, which was
moving away from traditional industry to tertiary and quaternary
activities. During the 1980s, the Thatcher decade, there was a
change of attitude, epitomising the values of the enterprise
culture. It is difficult to cite major Acts of Parliament which
brought the changes in, as the present government has often
preferred to introduce change through amendments, statutory
instruments and orders, and circulars, related to subtle alterations in existing legislation, rather than introducing clear-cut new
Acts. For example, both the Community Land Act, 1975, and the
office development permits were abolished by the Control of
Office Development (Cessation) Order in 1979, and in 1981
industrial development certificates were completely suspended.

In 1979 47 per cent of the population was covered by some

form of regional aid. By 1982 the extent of coverage had been reduced to 27 per cent of the working population, at which time a three-tier system was established of special development areas, development areas and intermediate areas, in which grants were available for plant and machinery at rates of 22 per cent, 15 per cent and on a discretionary basis respectively. But in 1984 aid was further drastically reduced, which led to a situation of 'less jam spread more thinly', as the late John Smith, then the Labour shadow Trade Secretary described it. The Conservatives clearly saw the inner city as a greater problem than the regions. Their strategy was based on the idea that there should be encouragement of private-sector business investment in the inner city. They saw this as a way of creating jobs and eradicating poverty and deprivation through private enterprise rather than through the state welfare programmes favoured by Labour. Changes in 1984 introduced a two-tier system of development areas which qualified for 15 per cent grants towards new plant and machinery and intermediate areas, which were eligible on a discretionary basis, with the areas themselves being greatly reduced. The emphasis had moved right away from regional planning to inner-city regeneration, with new legislation heralding Enterprise Zones and Urban Development Corporations.

For many ordinary people the regional dimension is still an important part of their lives, as manifested in the great disparities in house prices which built up throughout the 1980s. Also, even if our national government has down played regional issues, Britain is now subject to several EC Europe-wide directives and policies related to regional planning. In particular some areas have actually benefited from the European Regional Development Fund, although many people are still suspicious as to whether Britain is 'net', putting in more as a nation than it gets back from the complex system of EC finance. Nevertheless it could be argued that in a sense much of Britain is but one region on the margin of Europe and in competition with other member states, although London and the south-east are part of the Golden Triangle with Paris and Brussels, shortly to be further linked by the Channel tunnel, for better or worse. However, the government has retained some level of regional perspective, albeit at the 'sub-regional' level, in producing Regional Planning Guidance (RPG, 1989 and 1993) on the development of the regional conurbations in recent years, for example on Greater Manchester and Tyne-and-Wear. Recently signs of greater recognition of regional planning's importance have been emerging, particularly in respect of the balance between the congested south-east (SERPLAN, 1988 and subsequent reports) and the rest of the country. This was reflected in the 1995 revision of RPG3

(Regional Planning Guidance) *Strategic Guidance for London Planning Authorities.*

The inner city

In spite of continuing regional planning policy throughout most of the post-war period, by the 1970s inequality was visibly re-emerging in society and the economy, and social unrest was becoming manifest. Increasingly it was found that the tradition-ally depressed regions, which the post-war planning system had been geared up to deal with under the Industry Act, 1945, were not the only areas where there was poverty and unemployment. Also it was noticeable that the poverty and deprivation which were developing were not entirely explained by the rise in unemploy-ment, but were the result of other social problems such as racial discrimination, family break-up and an ageing population. The 'inner city' became the catch phrase to describe the collection of spatially identifiable groups and problems located broadly within the poorer inner urban neighbourhoods, corresponding to what traditional urban sociologists called the zone of transition (see Chapter 11).

Riots occurred in inner city areas, including Handsworth in Birmingham, Everton in Liverpool, St Pauls in Bristol, Tottenham in London and Sparkbrook in Birmingham. Some would say that the overconcentration on the development of new towns, and on new development in general, plus decentralisation of employ-ment to the regions through regional economic planning policy, had taken the guts out of the cities and actually created many of the problems. Others were warning, from a variety of political perspectives, of the potential problems of concentrations of deprived ethnic minority groups in inner-city areas. Enoch Powell in 1968 made his 'rivers of blood' speech, painting an inflammatory view of the future. The Commission for Racial Equality concluded that certain racial groups were actively kept out of all-white areas by racist estate agents and biased local authority housing managers, thus creating an enforced ghetto situation (CRE, 1989). Many estate agents pleaded that they simply had not realised, and so more sensitivity was needed all round.

By the 1970s the problem of the inner city had become firmly established in the public's conscience. The 1969 Housing Act, as stated, had given many of the older housing areas a new lease of life, but it had not necessarily solved the related social problems – indeed, as we have seen, the existing residents were often being pushed out as a result of its policies. In 1968 the Home Office initiated the Urban Programme with thirty-four pilot local authorities, to investigate the emerging problems of the inner city: note that this project was as much concerned with rising crime as with wider social issues. In 1969 the Community Development Programme was set up, CDPs running in twelve areas initially, with social workers rather than town planners taking the leading role. However, it was fashionable at the time to see the problems spatially as specific to and caused by a particular location, such as the inner city, without necessarily considering the social forces that brought people 'down' into such areas in the first place. For example, in 1970 'educational priority areas' were established where positive discrimination was needed – interestingly, towards the white working class rather than ethnic groups at this stage, as in the case of a scheme which was established in Everton in Liverpool.

In 1971 'comprehensive community programmes' were introduced in a range of areas, widening the concern to include education, health, social services and housing. In 1972 the emphasis shifted towards special policies within the realms of town planning itself, and the Department of the Environment established its Six Towns Study, focusing on areas such as Lambeth in southern inner London, and at last publicly recognising poverty near at hand. The 1974 Housing Act established another category of special housing areas known as 'housing action areas', which were smaller than general improvement areas but in which the emphasis was upon more concentrated immediate attention. Such schemes often seemed separate from or insensitive to other social problems in the areas chosen. For example, in one black inner city area in Birmingham where unemployment was high, white workmen were brought in by the council to repair black tenants' houses, causing considerable tension in community relations. In 1975 the Urban Aid programme enabled money to be allocated to other inner-city schemes, including community centres, and later law centres. In 1977 the Manpower Services Commission was set up with particular concern for enabling employment in inner areas. This was followed by the Inner Urban Areas Act, 1978, which as the name suggests enabled the creation of special inner urban area policies, this time under the control chiefly of the town planners. The Local Government and Housing Act, 1989, has introduced the concept of Renewal Areas which are like the old general improvement areas and housing action areas (which they replace) but the emphasis is on more partnership with the private sector in renewal, and grants to individual householders are means-tested.

The 1980s

Retrospect

The planners had done a great deal but had solved very few problems, in fact they had created many new ones. Perhaps they were going about it all from the wrong perspective. It all depends on what you see as the role of the planner. Some would say that inner-city problems are the result of deeper social and economic forces which can be solved only by dealing with unemployment and social deprivation, in which case the planner's role is limited to ensuring that land use zoning provides adequate employment. Others would say that the quality of the area itself does affect people's behaviour and life chances (as will be explained in Chapter 11). Indeed, some would blame the planners and their policies for inner-city unrest. For example, after the Brixton riots of the early 1980s Lord Scarman implied in his report (1982) that the planners were to blame. If this is so, then the planner has a major role in social problem-solving, offering 'salvation by bricks'. Indeed, many of the nineteenth-century visionaries believed that transplanting people into model communities with plenty of grass, trees and sunshine would change them as people.

Enterprise

The Local Government Planning and Land Act, 1980, con-solidated the legislation relating to policies which had come in during the late 1970s, moving resources and emphasis from the New Towns and regional planning to the inner city. But the approach, as stated, was to encourage private businesses to move back in, and so create jobs and prosperity, although there was no guarantee that other social problems would be solved as a result. In particular the government introduced enterprise zones and Urban Development Corporations. (See the current edition of Heap's *Outline of planning law* for lists of these.) The aim in both cases was to reduce planning controls by suspending ordinary planning law to some extent so as to encourage firms to move back into the inner city. All sorts of other grants, loans, rates 'holidays' and other incentives were introduced, including the City Grant for the redevelopment of areas and repair of buildings too far gone to be of interest to the developer (which can often be used with effect alongside Conservation Area policy). Although many firms took up the offer, as with old-fashioned regional planning, it is debatable whether new jobs and new prosperity were really created or whether firms simply moved across the boundary in order to claim the grant, thus depriving other areas of existing employment.

Enterprise zones are relatively small areas, the size of a small industrial estate, administered via the local authority, whereas UDCs are much larger, for example the London docklands or the Bristol Development Corporation. Urban Development Corporations are administered by a separate *ad hoc* governing development corporations (in a similar way to the old New Towns). Neither the enterprise zones nor the UDCs are meant to last for ever and have a life expectancy of around ten years, when they will be de-designated (it is already happening to some of the early ones), the aim being simply to give them special status whilst they are finding their feet. Considerable investment is put into infrastructure, as in the case of the Docklands light railway in London, and into road improvements.

Whilst the London Docklands Development Corporation has created a whole new area for residential and business use near the City of London, and so convenient for the yuppie business person, there is considerable resentment among some of the original working-class residents. Although the inner-city legislation was purportedly meant to be on their behalf, it has benefited middle-class people far more. People remember how difficult it was in the past even to get the council to put on an extra bus service to get them to work, whereas now expense is no object. Meanwhile, because of high house prices, and the lack of council or cheap rented accommodation, many working-class people who are employed in central London (on the Tube, in the hospitals, cleaning offices or shops) find they have to commute further and further out, whilst managers wonder why there is no longer a ready supply of working-class labour to do all the essential yet low-status jobs upon which the running of the capital depends.

In 1985 the government introduced White Paper 9517, *Lifting the burden*, which emphasised minimising the perceived restrictions on economic growth created by planning controls. Subsequently the Housing and Planning Act, 1986, introduced, among other things, simplified planning zones which supplement the enterprise zones and Urban Development Corporations but are smaller and the criteria for location are more flexible. Meanwhile, paradoxically (in non-special category areas) planning law itself has, if anything, become more complex, and the Conservatives introduced charges for planning applications in the late 1970s. In spite of gimmicky schemes such as garden festivals and other inner-city initiatives unemployment has continued to rise, inner-city problems continue, and regional disparities have become even greater. Many would argue that it is time to bring back regional planning (Hamnett *et al.*, 1989), provided it is based on more sensitive criteria than last time – for example, taking account of women's employment as well as men's, and showing awareness of the great social disparities which can exist within a region such as the south-east between run-down inner-city areas and the more prosperous suburbs and market towns.

The 1990s

Inner-city problems continue, and if anything have become worse because of the property recession of the early 1990s which followed hard on the heels of the 1980s boom. However, at least recession has meant a drop in house prices in some areas, allowing more people access to housing, and reduced some of the pressure for development on greenfield sites. However, housing seems to have replaced planning and the inner city as the major urban social problem in the eye of the media public. Homelessness has been a continuing problem, with large numbers of people sleeping on the streets, as is shown constantly on the news and documentary television programmes. The housing situation has become increasingly topical in the light of the swing in government policy away from state provision of council housing in the 1980s. Under the Housing Act, 1980 (followed by a series of Acts such as the 1985 Housing Act, further marginalising the role of public-sector housing management) tenants were given the right to buy their council house. This was all right for them, but it reduced the stock of housing available to people on waiting lists. At the same time very little new council housing has been built over the last ten years. However, there has been a revival of interest in the voluntary housing sector and the government has favoured contributing financially to the building and management programmes of housing associations (Smith, 1989), reducing local authority housing departments' role in the provision of social housing. Generally the government went for more targeting of special housing and planning schemes in the inner city and on problem estates in terms of finance and support (arguably thus reducing local government's say in the management of its locality).

Although there have been a series of new town planning Acts in the 1990s, dealing mainly with the format of the development system and the enforcement of planning control, there does not appear to have been, at first sight, any strong policy statement on national town planning policy as one would have expected from governments in the past, particularly Labour

ones seeking to demonstrate their commitment to state intervention. This is chiefly because the Conservative government of the
1990s favours the development activities of the private sector
rather than state intervention. Much of the legislation has been
concerned with tidying up and consolidating previous amendments rather than altering, or abolishing, the system. This is
because, whilst the Conservative government has sought to
promote the needs of business interests by reducing state
planning intervention, at the same time it is under pressure from
other groups to conserve and protect the environment from
further encroachment by development, particularly in the shire
counties. Indeed, there have been many demands for more, or
different, forms of town planning from a variety of interest
groups, ranging from the private property sector, which wants
more government investment in the infrastructure, even private
toll motorways, to various community groups who want more
'people-centred' planning and 'green' environmental pressure
groups. The government has suggested the idea of additional
motorways funded by the private sector, is building a second
Severn bridge, and has considered increasing both investment in
and competition on the railways. Better regional planning might
solve many of the traffic problems by spreading development,
jobs and houses more evenly and so reducing the pressure for
journeys in congested areas. However, as will be seen in the last
section, although the present government has been committed to
reducing state intervention and regional and urban planning, in
fact, rather like Topsy which 'just grew and grew', by the mid
1990s it had created at large collection of new initiatives and
programmes which together comprise a significant new 'block' of
planning policy.

New Times?

Many of the changes in approaches to urban governance, and
related urban economic policy making are reflective of new
philosophies and approaches to managing the national economy.
Many commentators consider we have now entered a post-fordist
and neo-liberal phase (Hall and Jacques, 1989). This means, that
traditional economic structures and 'ways of doing things' have
been replaced by a range of more experimental, entrepreneurial
initiatives and business enterprises (Atkinson and Moon, 1994;
Stoker and Young, 1993; Rydin, 1993). This is expressed in
the nature of the urban renewal initiatives now in place in the
mid 1990s. For example, many of these are targeted towards

encouraging a diversity of small businesses grouped within the quaternary economic sector (professional, retail, services) rather than concentrating, as in the past, upon attracting one large employer with a huge workforce skilled in secondary sector industrial production (manufacturing, processing, assembly).

As indicated in earlier sections, central, and increasingly local authorities have been bypassed in the organisation of new economic urban initiatives, with central government often making direct partnerships and linkages with the private sector: with business and property developers direct. (This is discussed in detail in Chapter 4 of Volume III.) In addition to the UDCs, there have been a range of other programmes and initiatives in which private developers dealt directly with central government to obtain funding as under the City Grant provisions introduced in the late 1980s. Because of the increasing diversity and complexity of government schemes, attempts were made to co-ordinate the various policies, firstly under 'headings' such as 'Action for Cities' and the 'Urban Programme', and in 1991 under 'City Challenge'. This was subsequently superseded by the Single Regeneration Budget (SRB) in April 1994. This combines over 20 existing programmes, such as Estate Action, City Challenge, Urban Programme, Safer Cities, TEC Challenge *inter alia*. The SRB also seeks to co-ordinate the input of different government departments, such as the DOE, Home Office, Employment Department, local authorities (significantly), and other bodies concerned with the social, economic and physical regeneration of inner city areas, through, interestingly, a system of integrated regional offices. It would seem that in order to manage such a vast initiative the government finds it cannot do without 'regional planning' (in all but name), and an increased role for local authorities.

This is but a brief indication of the changes which are taking place, because the newcomer is likely to be overwhelmed by the range of initiatives, programmes and details. (Readers should consult the current professional press for updates on the situation.) The cynical person has to ask how much of all this is merely publicity 'hype' just renaming tired programmes, and shifting limited funds around without necessarily creating new investment. In particular, local authorities are increasingly concerned that whilst local government finance has been restricted, in its place, central government has taken on a more direct role in allocating funds locally, often expecting local authorities and bodies to bid competitively for funds rather than receiving them automatically. However, it would seem that the government has now created such a diversity of programmes that they find they cannot do without the 'planning' and 'management' functions traditionally carried out by local government in order to implement central government policy at local area level, creating a new 'managerial localism'. However, local authorities, and especially town planning departments therein, have always sought to be more than mere agents of central government policy, but to have a policy making input themselves. It would seem SRB may provide opportunities for more input, and opportunity to tie these specialist high-level programmes back into mainstream statutory development plan-making. There has been concern that such a strong thrust towards property market-led initiatives within the inner city as SRB presents might weaken and marginalise traditional town planning functions in some areas, and imbalance the overall urban situation. In studying 'town planning' it is always important to look at the nature of the governmental structures through which town planning policy is implemented, as well as looking at the policies themselves (Healey, 1988). The themes of implementation, agency, regulation, management (and related managerialist perspectives), localism, and urban governance are developed further in Volumes II, and III in this series.

PART III

The visual and design aspects of planning

Chapter 8

The historical development of town planning

In this part the visual aspects of town planning are discussed. Cities are more than a collection of economic, social and physical factors: they are the visual setting to people's lives. There is a long historical tradition of town planning being aligned to architecture, civic design being seen as a branch of art. Firstly, in this chapter, the issue of townscape is considered, then an account is given of the development of the historical heritage. Secondly, in Chapter 9, urban and rural conservation is covered, and thirdly, in Chapter 10 planning controls and design standards for modern development are explained. One of the problems of post-war town planning is that it strayed too far in the direction of seeing cities in terms of function, disregarding matters of design, townscape and architectural detail, and of not appreciating the effects this would have on the well-being of the people.

Townscape: Prince Charles's ten principles

The general atmosphere and feel of an area (Lynch, 1960), the satisfaction of the residents and indeed the saleability and commercial attractiveness of a development may be influenced by quite small but significant details such as the colour of the brick. For example, red-brick buildings may look more homely than yellow London brick, and worse are grey slate roofs, which look very dull and chilly on a wet day (Prizeman, 1975). Traditional architectural detail, ornament and well-finished construction can create a sense of well-being, whereas functional concrete slabs can be stark, unfriendly, and invite graffiti. The original Corbusian idea of stark white towers rising under a blue Mediterranean sky, from which rain seldom falls, is inappropriate in Britain. Le Corbusier's flat roofs were a practicality in such climates rather than a constant maintenance problem as in Britain. The space around the buildings is equally important.

Sympathetic planting can soften hard layouts, add colour and interest, and trees increase privacy and shelter, creating a cohesive 'townscape' of buildings and their surroundings.

Topically Prince Charles (1989) has drawn attention to the deficiencies of modern town planning and architecture, but they have also been a theme stressed by leaders of the town planning profession itself. Prince Charles, significantly, has concentrated on the visual aspects rather than the functional or social aspects. In the second part of his book he presents ten principles. They are summarised here to be borne in mind as the different historical periods are discussed in this chapter. They are not tremendously earth-shattering but similar to other writings on design, and echo many of the ideas proposed by architectural critics from the early twentieth century such as Trystan Edwards, Clough Williams Ellis (of Portmeirion fame) and Osbert Lancaster. There have been many critics of Prince Charles's views, such as Max Hutchinson (1989), president of the RIBA at the time the book was published, whilst the principles were supported by (the late) Francis Tibbalds, the then president of the RTPI.

Prince Charles's ten principles are Place, Hierarchy, Scale, Harmony, Enclosure, Materials, Decoration, Art, Signs and Lights, and Community. The first principle concerns the importance of Place, that is, land, a need to respect what might best be described as the *genius* of the place, sensitivity towards the aspect, slope and character of the site – a theme which has run right through the landscape movement in Britain. The second principle stresses the importance of respecting the hierarchy of relationships between buildings, and of the components which make up each building, so that, for example, everyone is clear where the front door is (as the Prince points out, it is not always in the middle in modern architecture). The classical style of architecture, which was dominant for several centuries, had a clearly defined set of rules governing such matters. They were undermined firstly by the eclecticism of Victorian times, and later by the 'anything goes' anarchy of self-expression within the modern movement. The third principle stresses the importance of the human scale, and the fourth reiterates the importance of architectural harmony. The fifth emphasises the importance of enclosure, that is, sensitivity to the spaces between buildings, which was a major issue in Renaissance and baroque architecture, with its emphasis on perspective and illusions of space to set the buildings off in relation to each other. The sixth principle concerns the use of appropriate materials, particularly praising regional and vernacular differences in the use of building materials. The seventh principle raises the importance of decoration, which is seen as integral to the building and not something cosmetic added on afterwards to cover a bad design. Quite apart from the influence of the modern movement, architecture in the 1960s put little emphasis on good design or decoration, because of the cost. However, this was rather a narrow view, as buildings become more marketable if they are 'different', and therefore good design pays.

The eighth principle applauds the importance of seeing architecture as a branch of art (rather than as merely construction) and calls for a return to the classical *beaux-arts* tradition of drawing as part of architectural training. Subsequently Prince Charles established an Institute of Architecture housed in two Nash buildings in Regents Park, offering a range of short courses and one-year courses, separate from the RIBA (*Guardian*, 31 January 1992). The ninth principle seems to be more of a development control than a building design principle and concerns restrictions on signs, lights and advertisements within the street scene. The Prince amusingly states 'do not make rude signs in public places', alluding to tacky advertising and shop signs. The tenth and final principle is of a different genre altogether and emphasises the importance of community and social factors.

Whilst many of these principles are laudable, one should nevertheless adopt a critical perspective in evaluating their validity in respect of specific examples of architecture. It should be borne in mind that buildings are seldom seen solely as architecture, but more often as important financial components of property portfolios, as economic commodities within the market system. Also buildings are usually built for a purpose, for a client: that is, they do have a specific practical and social function, they are not just ornaments. However, one of the problems of the modern movement, which the Prince is reacting against, is the overemphasis on the function alone as encapsulated in such architectural slogans as 'form follows function' and 'function is beauty, beauty is function'. The buildings of the modern movement often proved very unfunctional, or were limited to a passing trend in function, thus rapidly becoming redundant. Some of the buildings from the 1960s cannot take all the modern cabling required for computerised office activities because they were built to minimum space standards internally. In contrast, older buildings with high ceilings can be refurbished to allow for all the ducting and technology with a false ceiling and still look good inside and out.

The Prince is somewhat silent on the question of the effects on town planning of people using the building in terms of the generation of traffic, car parking and pedestrian flows. Traffic is one of the biggest problems for town planners, and is generated anywhere people live, work or exist, regardless of the architectural style of the buildings they are using. To create a more pleasing townscape a more fundamental change would be to provide more investment in public transport to reduce congestion, building attrition and noise, and to decentralise many of the central area functions to the suburbs (as happened to industry). In the ideal approach to town planning for the next millennium, equal importance would be given to the social, economic, physical and visual aspects of urban development.

Historical development

A description follows of some of the main aspects of the historical development of town planning and architecture. This section is intended to provide a thumbnail sketch of each period, and further guidance and reading are given in Appendix I. The aim is to cover the main themes but not to enter into deep analysis at this introductory level. To reiterate, this knowledge is important, particularly because of the emphasis on urban conservation today, which requires a basic knowledge of why buildings are considered important. The main thrust of this section is in relation to Western European architecture, because that is the context of British town planning. At various periods Chinese, Arabic and Indian architectural styles have influenced British work, and of course there are many other urban civilisations and cultural traditions which are of great worth in their own right in other parts of the world. The following historical periods will now be covered: ancient (Egyptian), classical (Greek and Roman), medieval, Renaissance, Georgian, Victorian and modern (see Table 8.1 for dates).

The ancient world

Architectural features and town planning principles from ancient times have been a continual source of inspiration to designers, and, for example, one can see a certain 'neo-Egyptian' influence both in 1930s architecture and nowadays in postmodern architecture. In the world of ancient Egypt town planning and architecture had the role of reinforcing the power and importance of the ruling elite, e.g. the priests and pharoahs, by the creation of gigantic temples, pyramids and palaces (Mumford, 1965). These often had a mystical rather than practical

Table 8.1 Chronological development of architectural styles

Date	World	Europe	Britain	
BC				
5000	Ancient world			
3000	Egypt			
2000	Mycenae, Knossos			
1000	Early Greece			
500	Greek	Greek		
400	Roman	Roman	Roman	
50				
AD				
400		Byzantine		
600	Islamic		Anglo-Saxon	
900		Romanesque		
		Norman		
1066			Norman	
	Crusades			
			Gothic	
1200			Early English	1200
1300			Decorated	1300
1450		Renaissance	Perpendicular	1400
			Tudor	1485
1550		High Renaissance	Elizabethan	1560
	South America	Palladian, Baroque	Jacobean	1620
1600			Classicism	
			(Great Fire,	1666)
1700		Rococo	Queen Anne	
			Georgian	1714
1800	Colonial	Neo-Classicism	Adam	
	Eastern styles	Romanticism	Regency	
			Victorian	
			Neo-Classicism	
			Neo-Gothic	
			Arts and Crafts	
			Garden City	
			movement	
1900	American		*Edwardian*	
			Art-Nouveau	
		Futurism		
		Functionalism	*Modern Movement*	
1930		Bauhaus	Functionalism	
	International	International style	Mock-Tudor	
	style		suburbia	
			Art deco	
			Neo-Egyptian	
1950		Late international	Neo-futurism	
		style		
1960			Brutalism	
1970				
1980		High-tech	Neo-vernacular	
1990		Green movement	Postmodernism	

Also many examples to be seen of 'Neo-Geo', 'Pseudo-Tudor revival' and 'Essex Design Guide', 'Conservation Area', 'Brick is Beautiful' styles as designs become increasingly varied in both domestic and commercial architecture.

Note: The dates are approximate and refer to the beginnings of a particular style. The names are derived from the historical period in which they developed; however, they often continue in popularity and as a source of influence into subsequent eras.

purpose by modern standards, thus illustrating that planning is in a sense neutral: it can be used for a wide range of political and ideological purposes. In comparison it is interesting that both Hitler and Mussolini favoured heavy enormous classical architecture. Totalitarian regimes, political or otherwise, seem to favour megalithic architecture on a knock-out scale. Large Egyptian cities, such as Thebes, with great processional routes and geometrically laid out streets were designed chiefly to serve the religious and governmental role of the state. Planning does not have to have a social welfare function, or to be associated with concepts of equality and democracy.

Many of the early settlements were located where there were a good water supply, good transport routes and fertile ground to support the population. A river valley was an ideal location, with the town sitting at the narrowest, bridging point of a river. Nowadays towns and cities can be located virtually anywhere provided there is adequate technology to overcome natural disadvantages and enough money to pay for it. In Britain the development of the national electricity, gas, and water grids and road and rail networks reduced the geographical restrictions on location considerably. The main constraints on development nowadays are likely to be the result of planning controls.

Most of the ancient civilisations built their main public buildings in stone or other local materials. For centuries, right up to the industrial revolution, every region in every country in the world had its own local architecture, distinguished by its local building materials and its own style, which developed in response to the needs of the village culture and the constraints of the local climate. (This raises again the classic geographical determinism debate: is it the geography of the area which makes the people the way they are, or the people who shape the built environment?) With the coming of mass-produced materials and the spread of the international style of architecture, building materials have become much more similar in different countries in the twentieth century, and may be supplied by the same multinational suppliers. Indeed, it is now expensive to build in local stone.

Nowadays it is often quite difficult to get hold of the original materials for restoration work. Maintenance has always been a major problem in respect of ancient historical buildings the world over. The present-day emphasis on conservation has broadened the emphasis to not just preserving building as historical monuments but also restoring the surrounding context of the buildings which form the backcloth and setting to the main attractions. In the case of more recent (rather than ancient) historical buildings the aim is to ensure that they are conserved as part of the living fabric of the city, and are used rather than being just preserved as antiquities. Obviously the very ancient buildings are in another category, as they are no longer surrounded by the original settlement but stand in isolation. Or do they? In Egypt the pyramids are very near the growing outer suburbs of Cairo, but the tourist photographs always give the impression they are miles from anywhere in the middle of the desert.

The classical world

Classical Greece

Greek civilisation is the source of many of the ideas and philosophies of Western civilisation. The classical style of architecture, with its use of columns, topped by capitals in the three main orders – Doric, Ionic and Corinthian – are still seen by many as the only real architecture. (Basically the Doric has what looks like a spare tyre on the top of the column, the Ionic has 'two eyes' on it, actually a stylised depiction of curled rams' horns, and the Corinthian has decorative acanthus leaves above the column.) The Greeks developed theories on town planning many of which they put into practice in the building of their city states and colonial towns. Most Greek settlements were based on a grid layout (streets at right angles to each other) but they combined this with a flexibility of design which took into account the particular features of the site, creating natural amphitheatres in the hillsides. Greek settlements centred on the *agora* (market place), which was surrounded by the main public buildings such as the *stoa* (town hall), etc. Not only did the Greeks build magnificent streets and buildings but they took into account the needs of sanitation, drainage, water supply. Lewis Mumford (1965) stated that the quality of a civilisation should be judged by the way in which it disposes of its waste, which exonerates the Greeks but condemns our own society. The architecture of Athens has acted as a model for generations of architects. The Parthenon (a temple) on the top of the Acropolis (a hill in the centre of the city) has inspired many travellers and is generally considered to embody perfect harmony of proportion. It became fashionable in the eighteenth and nineteenth centuries to make the Grand Tour of Europe, and many of the features of Greek architecture were copied back in Britain, adding a touch of 'class' to the new industrial cities, e.g. Birmingham town hall (Briggs, 1968). Nowadays some of the buildings on and around the Parthenon are being restored, virtually rebuilt, a subject of much controversy. People are often startled by the fact that many of the Greek temples would originally have had red 'Roman' tile roofs.

Roman planning

The architecture and town planning concepts of Rome were highly influential on the work of subsequent centuries. Rome completes the classical period, with the emphasis shifting to a more decorative and ostentatious style, Greek architecture being purer and more simple. In fact throughout history it is noticeable how architectural styles go in cycles from pure classical simple buildings into more and more ornate styles → ostentatious styles → mixtures and novelties → over-decorative → reaction → return to classical simplicity. Some would say the modern movement towards plain abstract architecture was a reaction against the over-decorative styles of Victorian times. On the other hand the present emphasis on conservation and neo-vernacular and generally more traditional historical styles may be leading to another decorative phase of architecture that is about to emerge – or perhaps architecture will react violently the other way, back to modernism, or towards what is called deconstructivism, which is an attempt to get back to basics.

The Roman Empire was a vast city-building enterprise and 'Every Roman soldier had a town plan in his knapsack,' indeed, the army did most of the construction and many of the town planners, civil engineers and architects were military men. Roman towns were more standardised than Greek ones, and were based on a simple grid layout with a square in the centre, called the forum, and several other standard public amenities were provided around the town such as baths, latrines, an arena, etc. There was an element of land use zoning based on the social rank differences and occupations of the residents, with distinct retail (merchants) and industrial (artisans) areas. As in most ancient and classical civilisations a high proportion of the population would be slaves. It is important to remember that when the Greeks talked about the ideal city consisting of 5000 people they meant the people who mattered: slaves, women, tradespeople, etc., were marginal.

The greatest engineering achievements of the Romans were the perfection of the arch and the dome, elements that were not features of earlier styles. The Colosseum in Rome is a good example of arch construction, as are the many aqueducts and viaducts throughout the empire in Europe and North Africa. Fresh water, efficient sewerage and drainage and good roads were all features of Roman development, and in many respects they were never surpassed until the industrial revolution. The Roman town was an important colonising tool in the empire, acting as a garrison and an administrative centre in order to subdue the local population. Defensive walls were an essential feature of many Roman settlements. Indeed, for centuries most towns and cities had walls, and town planning was in certain respects a military exercise to ensure effective defensive measures. The Roman towns and interconnecting roads established the basic national land use and settlement pattern for Britain's subsequent development. Today many main roads follow Roman routes. Many of the main towns and cities (especially those ending in -chester, -caster or -cester) are of Roman origin. Some believe the Romans were in fact following earlier roads related to ley lines (prehistoric lines of terrestrial power) and that many of their settlements were based on earlier religious or tribal centres in what was a sophisticated but predominantly rural society that antedated urban civilisation.

Medieval development

Rushing through the centuries after the Romans left, there were a series of other invasions but in general Britain reverted to a more rural society in which towns functioned as market centres and local administrative centres rather than being part of the mechanism of a highly centralised empire. The Norman empire, which was extended to Britain by William the Conqueror in 1066, had a major effect on the land use patterns of Britain. It influenced the class structure and feudal foundations of society, in fact many families in the House of Lords today can trace their ancestors right back to their Norman roots when they came over with William the Conqueror. The Church was the main administrative arm of the state. The establishment of abbeys and the endowment of cathedrals led to a new spate of construction, and the development of new market places, squares and related buildings administered by the ecclesiastical powers. There were also some new towns built by Edward I (Bell, 1972) and castles built mainly for defence but in general towns grew and expanded naturally over the centuries in an unplanned, organic manner. For example, a small settlement might develop beside a river and gradually tracks would develop into roads that meandered down the valley side to a bridge. From time to time houses would be built alongside the roads where and when the residents felt the need. Bit by bit other facilities, artisan quarters, houses, paddocks and market places would develop, often centring round a well or a cross-roads. Roads would follow footpaths, creating the typically irregular street pattern characteristic of medieval towns. All this contrasts with the premeditated plan characteristic of Roman towns, and other periods of history when the design was imposed from above by a powerful empire, military force or ruler upon the subject population.

In medieval times the main architectural styles were of two types. Firstly, there was the official architecture of the church or cathedral. The Norman style (with a rounded arch) preceded the Gothic style (pointed arch), which went through various phases from a simple basic style to a very decorative, exaggerated style. The Gothic was a style much copied in later centuries, especially by the Victorians when building railway stations. The other style, or rather collection of styles, was the vernacular. It is not really a style at all in the formal sense, rather it is applied to the efforts of the local builders and carpenters who built the cottages and dwellings of the ordinary people. As explained in Appendix II distinct styles emerged in different parts of the country according to the availability of materials and local weather conditions. Thatch and half-timbering were not universal, indeed slate and stone were probably more common in some areas, and cob in others. Nowadays neo-vernacular is very popular but whether it is a genuine style is another matter. Mock-Tudor (pseudo-Tudor) is a variation of 'neo-veo' which has always been scorned by architects and loved by the people.

Left to themselves towns and cities tend to evolve naturally if somewhat chaotically and not necessarily in the best interests of all the residents. In recent years, almost in reaction against overplanning, there has been a return to enthusiasm for organic, natural town forms. Paradoxically, to achieve this effect nowadays – for example, on a new housing layout – requires forethought and planning to create a genuine quaint townscape! Another effect of current emphasis on the virtues of the past, and on conservation in particular, has been to stop the change that would naturally occur and to freeze it in a conservation area. Any normal street scene is usually made up of buildings from different historical periods cheek by jowl; some clashing and some complementary. Emphasis on design policy controls may lead to artificial sterilisation of the townscape.

The Renaissance

Towards the end of the Middle Ages in Europe the sway of the Church began to become less dominant in the more prosperous city states which were developing, particularly in Italy, where self-made businessmen and merchants rather than traditional feudal powers took control. There was a rebirth (renaissance) of interest in the ideas and culture of the classical civilisation of the Greeks and Romans, which were considered more appropriate to modern needs than the mystical other worldly emphasis of the Middle Ages. In architectural circles there was considerable enthusiasm for the use of classical features in new public buildings and palaces to express the wealth of the merchant princes e.g. the Medicis in Florence. Splendid new town planning features were introduced to Italian cities as in effect central area redevelopment occurred. Emphasis was put on the creation of a formal central square (along the lines of the forum or *agora*), the piazza. Most Mediterranean settlements have always had market squares which often act as 'outdoor living rooms' where people meet and eat in the pavement cafés and stroll in the cool of the evening. Many Italian cities at the time were built at a fairly high density owing to the need for defensive city walls. It was dangerous and expensive to extend them even if population growth occurred. The overall layout of many early Renaissance Italian cities was shaped by the need for defence, and one can see many examples, both in Italy and in the planning books, of geometrically laid out military settlements with octagonal, star-shaped or circular forms. The squares acted as important safety valves in providing communal open space, and areas for military parades and *festas* (religious processions and carnivals). Later Renaissance piazzas often incorporated a colonnaded walkway in the classical style along one side, and fountains and statues tastefully arranged in the centre.

Parallel to the developments in town planning and architecture, Renaissance art was also rediscovering the classical tradition and developing new ways of creating the illusion of space and three-dimensional illusions of reality. The use of perspective techniques to create space and depth in paintings was carried over into town planning. Long narrow squares with a statue or townscape feature placed strategically at the vanishing point drew the eye into a greater perception of three-dimensional space. Making the windows on a building progressively but imperceptively smaller as the upper floors were reached gave an illusion of height. In fact town planning and architecture had more in common with theatrical stage set design and 'art' than with modern-day 'nitty-gritty' practical functional land use planning.

Venice is one Renaissance city of particular interest to modern planners. It had all the features of piazza planning but also serves as an ideal example of complete pedestrian–vehicular segregation. This is because there are no roads, only canals.

Originally Venice consisted of a series of swamps and small islands that were reclaimed by the construction of drainage canals. Each small man-made island was centred on a well in a piazza, in which fresh water rose up from the artesian basin under the sea bed. A natural neighbourhood unit developed around each well which also acted as a model of the ideal community to planning theorists over the centuries. Another interesting feature of Venice is the unique architectural style, a combination of classical, Gothic and eastern Mediterranean Muslim influences. It was much copied, particularly by the Victorians for example, the Bristol 'Byzantine' style.

It was in Rome that the Renaissance style really developed on a magnificent scale as the High Renaissance style (quickly followed by the baroque and the rococo styles). Various Popes in conjunction with various great names in art and architecture, e.g. Michelangelo, Bernini, etc., progressively redeveloped the centre of Rome, creating magnificent squares and processional avenues. St Peter's itself was rebuilt in a style that resembled a pagan Roman temple, replacing the Gothic structure which was destroyed in a fire. The baroque style of planning and architecture made much of the space around and between buildings. An obelisk (pointed stone column monument) was often placed in the centre of a square to act as a pivot to the geometrical layout of avenues and buildings radiating from it. No expense was spared, but it should be remembered that the aim of this type of town planning was not to rehouse the poor, or zone industry, or solve traffic problems; such matters were of little interest. The grand manner of Renaissance planning gradually spread throughout Europe. It was the ideal style in which to express the power of the ruler and the state. Many European cities were replanned (some several times) with boulevards, squares, fountains, statues and triumphal arches. Town planning was essentially a form of art and aimed at meeting the aspirations of the rising merchant classes and affluent bourgeoisie. (This paragraph just about sums up European planning from the sixteenth century through to the nineteenth.)

Georgian planning

Georgian planning and architecture were the result of the impact of the Renaissance on Britain, but the style, scale and whole approach are significantly different from the grand manner in Europe (Summerson, 1986). The Georgian style (broadly contemporary with the reigns of the first four Georges) is a mixture of classical Italian Renaissance features with other influences from northern Europe. In particular the Dutch had developed (with their usual enthusiasm for frugality, cleanliness and puritanism) a distinctive domestic (housing) architectural style as expressed in the neat but restrained symmetrically proportioned brick town houses in Amsterdam, with sash windows and gabled facades. Brick was a relatively expensive building material in Britain and was usually only used in great houses, being imported from the Low Countries (Holland and Belgium). Following the Great Fire of London in 1666 (a landmark in British architectural history) there was an opportunity to rebuild the capital with a comprehensive master plan in the grand manner. But there was much opposition from landowners. The monarchy lacked the power of some of its European counterparts to impose a plan from above. Individual real property rights and a growing parliamentary democratic approach to government (which allowed for discussion and disagreement) meant that redevelopment was inevitably going to be piecemeal.

In fact a series of individual speculative developments emerged, many of which took the form of squares with town houses facing on to grass and trees in the middle of the square. The houses themselves, aimed at the new affluent classes, were a mixture of Dutch features and classical elements, with an emphasis on symmetry, sash windows and Greek pediments and columns (rather than gables). The squares were no doubt inspired by the Italian piazzas but had a soft grass centre rather than a hard paved surface (prefiguring the garden city movement's love of grass and trees). Individual front gardens were not favoured, being considered rather rural and peasant-like, but there were often long walled back gardens, and separate mews at the back for the servants and the horses. Names such as Bedford Square, Grosvenor Square and Sloane Square bear witness to the property development abilities of the ducal landowners who possessed estates in what is now the West End, Kensington and Chelsea. Today the Duke of Westminster is acknowledged the richest man in Britain, who happens to own (thanks to his ancestors' business acumen) some of the wealthiest square miles in London. The main City churches and St Paul's Cathedral were rebuilt following the fire by Sir Christopher Wren. St Paul's is in the style of St Peter's in Rome, whereas many of the other Wren churches are more English yet still classical in design.

Prior to the fire, Inigo Jones, the King's surveyor, had built the Covent Garden scheme, just outside the City of London. It was originally designed along the lines of an Italian piazza, with a colonnaded walkway and town houses facing the square. An opera house and theatre was also provided for the leisure and pleasure of the residents. A small market was held in the square from time to time. Over the centuries the market took over as the main fruit and vegetable market in London, and the area went downhill socially. In the early 1960s the market was moved to Nine Elms, Vauxhall, and the area seemed threatened with demolition by the planners and developers. Eventually, after an epic fight, it became a conservation area and was eventually turned into an up-market tourist attraction, being totally refurbished. Many of the original working-class residents despaired that they no longer fitted in and could not afford to live there any more. This example raises all sorts of questions about conservation and social issues. London continued to grow throughout Georgian times to develop eventually in the nineteenth century into a world capital of empire. This role was reflected in the architecture of individual buildings in Georgian and Victorian times, but with one exception there was no comprehensive replanning in the grand manner. In the early nineteenth century, when George IV was still Prince Regent, part of the Crown estates just north of the centre of London, now known as Regents Park, was developed as a series of up-market town houses by John Nash. Further developments occurred down Regent Street to Clarence House, a north–south axis on the boundary between Soho and Mayfair. Trafalgar Square, the Mall, Piccadilly Circus, Oxford Circus and Buckingham Palace were all part of this grand design. In fact the scheme developed over many years with the Victorians altering and enlarging various elements.

In Georgian and Regency times a whole series of provincial towns and resorts were developed to meet the needs of the new affluent leisured classes. The early ones were mainly inland and centred on spas where people could take the waters, e.g. Bath, Cheltenham, Harrogate (and also Epsom, hence the racecourse, Hotwells in Bristol, and Brixton in south London). Later sea bathing became the fashion, and a second series of resorts were developed, e.g. Brighton (with its Regency Pavilion), Skegness, Weston-super-Mare. It was not until the development of the railways that these became working-class resorts for the urban masses, by which time the upper classes were more likely to be found in resorts in the south of France.

Bath is one of the most famous spa towns. It was put on the map when Queen Anne took the waters for her rheumatism in the 1720s. But Beau Nash really popularised and publicised it when he was made Post Master. He has been compared with Billy Butlin in creating a holiday industry, in his case encouraging wealthy people to come for the 'season'. Bath is composed of a series of terraces, squares and crescents, all in the Georgian style. Even the smaller houses, back streets and mews are designed in a similar style, creating a co-ordinated 'designer' environment. Houses in those days were built to different maximum sizes which were taxed at different levels or rates and this was a considerable constraint on the design and density of housing. In Bath there were six main rating levels. Thus the colloquial phrase 'second-rate' originally meant housing of not quite the highest standard. Nash worked in conjunction with two architects named John Wood the Elder and John Wood the Younger (father and son), who created the illusion of refinement and classical culture in designing a city of uniform town houses.

All this was done entirely through private enterprise without government intervention or special powers (although there were some elementary by-laws and building regulations in some areas which influenced the architectural style to a small degree). There is no doubt that aesthetically Bath is a great achievement and that even today it has retained its 'status' as a desirable place to live, in spite of various attacks by bombers, planners and property developers. Whether it is real town planning is another matter, as it was designed predominantly as a pleasure centre for the middle classes. This is not to discount the fact that nowadays it is a surprisingly industrial city. It is still affluent but has a considerable measure of unemployment and homelessness which is often a surprise to outsiders.

This account has centred upon English towns, but it should be noted that both Dublin and Edinburgh, in the 'New Town', also provide magnificent examples of classical development. This chapter has also centred upon urban development. An account of the history of rural development is to be found in the next chapter, in the context of conservation.

Victorian architecture

Some of the main features of Victorian architecture have already been examined in Part II in the account of the industrial revolution. In summary, Victorian architecture was decorative and heavy in style, and eclectic, that is, it incorporated features from a range of historical styles, in particular the Gothic and the classical, but the Victorians also picked up all sorts of other features from the empire and other world cultures, including Hindu, oriental and Egyptian features. This type of architecture fell out of favour whilst the modern movement held sway, when the emphasis was on clear-cut lines and 'honesty' in building style. Nowadays it is recognised that Victorian architecture and townscape made a tremendous contribution to the urban fabric, as reflected in the listing of many buildings from this period. As explained in Part II, the Victorians built a whole range of sizes and types of houses, including villas and town houses for the newly affluent classes, as can be seen in large areas of the inner London boroughs today. Whilst many Victorian residential areas have been recolonised (gentrified) by the middle classes, and modernised with central heating and other mod. cons, people of a previous generation remember how cold and unpractical town houses from this period were to live in without servants. A certain income and life style are still required to keep the larger houses going. Some are still in multiple occupation and run-down, part of the 'inner city'.

The Victorians liked to build solid enduring public buildings faced with stone and often marble, e.g. Portland stone brought in from Dorset by the railways for use in London. As stated in respect of the industrial revolution, there was a strong sense of civic pride, and no expense was spared on public works (Dixon and Muthesius, 1978). The new wealth derived from the industrial revolution was used by the city fathers and urban benefactors to lend prestige and respectability to the new industrial cities such as Manchester, Leeds and Liverpool with impressive town halls, museums, libraries and art galleries. However, it should be remembered that society was socially divided, different classes lived in different districts and had different travel routes, so the working class mill hand might never visit the new central business district. If he did he would have been unlikely to gain entrance to the galleries.

Many industrial buildings, particularly warehouses, were also given the full architectural treatment, and there were many examples of magnificent buildings in a commonplace industrial setting among declining docklands and industrial zones, although many have since been renovated and incorporated into yuppi-fication schemes. Railway stations and other public buildings, workhouses, police stations, asylums, public conveniences, were all, however, more humble in design, but were still given some architectural embellishment, even if only, in the case of workhouses and prisons, to give the inmates a sense of the overpowering, fortress-like strength of the buildings and the harshness of their circumstances. Also because people were unsure about travelling on the new railways it was thought that if they were made to look like great cathedrals people would be less afraid because they would feel they were going to church. Compare this to the approach to airports nowadays. However, towards the end of the century a reaction was setting in against the excesses of Victorian architecture. Perhaps people had been looking at the wrong buildings. Wonderful structures in the form of factories, bridges, warehouses and train sheds (built by people such as Isambard Kingdom Brunel) were still relegated to the category of 'engineering' although in fact they proved to be the true forerunners of modern architecture.

Modern architecture

As explained in Chapter 6, early twentieth-century architects reacted against the excesses of decoration, eclecticism, and urban chaos of the nineteenth century and sought to create a style-less modern movement, based on function and the application of science and technology in the form of new building materials and methods. However, in the early twentieth century there were a variety of other architectural trends, such as Art Nouveau, which drew inspiration from trends in painting (and the broader Arts and Crafts movement) and was characterised by the use of traditional materials in an original manner, especially ornate ironwork. Other architects sought to return to a restrained, classical style, for example the famous architect Lutyens favoured a modest neo-Georgian style, using traditional brick in the building of many town halls and public buildings. His architecture also shows evidence of influences from India, which he became interested in in the course of designing the state capital, New Delhi. Also there was a new interest in eclecticism and escapism, as evidenced in neo-Egyptian and art deco architecture, much used in cinemas ('picture palaces') and influenced by the Hollywood stage sets seen in the films themselves. These styles were modern but they were fantasy.

In domestic housing pride of place was given to the garden-city mock Tudor style in the inter-war years, as explained in Part II. There were attempts to apply the ideas of the modern functionalist movement to domestic housing in Britain, creating 'sugar lump' houses of white concrete with flat roofs and metal window frames. These can be seen in many cities, thanks to daring builders, but they never caught on. With the Second World War utility and function came back into fashion. The Anderson air raid shelter was probably the most representative architecture of the time. Following the war there were continuing shortages, and rationing of building supplies, resulting in a functional modern style being adopted. One feature of interest is the pre-fab, an entirely temporary form of housing which stood the test of time.

In the 1960s the private property sector took off when the building controls of the 1950s were lifted, resulting in town centre redevelopments, new office blocks and high-rise housing schemes, discussed in Chapter 7. In the 1970s a reaction against the modern movement set in, and traditional styles grew in popularity. In the 1980s and 1990s the styles of 'modern', contemporary architecture have divided out between the neo-Georgian conservation movement styles, used in offices as much as in residential development; and the high-tech style used, for example, by Richard Rogers in the Pompidou centre in Paris (with exposed systems and structure all brightly coloured) and in his Lloyd's building in London. Whilst conservation policy controlled the march of high-tech buildings in many provincial city centres, the development of science and business parks on the edges, beside the motorways, allowed free rein to the new 'shed' architecture which has developed in the name of progress and technology. The current postmodernist mood is generating a variety of styles, such as deconstructivism, and it will be interesting to see what style becomes dominant in the next century. It certainly seems that the green movement is increasing in influence, requiring architects to produce 'sustainable architecture'. Also it would seem that there is more 'space' for a greater variety of styles, without the need for a slavish following of fashion which was a characteristic of earlier decades.

Chapter 9

Urban and rural conservation

It is an indictment of modern town planning, and a reflection of the unpopularity of modern architecture, that there is so much emphasis on the retention of the past, and on protectionist policies. In this chapter urban conservation, and secondly rural conservation and wider environmental controls, are considered. The two aspects of conservation are linked, as the greater the level of urban conservation and reuse of vacant land the less likelihood there is of further encroachment on the countryside for development.

Urban conservation

The development context

Conservation is not the same as preservation. Preservation conjures up images of buildings turned into museums and put in mothballs. Conservation contains the idea that the buildings in question remain part of the living fabric of the city, in daily use, for example, as houses or offices. Conservation should not be seen, either, as applicable only to stately homes or the *Country Life* type of up-market private house. There are many working-class areas and terraces which are conserved because they too are part of our heritage. Conservation policy, by means of the designation of Conservation Areas (as described in this chapter), covers large parts of our historic inner urban areas. For example, most of the centre of Bristol is covered by a mosaic of Conservation Areas.

People can get the wrong idea of what conservation is about, as in recent years with the growth of the tourism industry the past has been commercialised, even by respectable government bodies such as English Heritage. This commercialism may become worse, as the new Department of National Heritage is now responsible for aspects of listed buildings policy and conservation areas, and the National Lottery. A false 'Disneyland', stage-set image of the past can be created. Nevertheless, public awareness and concern with architectural and urban aesthetic issues, such as the design of new buildings, and the conservation of historic buildings, have increased. The general public may expect more, rather than less, design control from the town planners than in the past (provided it does not affect them personally, of course). Bad visual design is often accompanied by poor functional design, making buildings dull and difficult to live or work in. People like user-friendly buildings, and welcome interest and variety in the townscape as they go about their daily business (Punter, 1990).

A distinction must be drawn at the outset between the powers of the planners and those of architects or developers in conservation (Burke, 1976). Planners are concerned with the overall design and appearance of the townscape. They can influence the design of individual buildings only within the limited parameters of their development control powers. Architects are the first to take umbrage if the planners try to limit their 'creativity'. As will be seen, developers, architects and the clients for whom the building is designed often have a far greater say in the design of the building than the planners. For the developer the cost factor, and the aim of achieving the greatest possible amount of lettable floor space, are far more significant in the real world than the outward appearance of the building. The main aspects of policy and legislation on urban conservation will now be described, namely the listing of individual buildings and designation of Conservation Areas (Heap, 1995).

Listed buildings

The Department of the Environment lists buildings to provide guidance for local authorities and controls to prevent demolition or alteration without notice, to prevent neglect by owners and to benefit the general public. English Heritage, a quango of the DOE, is the body responsible for listing buildings. The DOE now liaises with the new Department of National Heritage on listing, tourism, and conservation policy. English Heritage advises the DOE on listing, finance, Conservation Areas and town schemes. The DOE co-ordinates conservation with policy related to inner-city initiatives, City Grants, housing improvement funds, all of which also deal with old buildings. Private development companies often have a conservation section and seek to liaise with the DOE, English Heritage and the local authorities on larger schemes, to maintain a good 'image' with the planners and the grant-givers.

Buildings are listed if they are seen to be of outstanding historical or architectural interest, all buildings before 1700, most from 1700 to 1840, some from 1840 to 1914, a few from 1914 to 1939 and even a few after that. In some countries buildings are given the equivalent of a listing 'at birth', if they are considered to be of exceptional architectural merit (although these are likely to be the least endangered). Listing is likely to increase the value of the property. In England and Wales (things are slightly different in Scotland, which has a similar but separate planning system) there are three main categories of listing. Grade I buildings must not be removed in any circumstances and are of national, even international importance: if a motorway is to be built the motorway has to go round them. Grade II comes in two sub-categories. Grade II* (starred) buildings cannot be removed without compelling reason, and are usually of significant regional if not national importance; they include set-piece Georgian houses in some of the main terraces and squares in cities such as Bath. Even with a compelling reason consent to removal is highly unlikely to be given. Grade II unstarred buildings are more ordinary structures such as typical Georgian or Victorian town houses of more local importance. There is also a non-statutory category, Grade III, which is not actually on the central government list but on a list compiled by the local planning authority. This list is advisory, but there are powers to upgrade buildings on it to Grade II if they are threatened. Conservation control is particularly concerned with the external appearance of buildings but in the case of Grade I and Grade II* there are additional controls on internal features. There are around half a million listed buildings in England and Wales, of which 5800 are Grade I and 15 000 Grade II*, and there are over 6000 Conservation Areas (Moore, 1987 with 1991 supplement: 249).

As stated, a listed building may not be demolished or altered without building consent, but in the past some people just left the building to fall down, particularly if it was in the way of a new development scheme. However, if a building is not properly maintained a repairs notice can be issued, and after two months a compulsory purchase notice can be served by the local authority. The owner can issue the local authority with a listed building purchase notice to buy the property if the upkeep is too much for him or her. Although there are considerable negative powers associated with conservation, there are limited positive financial incentives. The assumption that listing will increase the value of the property may be questionable. However, the local authority may impose additional burdens by stipulating in renovation work the use, say, of genuine slate tiles on the roof or hardwood sash window frames (not aluminium double-glazed ones, a bone of contention with many owners).

As more and more Victorian and Edwardian areas come within the scope of conservation policy some poorer or working-class people find they are faced with an impossible burden and may simply move out to avoid the cost of upkeep. Further, some of the design controls on listed buildings actually contradict the rules of public health and building regulations, e.g. on the height of ceilings or the design of windows in relation to conversion and modernisation work. Basically there is more flexibility if it can be shown that the developer is seeking to return a building to what is agreed was its original design. A building can be listed without the owner's consent, and there is limited appeal (s. 21.4, 1990 Act), but a five year certificate of immunity against listing may be granted. Whilst conservation is a worthy object in protecting the visual quality of the townscape, many would argue that it involves greater infringements of personal freedom and rights in property than ordinary planning law. One has to apply for 'listed building consent' on a special planning application form if one wants to alter, extend or demolish a listed building, and must apply for planning permission in the normal way if the proposal involves wider planning matters such as a change of use. Non-listed buildings in Conservation Areas are also subject to special controls (see Chapter 10 on development control) and may require Conservation Area consent.

Limited financial aid is available under the Historic Building and Ancient Monuments Act, 1953, which empowers the Minister to make grants for the maintenance and guardianship of properties, but this is aimed more at the tourism side of the problem. Also, under the Act the Minister is empowered to designate 'town schemes', which are usually small areas such as a town square, a high street or a village green, for which the following grants are available; 25 per cent from central government and 25 per cent of the cost from local government, the rest being supplied by the owner. The current legislation on town schemes, and the limited availability of grants and loans related to conservation, are set out in Sections 77–80 of the consolidating Act on conservation, the Planning (Listed Buildings and Conservation Areas) Act, 1990. City Grants are also available in some cases under Part III of the Housing and Planning Act, 1986, and are part of the Action for Cities programme. Under the Local Authorities Historic Buildings Act, 1962, local authorities can make grants and loans towards conservation but in view of the present state of local government finance and cut-backs it rarely happens nowadays. Many listed buildings are also used as houses and therefore people have been able to claim housing improvement grants under the Housing Acts (1969 onwards). In the 1970s these were easier to obtain, as more money was available, indeed this provision contributed to the process of gentrification, although the original intention was to help poor working-class areas. In some cases areas worthy of conservation were also designated as general improvement areas or housing action areas too. There are so many listed buildings nowadays that buildings are no longer considered so special and worthy of financial support just because they are listed. Housing grants are available for a limited range of improvements. But World Heritage sites may receive international funding (PPG15).

Conservation areas

Whilst listing dealt with individual areas it seemed more logical to plan for historical areas as a whole, to enable increased control, not only of individual buildings but of the surrounding townscape, trees, street appearance and incidental non-listed buildings which together formed the backcloth against which the listed building stood. The Civic Amenities Act, 1967, established the category of Conservation Area. Such areas are designated and controlled by the local planning authority. The aim is to maintain the overall visual quality and character of the area. New buildings can be constructed but they must fit in with the historical style. This is why in many towns there has been a proliferation of neo-Georgian office buildings with sash-like windows and Mansard roofs. Some architects have criticised Conservation Area policy for preventing the spread of more modern styles and sterilising the built environment against further change. Since the aim is chiefly to protect the external appearance of the buildings, in fact, some are quite modern inside. This has led to accusations of 'façadism', adopting a false historical style externally which gives no indication of what the building is like inside: hardly in the spirit of the modern movement in which 'form follows function'.

The Town and Country Amenities Act, 1974, gave increased powers of control in Conservation Areas, preventing the demolition of any building and protecting, further, plants, trees and other townscape and street features, e.g. walls, fences, etc. Local planning authorities can protect trees anywhere by tree preservation orders under Section 198 of the Town and Country Planning Act, 1990, making it illegal to lop or prune them without planning permission. As stated, all the conservation legislation is now consolidated in the Planning (Listed Building and Conservation Areas) Act, 1990. This has not, of itself, introduced any significant new measures but it has tidied up existing legislation. Many planning authorities found that the designation of Conservation Areas (often on the rather questionable grounds of protecting marginally important buildings) was a means of increasing development control and reducing rights under the General Development Order, for example in respect of demolition, which had not counted as development. Following the Planning and Compensation Act, 1991, under Section 13 the demolition of certain buildings is brought within the control of planning (whether or not they are in a Conservation Area). There are already additional powers by which the minister can introduce special planning controls which suspend the rights under the GDO. These are known as Article 4 directions. In fact there are a range of special controls (see Section 102 regarding special control orders under the Town and Country Planning Act, 1990). An Article 4 direction can be used to increase the level of control in an area which is not in a Conservation Area, for example to preserve the architectural features and layout of a housing estate – to retain open-plan front gardens. Or it can be used to increase powers in Conservation Areas, although this has become less necessary as the legislation (and case law precedents) have tightened up the controls over the years. There are a range of Special Development Orders which can also be introduced to protect areas in the countryside and in other special circumstances. Compensation is payable in some cases for loss of development rights under the General Development Order.

Control of advertisements is also increased in Conservation Areas. However, local authorities also have the right to designate areas of 'special advertisement control'. Note that in order to display an advertisement, whether or not it is in a Conservation Area, requires a special planning application under the Town and Country Planning (Control of Advertisements) Regulations, 1984. When designating a Conservation Area the local authority needs to be concerned about traffic movement, parking and pedestrian circulation. In some cases streets are blocked off, or one-way systems introduced to control traffic movement. The environmental impact of traffic has to be taken into account in terms of both the effects of attrition on the building fabric and the overall visual impact. However, most Conservation Areas are localities where people live and work, and so a compromise must be reached between the need to protect the area and the need to enable people to carry on their businesses and daily lives there. In some cases Conservation Areas are also designated as Local Plan areas in the development plan, because this enables the comprehensive planning of the area on the statutory basis of the approved policies enshrined in the plan's written statement and land use plans. There has been much controversy about car

parking restrictions and through traffic controls in Conservation
Areas. Whilst these no doubt improve the quality of the
Conservation Area, some community groups living in nearby
working-class districts are of the opinion that such policies can be
class-biased, pushing the commuter traffic and on-street parking
into poorer neighbourhoods where residents are less articulate.
Further, from the suburban commuters' viewpoint, faced with
reduced car parking space in central areas, residents of
Conservation Areas may seem to project a fortress mentality in
protecting their area from urban transport pressures generated
by adjacent Central Business District expansion.

Urban conservation bodies

There are several non-governmental bodies which have acted as
powerful pressure groups in bringing about the current emphasis
on conservation. Voluntary bodies include the National Trust,
which, amongst other matters, is concerned with the fate of
stately homes and large country houses, and its urban relative,
the Civic Trust, founded in 1957 and entirely independent of the
government. There are a series of voluntary bodies representing
the needs of buildings from different historical periods, such as
the Georgian Society, the Regency Society and the Victorian
Society. In recent years societies defending buildings of the 1920s
and 1930s have grown up, and even a 1950s society is now
established. In addition there are government bodies such as the
Royal Fine Arts Commission and various other design bodies,
including the Design Centre in London, which, among other
functions, has a particular concern with the design of street
furniture (litter bins, lamp posts, seats, etc.).

There are a number of categories of historical buildings,
especially buildings associated with royalty and the Church, which
are not currently subject to normal conservation policy, but their
guardians take their custodial role seriously (no doubt
encouraged by the example of Prince Charles himself). Normally
agreements are concluded in respect of Crown land (Section 293
of the Town and Country Planning Act, 1990), as the Act does
not bind the Crown. Similar exemptions may apply to land and
properties under the control of the Ministry of Defence, the
police and a range of statutory undertakers related to gas,
electricity, water, etc., some bodies having a better reputation
than others in respect of environmental sensitivity. Many would
argue that there is a case for a complete overhaul of the powers
of the planning system as it affects these bodies. However, there is
a provision that, on the disposal of land by these bodies, planning

permission can be given before the sale, which enhances its value on the market (e.g. in the case of property in a Green Belt).

Rural conservation

Green issues

Nowadays the traditional boundary between town and country has become blurred, with the rise of car ownership, demand for out-of-town sites and growing pressure on the Green Belt and the open countryside. Town and country planning has always been concerned with the countryside as well as the towns, in particular with protecting the countryside from the spread of the towns. There is an anti-urban theme running through much of British town planning which sees towns and townies as bad, and the countryside and farmers as good. When the post-war planning system was established it was assumed the farmer knew best, and that there was little need to control his activities. The effects of modern farming practices, the Common Agricultural Policy (CAP) of the European Community and wider concern among the general public about 'green' issues have raised the profile of rural planning as an issue and cast doubt on existing attitudes to the countryside. Reconciling the demands of conservation, agriculture, recreation and development is a major task for planners (Countryside Commission, 1990). One of the most informative (and controversial) authors on countryside planning is Marion Shoard (1980, 1987). Before discussing the present-day situation a potted history of the development of the countryside and of the landscape (Hoskins, 1990) may be useful.

Historical development of the landscape

As the demand for greater planning control in the countryside, especially conservation of (what are imagined to be) traditional natural features, increases it becomes vitally important to understand the historical nature of the factors which have shaped the countryside as it is today. People often assume that the countryside is natural and not man-made; however, there is hardly any part of the landscape which has not been touched in some way by human activity. Nowadays many complain about the loss of traditional field patterns and hedgerows, but in fact those hedgerows were not always there, and much of the land has been brought into cultivation either from forest or from heathland. Likewise there is much concern about the natural habitat of wildlife being destroyed as a result of the draining of the wetlands in Somerset and of the fen in East Anglia, but again these only exist because of man-made drainage schemes in the past, which the fauna have adapted to occupying.

Before the Romans there was fairly limited cultivation in Britain; settlements tended to be on the higher land and lowlands were left undeveloped. One can still find many examples of hill forts, standing stones, ancient trackways (often aligned along ley lines) and earthworks from earlier times, some of which are protected as ancient monuments. The Romans had a tremendous impact on land use, urbanisation, road construction, land drainage and cultivation patterns. The decline of the Roman Empire was followed by a series of invasions by European tribes, each contributing in its own way to farming and to place names and local cultures.

The Normans arrived in 1066, and established a programme of colonisation and plantation development. The land and society itself were divided up and organised on the basis of the feudal system. In the Middle Ages the population was over 80 per cent rural, mainly located in small villages with agricultural activity based on what was known as the three-field system of crop rotation, with each peasant farmer having his own strips of land within this framework. Increasingly the more remote areas were brought into cultivation by the monasteries, which introduced sheep to the Pennines. Other improvements were made by the monks, for example the abbots of Glastonbury in Somerset had Sedgmoor partly drained. Britain was relatively peaceful and unified, allowing expansion of agriculture into the more remote areas, whilst many other European countries were not unified, with walled cities providing shelter from which the inhabitants would cautiously venture forth to tend the adjacent farmland.

The development of wealthy city states in Italy provided the seedbed of the Renaissance. Formal gardens of huge dimensions were laid out according to classical architectural principles, purely for the pleasure of their owners and as a sign of 'conspicuous consumption' (wealth). (Flowers and vegetables had little place in these gardens, and were relegated to the servants' area.) These ideas spread to Britain, but had to compete with an already established traditional form of garden which was on a more intimate and functional scale, as typified by the Shakespearean knot gardens with their box hedges and beds of herbs, flowers and vegetables.

By the seventeenth century there was a gradual move

towards a more 'grand manner' approach to gardening which in Britain took the form of the landscape movement with its emphasis on earth modelling on a huge scale, creating lakes and vistas, accompanied by extensive tree planting. This was linked with the growth of the English country house, set in its own grounds, without fortifications and without the estate farm, kitchen gardens or tenants in sight. There had always been a great interest in arboriculture, as evidenced by the cultivation of the royal forests of oak for ships and also as hunting parks. For example, in 1664 John Evelyn wrote Sylva on tree cultivation. Art and literature influenced people's ideas about the landscape too. Milton's poem *Paradise Lost* describes a beautiful natural wilderness. French artists such as Claude, Poussin and Lorrain painted naturalistic landscapes, presenting an idyllic image of pastoral life. This romantic view of the countryside was chiefly for the upper class and bore little relation to the harsh realities of farming for ordinary people. In 1720 Bridgman designed an estate at Stowe in Buckinghamshire on which he created 'a little gentle disorder' as he put it. One could look out of the windows of the big house and see the pastoral landscape stretching into the distance with cows grazing and 'figures in the landscape', that is, picturesque peasants going about their work. Stock were prevented from straying up to the house by Bridgman's invention of a hidden ditch, called a *ha-ha*. Other landscape architects of the time include William Kent, who, it was said, was 'the first to leap over the fence and to show the whole of nature is a garden', and Lancelot (Capability) Brown, the most famous of the landscape gardeners, responsible for schemes such as Blenheim Palace, and Longleat at Wiltshire. Humphrey Repton created a more contoured approach and incorporated artificial grottoes and follies (pretend ruins). In all these estates the emphasis was upon grass and trees and features in the landscape rather than on details of flowers and colours.

The agricultural revolution which preceded the industrial revolution was based on many innovations in agriculture which increased yield whilst reducing labour, by people such as Jethro Tull, Turnip Townsend, who perfected crop rotation (nowadays his work would be seen as organic farming but it was science then!), and George III himself, who was known as 'Farmer George'. The need for larger units for efficient rotation, and the extension of sheep farming, led to the general enclosure Acts of the early nineteenth century, reducing grazing and common land rights for the rural population who increasingly migrated to the towns. The industrial revolution itself, and the urbanisation, canal and railway building, mining and factory development which accompanied it, had a major impact on land use patterns, and created large amounts of derelict land, spoil tips and pollution.

The Victorians were keen gardeners (as an escape from industrialisation?). The science of horticulture and cross-breeding developed, accompanied by the introduction of exotic species from all corners of the empire. Botanical gardens and greenhouses, as at Kew, became popular. Formal public Victorian parks were laid out in the new industrial towns. These were characterised by formal beds containing flowers in primary colours, floral clocks, as in Edinburgh, and adjacent playing fields for recreation. Domestic gardening by individual householders also became popular (now that most people no longer worked on the land). Indeed, the development of the Garden City movement reflects this trend, with the emphasis on a large individual flower garden for each house.

Carefully designed cottage gardens for the more discriminating and affluent members of society became fashionable, as popularised by the work of Gertrude Jekyll (1834–1932) (Massingham, 1984), who, in conjunction with Edwin Lutyens, the architect, developed several gardens around the turn of the century in country houses, her hallmark being the use of subtle blue, silver and white flowers and foliage, as at Sissinghurst, and at Hestercombe in Somerset. In contrast, in the early twentieth century there were still landscape architects designing in the grand manner, such as Jellicoe (who even admitted he knew nothing at all about flowers), who was a founder of the Landscape Institute. Landscaping of municipal and public-sector schemes, for the new universities in the 1960s, the New Towns and motorways, rather than for individual houses, became the main source of work in the post-war period. In more recent years concern with the environment and 'nature', rural estate management, afforestation and planning for recreation and leisure are all leaving their mark on the countryside. Most large developments are now 'landscaped' but if it is done well people do not even notice. There was also a tremendous growth of interest in gardening for the masses, as evidenced in the proliferation of television programmes, books and gardening centres.

State intervention in the countryside

Post-war reconstruction planning was more concerned with keeping the town out of the countryside, and protecting remote or scenic areas from development, than worrying about extending development control to the activities of farmers. The provisions of the Agriculture Act, 1947, were based on the assumption that the farmer should not be hindered from increasing agricultural production. There was pressure from the urban population, and from groups such as the Ramblers' Association, for the countryside to be opened up for recreational purposes. The National Parks and Access to the Countryside Act, 1947, as its title suggests, set up the National Parks and opened up a series of footpath networks throughout the countryside. The National Parks were administered by *ad hoc* bodies, by means of joint boards and committees, and overseen by the National Parks Commission. In 1968 the latter became the Countryside Commission, with a broader role, including concern for agriculture, leisure, recreation and landscape as well as the parks. In the post-war period car ownership was low and some areas were still quite inaccessible by road, so the Bank Holiday traffic jams now found on Dartmoor or in the Lake District were undreamt-of. The aim of the National Parks was to preserve the natural beauty of the countryside and to provide access for the general public, in line with the recommendations of the Scott, Dower and Hobhouse reports (Hall, 1994), and so they were part of the post-war national land use planning strategy described in Part II.

The 1949 Act also established Areas of Outstanding Natural Beauty (AONBs), which are smaller and more accessible than the National Parks, e.g. the Quantocks in Somerset. Seventy-five per cent grants were available to the local authorities whose job it was to administer them, for the maintenance and improvement of amenities. Both in National Parks and in AONBs there are strict planning controls on new and existing development (comparable to the situation in urban Conservation Areas). For more legal details see Heap (1995) and for a current list see Grant (1990: 311).

In addition to these main post-war provisions, under ordinary planning law there were further controls which applied to all agricultural areas in respect of new residential buildings. New residential development was and is not allowed in the countryside unless it is specifically for agricultural works in relation to a farm. However, all manner of other agricultural buildings are allowed. People have spent years trying to find ways around these controls. There have been examples of spurious agricultural workers, and of people building rather large 'stables' complete with horses which can readily be converted into a house (thus getting around restrictions on house building on farmland). Around urban areas there are additional controls under the Green Belt legislation.

Green Belts were given a new impetus in the 1960s under Duncan Sandys, the Conservative minister responsible for town planning, under Section 4 of the Town and Country Planning

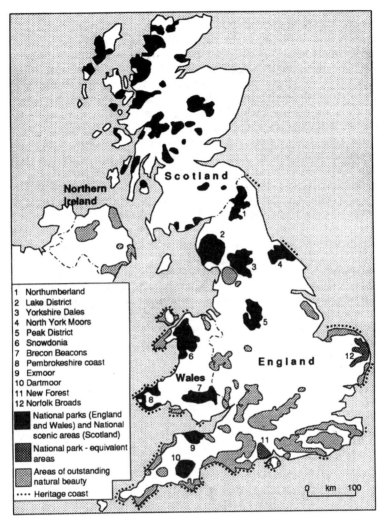

1 Northumberland
2 Lake District
3 Yorkshire Dales
4 North York Moors
5 Peak District
6 Snowdonia
7 Brecon Beacons
8 Pembrokeshire coast
9 Exmoor
10 Dartmoor
11 New Forest
12 Norfolk Broads

■ National parks (England and Wales) and National scenic areas (Scotland)

▦ National park - equivalent areas

▒ Areas of outstanding natural beauty

•••• Heritage coast

Figure 9.1   Areas of rural control. *(Adapted from Burton (1991) in Tony Scrase and Martin Chick 'Agricultural Diversification and the Planning System', Pickup: University of West of England, 1990)*

Act, 1962, and they have gone from strength to strenght since. Green Belts are designated not for their landscape value but to prevent urban sprawl in areas of development pressure. More broadly, they have also been seen as the green 'lungs' of the city and as having recreational and agricultural value too. In fact substantial parts of approved Green Belts are not really very green, more brown, with a diversity of gravel workings, glass-houses and infill sites, yet they still contain 20 per cent of all agricultural land. Certain uses are regarded as suitable for Green Belt location, such as golf courses, hotels and leisure facilities nowadays, and hospitals and similar government institutions in the past (indeed, Ebenezer Howard located asylums in his green belt encircling the Garden City, but in general he envisaged the Green Belt as much more agricultural than the present versions). Although Green Belts are intended to be permanent, bits are occasionally chipped away from the inner circumference, and extensions are not infrequently added on the outer edge (Elson, 1986; Herrington, 1984).

'White' land, as Grant explains (1982: 309), is a term with no legal significance, denoting land that was not designated for a particular use under the old style of development plan, and which is often on the inner edge of the Green Belt. Developers saw such areas as ideal for housing, and in some cases the government appeared to go along with the presumption in the past. Nowadays most white land areas have been covered by Structure Plan policy. In addition there are lots of bits and wedges of land marooned on the urban–rural interface which would nibble away at the countryside if developed. For example, awkward little bits are often left between the edge of an urban area and a passing motorway – a prime site for development if there is also a motorway intersection near by. Motorways themselves cut right through established Green Belts, often attracting a corridor of planning applications along their path. Some would argue that Green Belts do not prevent development, in any case; all that happens is that development leapfrogs over the Green Belt, leading to a second ring of housing and greater commuting distances for its inhabitants (Pahl, 1965; Newby, 1982).

Continuing pressure for rural recreation, combined with growth in car ownership, led eventually to another category of special area being introduced in 1968 under the Countryside Act. It followed the recommendations of the White Paper *Leisure in the countryside*, which marked a change of attitude in laying more emphasis on non-agricultural uses and ecology. The 1968 Act established Country Parks, intended to enable people to enjoy the countryside without having to travel a long way, to ease pressure on remote and solitary places and to reduce the risk of damage to the countryside. This was achieved by creating small, managed park areas near urban concentrations, with ample provision of car parks, toilets and amenities such as picnic sites and transit sites for campers and caravans (for which local authorities received 75 per cent grants from central government) to create what were seen as 'honeypots' drawing people away from a more dispersed use of the countryside.

Emphasis was increasingly put upon the need to protect small special areas of the countryside, for example where a rare wild flower or species of butterfly was to be found, or where there were other interesting features. Under the 1949 Act provision had been made for the identification of Sites of Special Scientific Interest (SSSIs), which are administered by the Nature Conservancy Council. However, many such sites were right in the middle of farmland and it was difficult to enforce the controls, indeed a site could be ploughed up overnight. Farmers were, however, compensated for the loss of the right to farm parts of their land where SSSIs were located. However, such sites could also be endangered by careless tourists and, more recently (as a DOE consultation document pointed out in 1991), by war games! Stricter controls were introduced over SSSIs, nature reserves and a range of other ecological issues under the Wildlife and Countryside Act, 1981. In recent years there have been other moves towards greater protection of the ecological aspects of the countryside, the farmer rather than the day tripper nowadays being seen as the villain. Indeed, many consider that the government should introduce a new green Act which would extend full planning control powers to farmland and the countryside.

There has always been a major division between the aims of the DOE and those of other government departments such as the Ministry of Agriculture, Fisheries and Food. MAFF has for example given grants for ploughing up moorlands and for the grubbing up of hedgerows (as they did in 1979, contrary to the policies of other government departments: Shoard, 1980). There has been considerable concern about the effects of other subsidies for industrialised farming methods which have led to the creation of prairiescape, flatscape in some lowland areas, and the subsequent demise of various species of wildlife. All this has been done in theory to increase food production, but under EC policy CAP farmers have been subsidised to produce more than they can sell. Planning has very little control over the countryside itself, and many people believe that there should be more on the use and development of farm buildings, field patterns, ponds and farm-related businesses, particularly industrial agricultural buildings such as silos and battery hen units. Planning has nevertheless been very powerful and negative in forbidding non-agricultural building in the countryside because of the historical need to conserve agricultural land.

The 1980s marked the culmination of the effects of many forces which were changing the countryside. In 1981 the census showed for the first time that rural villages were actually gaining population rather than losing it. In the 1960s, because of the decline in the rural population, some county planning authorities had designated villages as Category D, to be allowed to die, the view being that it was better to concentrate resources on the more populated Category A. But many people moved back into the countryside, either to retire or because, with the development of the motorway system, they were happy to commute longer distances to work. Ironically by then many of the local facilities and shops were in decline, a process which had not been helped by the Beeching cuts in the railway network back in the 1960s. In fact many without cars are suffering from 'rural deprivation' through the loss of local transport, schools, shops and community facilities, which can be as devastating as the deprivation experienced by their urban cousins. Many people on low incomes in rural areas felt compelled to move out, particularly young couples who could not possibly compete with the newcomers in the housing market. The availability of housing was further reduced by the planners' policy of restricting growth in rural settlements to a limited amount of infill. There had been no provision in planning law for specifying the tenure or category of occupants of housing developments. However, in circular 7/91, 'Planning and affordable housing', for the first time the DOE stated in 1991 that the provision of low-cost housing for *local* needs should be taken as a 'material consideration' in development control. This may prove a double-edged sword. There is a danger of an over-romanticised view of the situation; even if people get low-cost housing they still need shops, schools and jobs, which for wives might mean working in the local chicken processing plant (7/91 has now been updated by PPG3).

The Conservative government in the 1980s sought to loosen planning controls in the interests of the developer, both in the town and in the countryside, although, interestingly, it was often Conservative voters in the shires who objected to the change the most, fearing that their areas would be swamped by people from the towns. A series of circulars, 14/84, 'Green Belts', 15/84, 'Land for Housing' and 22/84, 'Structure plans and local plans', all set policy directives which leaned towards allowing development in the urban–rural fringe, especially on the immediate edge of urban areas. It was calculated that less land was now needed for agricultural production because of the enormous surpluses which had built up in the EC. Two and a half million acres, that is, the size of Devon and Cornwall, were seen as no longer needed for agriculture. The emphasis shifted from seeking to protect the countryside for the sake of agricultural productivity to protecting it for its own sake as an environmental resource. Farmers were expected, by some, to take on the role of park keepers rather than food producers. Farmers increasingly entered into land management agreements in relation to the preservation of certain sites, for which they are compensated. Related to this is set-aside policy, derived from EC policy, which has become increasingly controversial in the 1990s because of the potential for abuse by farmers. It enables them to take land out of agricultural use, with the proviso that interim uses should not prevent the ultimate return of the land to full agricultural use. Relaxations of controls were proposed, to enable farmers to engage in countryside-related businesses to enable them to stay on their farms. Circular 16/87, 'Development involving agricultural land', and PPG 7, 'Rural enterprise and development', reflect this new philosophy, and farmers were encouraged to diversify within the rural economy. However, business activities were still meant to be related to agriculture, and there was a fine dividing line between selling home-produced jams in a farm shop and setting up an industrial plant on the farm – although some saw this as the logical conclusion, and argued that it would also ease rural unemployment. Town is still town and country still countryside (rural gentrification notwithstanding).

The Countryside Commission, an arm of the Department of the Environment although it often seems to operate independently, produced two significant documents reflecting this new strategy, *Shaping a new countryside* in 1987, and *Planning for a greener countryside* in 1989. The commission believes that the old reason for adopting a restrictive approach to development in the countryside, shortage of agricultural land, no longer holds in the light of changing economic circumstances. Therefore there is a need for acceptance of some development in the countryside provided it is done in a constructive and controlled manner. The question follows of whether development can actually enhance the rural scene with suitable landscaping. The commission proposes that Green Belts should be seen as having a wider purpose and should be viewed more positively in their own right. In fact the government produced a consultation paper early in 1991 which proposed that fewer limitations should be put on the reuse of redundant buildings such as mental homes and hospitals in the Green Belt. For example, business uses would be acceptable provided the development fitted in to the 'footprint' of the existing building stock and site layout. The Countryside Commission also recommends that the idea of new settlements in the countryside should be viewed more positively. This ties in with widespread support for private New Towns, an idea which Peter Hall (1994), the influential urban geographer and planner, also supports, seeing it as a continuation of the ideas of Ebenezer Howard. The commission itself, to a degree, favours accepting more urban development in the countryside, provided adequate design and landscaping measures are guaranteed. But it is also emphasising the 'greening' of the city in the sense of bringing the countryside into the town, thus breaking down the urban–rural dualism further. The creation of new countryside on derelict land is suggested, as is the planting of urban forests on the edge of cities, within the Green Belt, as is already being put into effect north of Bristol, and there are other proposals affecting cities in the Midlands. Special areas for horses might also be considered, indeed there is already a thriving unofficial 'horsiculture' sector on the edges of many cities, providing grazing and shelter for ponies and horses.

Rural conservation bodies

There are other voluntary and government bodies which have a continuing impact on the nature of the countryside but are beyond planning control. Various statutory undertakers, including electricity and water authorities in the past, have always had the right to develop, the latter being infamous for screening their reservoirs with trees and painting everything green, which draws even more attention to the developments. The electricity companies now often route cables underground, particularly in environmentally sensitive areas, but the predecessor boards were notorious for their pylons striding across the landscape. By comparison controls on private developers and individuals seemed draconian. As mentioned in Part I, the Ministry of Defence owns over 90 000 acres of forest and vast amounts of land, for example over 10 per cent of Wiltshire is MOD property. The Forestry Commission, which one would imagine green and environmentally friendly, has had a tremendous influence through reafforestation. However, many criticise the rows of Scandinavian conifers, and the ugliness of miles and miles of standardised plantation relieved only by linear firebreaks. There is pressure for more use of native deciduous trees, so vital to many creatures in providing a natural habitat.

The Country Landowners' Association, founded in 1926, is a powerful pressure group supporting the needs of its members, who no doubt influence legislation through links with the House of Lords, and with the National Farmers' Union. In 1986 it published *Land: new ways to profit*, a 'handbook of alternative enterprises' which echoed many of the government's own proposals. The emphasis in this document was more on clay pigeon shooting and golf courses than on small farm shops or crafts. The National Trust, founded in 1895 (Gaze, 1988), is independent of the government but has a powerful voice in countryside matters, and in the protection of individual houses and areas of landscape. Enterprise Neptune is a branch of the trust which offers protection to over a third of the coastline. The Council for the Protection of Rural England was founded in 1926 and campaigns for the preservation of rural amenities and scenery. Many other local voluntary bodies play their part in influencing policy at both central and local government level. In recent years, urban bodies concerned with food production and prices from the shoppers' viewpoint have had increasing influence on rural matters, in particular the Consumers' Association (which publishes *Which?* magazine). For years the government and the EC encouraged farmers to modernise the countryside; now they are paying them to stop producing under EC 'set-aside' schemes and to put the countryside back as it was.

Environmental groups such as Friends of the Earth are concerned about the use of chemical fertilisers and pesticides. Animal welfare groups, including the long respected RSPCA (Royal Society for the Prevention of Cruelty to Animals), are concerned about factory farming methods and the quality of life of farm animals in general. Also, in respect of pets, welfare groups are concerned that the increasing tendency to ban dogs from public parks and beaches (whilst understandable, on account of the health hazards to children) is reducing domestic animals' access to the countryside (farmers have already put increasing numbers of farm animals indoors). If there is to be a surplus of agricultural land it would seem logical to solve the growing problem for dog owners of where to go 'walkies', and the potential cruelty of keeping dogs inside, or locked in hot cars on family outings, by introducing 'dog only' exercise fields and areas of public open space (as is already the case in some special public parks in Switzerland). Planning must take into account the needs of all users, human and otherwise, and introduce policies which provide for greater differentiation between types of open space, including specialist use by potentially incompatible groups, rather than having a blanket 'open space' or 'countryside' policy (the 'colour it all green' mentality) as has been common in the past.

Other environmental controls

Vacant and derelict land

There are vast areas of spoilt land in both urban and rural areas which are increasingly the subject of planning initiatives. The government, and indeed the EC, appear to favour the use of waste land within cities for new development rather than greenfield sites, as set out in the European Commission Green Paper on the urban environment of 1990 (*Planning Bulletin* 42, 9 November 1990, p. 153). As was indicated in relation to regional planning, there are a range of policies, incentives and grants to encourage the reuse of derelict land.

The Department of the Environment keeps a register of publicly owned underused or underutilised land under the Local Government, Planning and Land Act, 1980 (not to be confused with other registers such as the register of planning applications or the Land Registry, which is related to the ownership and transfer conveyancing of land). On average there are 100 000 acres on around 8000 individual sites per year identified on this register (Hansard, debate on greenfield sites (development), 27 July 1989, p. 1342). Around 25 per cent of such land has been vacant for over 20 years. Interestingly, much of it is owned by statutory undertakers, local authorities or nationalised industry, British Rail having a particularly bad record in this respect. Ironically, under Section 215 of the Town and Country Planning Act, 1990, local authorities have power to require the proper maintenance of land by private owners, and there are additional powers under the Public Health Acts. However, if the owner considers his land to have been blighted by adverse planning decisions he has the right to serve a blight notice on the local authority, which must purchase the land under Section 150 of the Town and Country Planning Act, 1990 (and will probably let it decay into an even worse state). Some areas can get into a terrible mess just through neglect and lack of management, without any mining or industrial activity taking place.

Under the Derelict Land Act, 1982, money was made available to improve such areas, being augmented by urban development grants and urban regeneration grants under the Inner Urban Areas Act, 1979, and the Local Government, Planning and Land Act, 1980. In 1988 these grants were replaced by a single category of City Grants. Money is also available within the ambit of the enterprise zone and Urban Development Corporation legislation, and the Single Regeneration Budget provisions, discussed in Chapter 7. The National Land Utilisation Survey, originally undertaken by the geographer Sir Dudley Stamp and continued by Professor Alice Coleman, has shown, in spite of the introduction of town planning over the last forty years, that the rate of loss of agricultural land to development has not been reduced, indeed it has continued to grow. In order to prevent at least some types of dereliction increasing in the future, the government has sought to increase controls over mining activity, especially open-cast mining, which causes some of the most visible problems.

Minerals planning

Mining counts as a form of development, and is subject to control under the planning Acts. The planners are concerned about how extraction will limit future uses, for example open-cast mining can sterilise wide areas for future development, whilst underground mining may render surrounding sites unsuitable for subsequent development because of the danger of subsidence. Both types of mining create major environmental problems, especially quarrying, with heavy lorries inflicting noise, wear and tear on local roads and communities.

Planners are concerned about ensuring long-term supervision of mining activities. A site will need to be reinstated when mining has ceased, perhaps in thirty years' time, and planning conditions may be laid down to this effect with varying success. In the past some successful agreements were entered into with the National Coal Board which were subsequently honoured, ensuring a measure of landscaping and environmental control.

The 1947 Town and Country Planning Act first introduced controls over mining. Guidance on the control of minerals was found in what were known as 'The Green Books' produced by the (old) Ministry of Housing and Local Government in the 1950s and 1960s, whose influence is still to be felt. From the 1970s minerals control became the responsibility of counties and other first tier authorities. Where local government reorganisation has taken place, for example in Wales in 1995, the new unitary authorities are now responsible for minerals (1994 Local Government (Wales) Act). All minerals authorities are required to prepare Mineral Subject Plans alongside their other statutory development plans. Under the 1981 Town and Country Planning (Minerals) Act powers were increased, especially in respect of restoration and aftercare of sites, and limitations on the duration of planning permission. Typically mining permissions will contain far more 'conditions of permission' than other planning permissions, and generally take longer to go through the system. In 1988 MPGs (Minerals Planning Guidance Notes, like PPGs) were introduced (see Government publications at back of book). In the same year controls were increased because of European Directive 85/337 (see list of government publications) requiring environmental assessment of minerals applications.

Although there has been an improvement in modern controls, there still exist many pre-1947 permissions (Cullingworth estimates over a thousand nationwide, Cullingworth and Nadin, 1994: 92–4). Such permissions were meant to be registered formally with the local planning department by March 1992, for consideration of imposition of modern conditions on the permissions, or they would cease to exist. In fact, in spite of considerable pressure from environmental groups, the process has not been straightforward as there are legal complexities involved in determining whether a permission is still extant or can be extinguished, and in some cases reliable records no longer exist. Such sites, nowadays, find themselves alongside gentrified rural settlements or in what are nowadays seen as environmentally sensitive areas. Such environmental considerations must be weighed against the importance of ensuring adequate provision of raw materials for industrial and construction purposes. The 1995 Environment Act introduces new controls on abandoned mines and contaminated land. Minerals planning is discussed in detail in Volume III in this series.

Environmental impact assessment

Concern with conservation is moving from matters related to specific buildings and land towards concern with the eco-system itself, with the new 'green' environmental movements having an impact on the scope and nature of town planning (for example, as reflected in PPG 9 on nature conservation). In particular Friends of the Earth and other pressure groups have drawn attention to deficiencies in policy and legislation in Britain, while internationally groups such as Greenpeace have alerted people to the global implications of the greenhouse effect, the holes in the ozone layer, pollution and diminishing natural resources. More broadly, the concern with the environment has come from diverse sources, including those traditionally concerned with recreation and leisure (Arvill, 1969); farming (Shoard, 1980, 1987); transport (as in the case of the Bristol-based groups such as the cyclists' pressure group Cyclebag and also SUSTRANS) and ecology in general (there are countless books and groups). Interestingly one finds overlapping interests in this field among diverse pressure groups, for example the women's movement has often been in the vanguard of the ecology movement, particularly in respect of the negative effects of aspects of science and technology, and the potentially polluting and carcinogenic effects of manufacturing practices (Carson, 1962; Griffin, 1978; Collard and Contrucci, 1988).

The EC now requires Environmental Impact Assessment to be undertaken in relation to the granting of planning permission on larger industrial toxic developments (Fortlage, 1990) the rules emanating from EC Directive 85/337 with instructions to local planning authorities on how to apply them in the 1988 Town and Country Planning (Assessment of Environmental Effects) Regulations, No. 1199. The emphasis has been strengthened by the Environmental Protection Act, 1990 and the Environment Act, 1995. In the future some see the planners' role extending beyond concern just with land uses and development, as under the British system, towards a role closer to the European model of 'environmental policing'. Uses such as salmon fishing and forestry which in Britain would once have been seen as good because they are rural are now subject to such legislation (for further examples see Grant; *Planner* **77** (33): p. 4–6.) The green intentions of the government were further expounded in the White Paper *This common inheritance: Britain's environmental strategy*, Cmd 1200 (1990). It should be stressed that EC law cannot be ignored, as it takes precedence over planning law. More broadly, the traditional division between public health law and town and country planning law is tending increasingly to be overarched within the broader category of environmental law and conceived of as two aspects of the broader green policy area. In particular there is increasing emphasis on 'sustainability' policies (Blowers *et al.*, 1993, produced in conjunction with the Town and Country Planning Association and Earthscan). Sustainability policy, generally, has four elements, to conserve stock of natural assets, avoid damaging the regenerative capacity of ecosystems; achieve greater social equality; and avoid imposing risks and costs on future generations.

The government (DOE, 1994) in a document on *Sustainable Development: The UK Strategy* covers issues such as global climate and air quality, and discusses policy towards non-renewable resources such as water, earth (soil) and minerals, in seeking to achieve sustainability. As stated, minerals is already the subject of town planning policy but some of the other issues have only been taken into account in British town planning in recent years as a result of European directives and the influence of the environment movement. Concern with sustainability became a higher government priority as a result of international influences such as the Brundtland Report in 1987 (*Our Common Future*) and the Earth Summit in Rio, in 1992. Following Rio, the Agenda 21 programme was established which required all signatory states to draw up national plans for sustainability. Chapter 28 of the Agenda agreement required local authorities in each state to produce 'Local Agenda 21' initiatives for their areas. DOE policy guidance, as embodied in the PPGs, has also begun to include sustainability related guidance, PPG 12 being particularly strong on this, with PPGs 1, 6 and 14 also touching upon it. Since consideration of sustainability is a new component in the statutory planning system it is proving difficult to determine its 'materiality' (legal relevance) and 'force' in planning appeal situations. However, as stated earlier, permitted development rights under the 1995 revision of the GDO are now amended, in some cases, owing to EIA compliance requirements (DOE, 1995).

Unless there is a tremendous shift in central government attitudes, funding, and regulation towards public transport, motor car usage, pollution control enforcement, building design, energy policy, and waste disposal practice, the planners, alone, have inadequate powers to achieve sustainable cities. Indeed, to achieve sustainably planned settlements the planners would need increased powers to achieve the fundamental structural shifts in land use patterns, densities, traffic management, and layout patterns (Barton *et al.*, 1995). At present, environmental principles are influencing society's attitudes, to a degree, rather than totally revolutionising town planning or city form. However, as with most urban policies, change is likely to be gradual and long term, as it is no simple task to change urban structure, provide people with a viable alternative to motor cars, and deal with all the related social and economic effects of environmental change. Sustainability and environmental planning are discussed in greater detail in Volume III. Readers should consult the 1995 Environment Act (Ball and Ball, 1995; Lane and Peto, 1995). It increases local authority powers to control pollution, strengthens recycling measures and increases grants for conservation. It also introduces measures relating to abandoned mines and contaminated land, and a new regime for reviewing and updating longstanding mineral planning permission. The Act also introduced changes to the authorities responsible for National Parks, strengthened control over water resource management, flooding and pollution, and established a National Environmental agency.

Other eyesores

A specialist area of planning law deals with advertisements. There are a range of controls over caravans and camping sites. Many of these uses are temporary, and permission is often granted on a seasonal basis, the aim being to prevent not only visual intrusion but the insidious and gradual use of holiday facilities as year-round housing. Mobile homes (usually far from mobile!) are a particular problem. Planners have control over temporary uses such as fairs, circuses, sport-related marquees and markets. These powers are administered in conjunction with the magistrates and public health officials. Land may also be 'set aside' from agricultural use for a limited period under EC law, provided it is returned to farming eventually, undamaged.

Chapter 10

Development and design control

The purpose of this chapter is to consider the means by which planners can control development, and thus influence both land use and design. Firstly, the development control process is considered. Secondly, the question of design standards in relation to residential estate development is discussed. Development control and planning law are complex legal areas. There are exceptions to almost every rule, as decisions are frequently challenged on appeal, and the legislation is constantly changing. There is a vast body of planning case law which is not incorporated into this introductory text but can be investigated in the planning law textbooks (Grant; Heap; Denyer-Green; Telling; Moore).

Development control

Planning permission

Before carrying out development, which (as defined in Part I) includes both new development (building, alteration and mining, and from 1991 certain incidences of demolition) and a change in the use of existing buildings and land, planning permission must be obtained. There are two types of planning permission, outline and full (detailed). Outline permission establishes the broad principles on which development of a certain type is allowed, whereas the full application deals with the specifics. Normally small householder-type applications, e.g. kitchen extensions, go straight to the detailed stage. For larger, more complex or controversial schemes, e.g. a new housing estate or an out-of-town shopping centre, it is normal to agree the principles at the outline stage. The planners and developers may meet for discussions long before the application form is filled in. It is likely that what are known as 'reserved matters' will be held over for consideration at the detailed stage. These are usually shown under five headings on the planning application form: siting, design, external appearance, access (including car parking) and landscaping. There is no single standardised planning application form at present; forms vary from local authority to local authority (and, for example, may in be Welsh). It is normal for the larger authorities to have a separate form for the small householder as distinct from the large developer applicants.

To submit a householder application, or full planning application for other uses, the applicant is required to complete four copies of the forms supplied by the local planning office, plus four copies of the plans. It is not uncommon for the Building Regulations application (which must be submitted as well) to be combined with the planning application, but it is passed on to a separate department. The plans consist of a site plan, normally to the scale of 1 : 1250, showing the buildings (proposed and existing) in and around the site, with a red line around the whole plot. An Ordnance Survey grid reference may be required, which is shown as follows. First (with the north at the top) the 'easting' is given, which is the number (found on the top or bottom margin) of the vertical line to the left of the site, followed by the 'northing', which is the number of the nearest horizontal line below your site (shown on the sides of the map e.g. L. Building plans should also be provided, showing the plan (floor layout) and elevation (external appearance) plus a section through the building showing annotated details of the construction and materials to a scale of 1 : 50 or 1 : 100 approximately $^1/_4$ in. to 1 ft or $^1/_8$ in. to 1 ft respectively. The north point, scale and key, if used, should be included on the plan. Charges are made nowadays for both planning applications and Building Regulation consent (check the current cost from local authority).

Conversion

Although the above example was in imperial measurements for illustrative purposes, it should be noted that from 1995, as a result of EC regulations, all planning applications must now be submitted in metric measurements, or they may not be processed by local planning authorities. Non-metric planning submissions, for example produced in relation to a planning appeal, will not be accepted by the Department of the Environment. Conversion for dimensions is as follows. To convert inches to centimetres multiply by 2.54; feet to metres multiply by 0.3048; yards to metres multiply by 0.9144. To convert centimetres to inches multiply by 0.3937; metres to feet multiply by 3.2808; metres to yards multiply by 1.936. For area measurements which are used in indicating floorspace, for example for retail development, 1 square foot = 0.09 square metres; and 1 square metre is 10.764 square feet, i.e. divide or multiply by ten approximately plus or minus a bit. Cubic measurements which are of relevance to development control for example when assessing the size of house extensions, are as follows. To convert cubic feet into cubic metres multiply by 0.3048, and to convert cubic metres into cubic feet multiply by 35.315.

Planning applications

When submitting a planning application a certificate must be completed which records the ownership of the property, this is known as a Section 66 certificate (Section 27 under the 1971 Act). Certificate A is completed by a sole owner. Certificate B is completed if the ownership is shared with others, then Notice 1 (given out as part of the application form) is sent to each owner. Certificate C is used where the applicant is unable to discover all the names of the owners, or certificate D where the applicant is unable to discover any of the names of the owners. The application will need to be publicised in cases C and D. However, the situation is under review, and it is likely that in future all planning applications will have to be advertised (and neighbours notified). In general at present certain other types of planning application are advertised by the planning authority in the local newspaper and on-site notices, and twenty-one days are allowed for people to inspect the plans and make written representations if they are unhappy with the proposal. Written representations are taken into account at the decision-making stage when the local planning committee (of councillors) decide whether or not to approve the scheme, taking into account the professional advice of their planning officers. The planning authority is required to keep a register of planning applications (Section 69 of the Town and Country Planning Act, 1990) which is open to the public and may be consulted without charge. (This is a separate register from the local Land Charges Register, which gives information on other relevant matters, such as road widening which would affect a piece of land, over and above planning issues *per se*.)

If the property is in a Conservation Area or is a listed building, in addition to the ordinary planning application, listed building consent may also be needed, and the local authority will advertise the application. Normally in Conservation Areas, and for listed buildings, a full planning application must be submitted (not an outline) because the planners will want to know what the scheme will look like, in terms of façade, townscape and matters of car parking, access, etc. Of course, listed building consent may also be required on its own, in cases of alterations to the building which do not actually constitute development. Conservation Area consent is required for the demolition of an unlisted building in a Conservation Area. In sensitive cases the developers may well produce a short report in addition, with annotated diagrams and plans, photographs and further explanations of exactly what is intended, e.g. whether a wall is going to be demolished, what the planting is going to be made up of. The planners and developers are likely to have a meeting about building materials at the detail stage, and samples will be discussed.

It may be that the applicant does not require planning permission. Under Section 10 of the 1991 Planning and Compensation Act, revising the provisions previously under Section 191–4 of the 1990 Town and Country Planning Act, an applicant can apply for a certificate of lawfulness. These are of two types, the 'Certificate of lawful use or development' for existing development, and the 'Certificate of lawfulness of proposed use or development' for proposed development (see Cullingworth and Nadin, 1994: 82 for history of past versions such as 'certificate of established use' and 'determination of need for permission of proposed development').

The planning authority makes its decisions on the basis of national planning law, that is, the planning Acts, and rules in the orders, such as the Use Classes Order and General Development Orders, deriving from the 1990 and 1991 Acts, and various other directives, statutory instruments, circulars, White Papers (Command Papers), PPGs and other guidance notes. These are all a reflection of the Secretary of State's policy and therefore, should a particular planning decision go to appeal, the decision may be determined in accordance with specific aspects of their content. In addition to these ministerial documents, case law and appeal decisions are major indicators of current policy as to what is permissible, almost more so than all the other factors mentioned. The local authority also takes into account its own policy statements, which may have the force of law as enshrined in the approved Structure Plan and especially in the Local Plan (Section 26 of the 1991 Act), and also, to a lesser degree, in planning-committee approved non-statutory plans and statements. Many planning authorities produce design guides which set out the acceptable standards of design, car parking, density and estate layout, which are also material considerations. As stated earlier, the application of planning standards and design principles in respect of a particular site should be seen not as absolutely fixed but as subject to a certain amount of negotiation and 'trading' to get the best solution for the site, all things considered. On some small inner-city sites it would be practically impossible to achieve the fixed standards. For example, the planners and developers might find their decisions constrained by the presence of underground sewers, unstable land, soil contamination, restrictive covenants or the height and effects of neighbouring development (not forgetting the possibility of the existence of archaeological remains; PPG 16).

The city-wide level policy statements found in the Structure Plan (or Unitary Development Plan) are of major importance when deciding whether a development should occur at all on a particular location in the case of the larger planning applications, as it must tie in with proposed development allocations for the area. Even before a request for outline planning permission is submitted, the developers may enter preliminary negotiations and discussions with the planners to sound them out, and either side may produce a planning brief, a document for discussion, setting out how the area is envisaged as developing. For example, for the planners the location of large housing estates may have strategic implications for the future structure of the whole urban area, the future infrastructure, bus routes, schools – everything. On the other hand, developers stand to make or lose millions, depending on the planners' decision. Some will try various tactics to speed up the planning process, and may offer, early on, to enter into a generous planning gain agreement (see 'Planning obligations' under Section 106 A and B of the 1991 Act). Circular 16/91 (which updates circular 22/83) sets out the parameters of what the DOE considers 'reasonable' factors germane to a planning gain agreement.

Local authorities are required to make a decision within eight weeks of the application being received, but on average decisions are given within fifteen weeks. If applicants are unhappy about the decision they have, in some cases, six months to appeal to the Secretary of State. However, they also have the right to lodge an appeal within a mere eight weeks if they have not got a decision by then. Some developers have gone in for 'twin-tracking', putting in two identical applications and then appealing on one if they get a refusal on the other. The big developers have all sorts of ways of harassing a small local authority, e.g. trying to push the planners into a favourable decision to avoid legal costs incurred by appeals in these times of government cut-backs. Likewise the local authority can cause delay by means of bureaucratic procedures to frustrate the developer! All this is in a quite different league from ordinary householder applications. Planning consultants and planning lawyers working for the private sector know how to play the game and how to submit the application in the manner most likely to achieve the desired result for their clients.

Planning applications (like prayers) receive one of three answers – yes, no or yes but. Planners are entitled to impose 'such conditions as they think fit' (Section 29 of 1971 Act, now Section 70 of the 1990 Act). Circular 1/85 sets out six tests as to the validity of conditions of permission, the basic principle being that the conditions must be for a planning reason related to the site, and not for some broader environmental or social policy reason. The local authority may accept the development in principle but require modifications, or it may choose to limit the permission to a period of years (an increasing trend in the case of a change of use, to see how it works out). In the case of new building development matters such as landscaping, car parking and access may have to be altered, for example screening with trees might be required. The highway authority will also have had a say in the decision, and will obviously be concerned with traffic generation, and the question of the need for new road development. Until recently the developers would enter into an agreement under Section 38 of the Highways Act, 1980, which allows the developer to undertake the construction of the roads (or pay for it) in return for the local authority adopting them and maintaining them in the future, or alternatively advance payments were made by the developer to the local authority under Sections 219 and 228 of the Highways Act before the site was 'released' for development, with Sections 38 and 278 also allowing for an element of 'highway gain' over and above the minimum to facilitate site development. The New Roads and Street Works Act, 1991, modifies the legal mechanics of these methods to a degree (Section 22) but the principle remains the same. Other negotiations are entered into between the developer and the statutory authorities for the provision of the other infrastructural services. In addition to all this, it must not be forgotten that there are additional hurdles in respect of public health and Building Regulation consent, and nowadays EC environmental assessment, before development can commence.

There is a great deal of legal debate as to what constitutes the commencement and indeed the completion of development (and now 'demolition'), with planning law cases abounding of men digging one trench and declaring development has started or leaving out a window in a house and declaring that development is not complete, for a variety of planning, taxation and other legal reasons. All planning permission should normally be taken up within five years of being granted, and in the case of outline permission the full application should be submitted within three years of the initial permission, and development should commence two years after the approval of detailed reserved matters. In some cases a completion notice may be served, once building has started, if the development work is slow. However, once planning permission has lapsed without being acted upon it may not necessarily be renewed, the idea of a time limit being to allow for changing circumstances and flexibility.

Use Classes Order and General Development Order

These were updated under the Town and Country Planning Use Classes Order, 1987, and the Town and Country Planning General Development Order, 1988, and minor revisions take place from time to time, so readers should check the current situation in the *Encyclopaedia of planning law.*

The Use Classes Order

The classes may be summarised as follows.

Class A1. Shops of all types, including superstores and retail warehouses; also includes hairdressers, sandwich bars, etc., but not car showrooms.

Class A2. Financial and professional services, including banks, building societies, estate agents and betting offices.

Class A3. Food and drink, including restaurants, pubs and take-aways.

Class B1. Business use, including offices, research and development, and general industrial use, provided it is not detrimental to the area.

Class B2. General industrial use.

Classes B3–7. Special industrial uses.

Class B8. Storage and distribution, including wholesale cash-and-carry.

Class C1. Hotels and hostels.

Class C2. Residential homes and institutions, use as a hospital.

Class C3. Use as a dwelling house (a) by a family; (b) by not more than six persons living together as a household (including those under care.)

Class D1. Non-residential institutions, including religious buildings, museums, medical clinics, public halls, creches, nurseries.

Class D2. Assembly and leisure facilities, such as cinemas, bingo halls, casinos and indoor sports.

Sui generis. Many uses do not fall into any class and are therefore literally in a class of their own. For example, theatres, car hire offices, petrol stations, car showrooms and various innovative uses have been seen as *sui generis* (of its own kind). This category is subject to interpretation, allowing the planning office discretion to decide on the basis of planning policy whether a change of use has occurred or not. The planning authorities must also take into account the zonings shown on the approved plans for the area. (The old-style land use zoning colours, which appear to be making a comeback under the unitary system, show the 'predominant' land uses, as some of the areas will be fairly mixed). If all changes of use were set out in the Use Classes Order planning would become very mechanical and there would be no professional judgement involved. Also the extent and intensity of the change has to be taken into account to determine whether it is a material change of use or just a temporary, or ancillary (secondary) use.

The General Development Order

The General Development Order, 1988, sets out which matters do not require planning permission. However, beware, because under Article 4 of the order the Secretary of State and the local planning authority can withdraw some or all of the rights in the order, and the rights may also be reduced through planning conditions being imposed. Local authorities themselves have power to suspend rights under Clauses I–IV of the schedule in cases where the development proposed would be detrimental to the proper planning of the area, or a threat to the amenities of the area, but this direction can remain in force only for six months, unless approved by the Secretary of State. Article 4 decisions remain in force indefinitely. Check the order in the *Encyclopaedia of planning law*, as it is subject to revision, and the list of changes is extensive. One of the more interesting points is that agriculture (class VI) has until relatively recently been subject to fewer planning controls than urban development. For example, farm buildings come under control if they are near an airport (if they are more than 3 m high within 3 km of an airport or 12 m elsewhere) but the trend is towards increasing control in view of pressure from environmentalists and the green movement in general. The GDO was last revised in 1988, but there have been procedural changes and other amendments in 1995, and loss of exemption of permitted development rights in some instances owing to the effects of EU environmental impact assessment directives (see DOE, 1995). Changes are detailed in the Town and Country Planning (General Development Procedure) Order 1995 and the Town and Country (General Permitted Development) Order 1995 and the 1995 Environment Act.

In class I there are various small-scale aspects of householder development which do not require permission, which are known as permitted development. For example, one can build a porch provided it is less than 3 m^2 in area, less than 3 m high and more than 2 m from the boundary of the road. At present householders are allowed one satellite dish provided it does not exceed 60, 70 or 90 centimetres in diameter depending upon the location, and area designation in question (DOE, 1995, b) and is no higher than the ridge of the roof. A loft can be built provided it does not increase the total cubic content of the house itself by more than 50 m^3 or 40 m^3 for a terrace in terms of loft extension. (This is not in addition to overall permitted house extensions but must be deducted from it.) The loft extension should not be above the ridge of the roof, and normally it should not face the road.

House extensions can be up to 15 per cent of the original current cubic volume on a semi or detached property or 70 m^3, or 10 per cent in a terrace, or 50 m^3, whichever is larger, both up to an overall maximum of 115 m^3. Note that in respect of getting permission for extensions all measurements relate to the house as originally built, or as it stood at 1 July 1948, and are related to the external cubic volume. The extension should not be in front of the front wall of the house except where the house is set further than 20 m from the boundary. (Many of the rules seem to favour large houses over small ones.) Neither should it rise above the ridge of the roof. No part of the extension should be higher than 4 m and it must lie within 2 m of any boundary. Along with outbuildings the extended house must not occupy more than 50 per cent the area of the garden (planners are very conscious of plot ratios in some areas, i.e. how much of the site is covered by buildings). (See *Which?* magazine, June 1990, p. 339, for a people's guide to planning applications and check for annual updates.)

All the above statements should be treated with caution, as general principles only, because local authorities have their own additional policy statements which apply to special situations. For example, a particularly sensitive area may be subject to an Article 4 direction which removes the normal rights under the General Development Order, or the house may be in a Conservation Area where there are additional controls. In addition to getting planning permission, as stated, permission under the Building

Regulations is also required, involving a separate department with its own forms and charges. The system is meant to be nationally consistent but some planning authorities are more strict than others. In London there are many additional controls on building construction. Also AONBs and Conservation Areas are subject to somewhat different General Development Order rules.

Any development which requires access on to a trunk or classified road requires permission from the county highway authority. However, if permission is given for car access the local authority is happy to permit access by dropped kerb on the site (subject to notification and the householder paying for the work). Classified roads are not only A and B roads but also C roads, which are not shown distinctively on Ordnance Survey maps but are coloured yellow like unclassified roads. Most bus routes are along classified roads. Planners are particularly concerned at retaining what are known as visibility splays on corners and intersections (as explained further below).

Otherwise any extent of hard standing or patio is allowed, and anything can be planted in the garden, provided it is 'incidental to the enjoyment of the dwelling', but even these factors may be covered by special controls. Students always ask about that hypothetical car port without walls in the front garden. If it is joined to the house it is development in any case, and if it is in front of the front wall of the house and/or over the building line the local authority is likely to act (if the authority notices it). Some local authorities have additional controls about parking caravans in front gardens, and any caravan which is permanently occupied within the curtilage of a dwelling is bound to attract the wrath of the local authority. Working or running a business from home may be construed as a 'change of use', unless the use is 'ancillary' to the main residential use. There is the principle that the 'intensity' and 'predominance' of the use should be taken into account, and a use which is ancillary or secondary to the main use is not necessarily a change of use. Planners are more concerned about external effects such as car parking, noise, disturbance, than the turnover of a business or how much disruption it causes within the household (Thomas, 1988).

Another tricky issue is the question of greenhouses, outbuildings, garages, lean-tos and conservatories (not to be confused with glasshouses, which are horticultural greenhouses and permitted in agricultural areas and Green Belts). Conservatories count as extensions if attached to the house, or if they stand within 5 m of it, and similar rules apply to garages. But greenhouses are part of the enjoyment of the curtilage of the dwelling and permitted under the General Development Order. (But for listed buildings anything within the curtilage of the dwelling is subject to additional planning controls.) New balconies jutting out from upper floors, even with no extension beneath them, are also likely to be counted as development. It is these very detailed, and debatable, aspects of planning law which generate most discord with the general public. Athough there are clearly some implementatory links with development plan policy, one could argue that this level of planning is a completely different matter altogether from strategic urban plan making.

Admittedly some of the rules do seem illogical, particularly in relation to gardens, as one can plant Leylandii trees which can rapidly form a high 'wall' without planning permission being involved. Hedge and plant height is not controlled by planning law (but may be the subject of other local authority controls if plants affect people's use of the adjacent pavement). Also, as stated in the last chapter, some individual trees are protected under preservation orders and permission is needed to lop such a tree; if felled it must be replaced with a similar species. Article 4 directions may be used to impose controls on planting on open-plan estates, and in Conservation Areas trees and hedges are subject to special controls. Fences and walls are normally permitted up to a height of 2 m, or 1 m if next to a classified road (except in Conservation Areas and other areas of special protection). There are additional design controls on the layout of housing at corners. Normally the developers have to leave a visibility splay (a triangle of undeveloped land allowing a clear view along the road at junctions). Standards for these vary according to the area in which they are located, and the category of road.

Confusion as to what is or is not allowed under planning law arises because some local planning authorities enforce the rules more rigidly than others (and some frankly have been known to 'try it on' in over-zealous authorities). Indeed, if they are short-staffed and no one notices illegal development it may appear that it is acceptable. But it should be pointed out that planning authorities do have powers to require the demolition of unauthorised developments, and it is a criminal offence not to comply with an enforcement notice. The Planning and Compensation Act, 1991, has increased the penalties and the related enforcement powers. However, if, for example, the alterations to a house would have been permitted in any case had the owners applied for planning permission, there are means of granting it retrospectively. This may be necessary if the irregularities show up at the time when a house is being sold, during the process of conveyancing. (In this day and age of do-it-yourself conveyancing it may go unnoticed, with dire consequences for the next owner down the line when a keen new planning officer does track it down.) Under the 1991 Act the four-year rule granting immunity to development without permission which has not been noticed in that period is accompanied by a new ten-year rule which gives immunity for changes of use effected without planning permission.

Planning standards and design principles

The principles behind, and present guidance on, some of the main planning standards will now be considered, within the context of the design of a housing estate, but many of the principles could be applied to other types of development too. Some additional material will be given, where appropriate, in relation to other sorts of land uses. Students sometimes imagine that there is one right technical answer to the question of how to design a housing layout. As with much of town planning, it all depends on what one wants to achieve, and where the development is located. For example, if an estate is designed with wide roads they might speed the traffic up, but they would also be likely to reduce the level of safety within the estate. However, different planning authorities adopt different standards for the purposes of development control and once the standards are adopted they enjoy a legal status in respect of the area in question. Even then, sites and circumstances vary considerably, so there always needs to be a measure of flexibility. Some local planning authorities produce design guides, e.g. the popular one produced by Essex (1980).

Site and client considerations

Some firms of private house builders, and some local authority housing departments, have a standard pattern of house type and estate layout which they will seek to impose whatever or wherever the site. However, good design should take into account the characteristics of the site in question and seek to maximise its good points. First is the question of who the development is intended for, and in the private sector this is directly linked with who it is going to be sold to, in terms of class, income, family size and age group. For example, in a desirable area near a golf course it would be possible to build a few really expensive houses on the site at low density and get a good financial return. In an inner suburban infill site the best market to go for might be young married couples wanting starter homes at the cheaper end of the price range, and so more houses could be built at a higher density. This is, of course, looking at it from the developers' viewpoint. The planners might also have specific policies in the Structure Plan, and in greater detail in the Local Plan as to the social mix (Chapter 11), density and land use combinations sought in the area. They may look favourably on a planning application for the development which includes a shop or pub, or a scheme which does not develop the whole site but leaves some land undeveloped for amenity purposes (all of which will have to be negotiated and may be the subject of planning gain agreements). How far the developer will go depends on how anxious he is to develop and whether he has his eye on another site where the planning authority is less fussy. After all, the developer is in it essentially for the financial return, not because he is necessarily interested in good urban design or housing the homeless.

In designing a scheme an initial site analysis must be undertaken of the main natural and man-made characteristics. The slope and aspect of the site need to be noted, in particular whether there are any good views that might be capitalised upon. The planning authority may be more concerned about the views in the sense that it will not want a development on the skyline or half-way up a hill which constitutes an eyesore. In the past developers used to be unwilling to build on a slope steeper than 1 in 7, but nowadays much of the land available is sloping and so a range of styles of split-level housing has emerged to make use of it. The level of the water table should be investigated and whether there are any areas liable to flooding. Attention should also be paid to the micro-climate of the site, in particular whether there are any frosty hollows to be avoided, and any areas which get the sun towards which the houses might be oriented. It used to be said that the bedrooms should face the sun in the mornings and the living rooms and the back garden should get the sun in the evenings. This is impossible to achieve on more than half the houses on an estate if the houses are built facing each other along a road (unless the internal layout is reversed). Wind direction is another important factor that should be taken into account, especially on exposed ground. This affects the orientation of the road layout in residential areas, and passageways which might become mini wind tunnels. The power of the wind is an even greater problem in city-centre commercial developments of high-rise office blocks which can increase the effect of wind eddies and air streams around the buildings. Everyone has had the experience of fighting their way through the elements along the pavement at the bottom of a high-rise building on a windy day. The principle also applies to high-rise blocks of council flats, which are notorious for being windswept, with accompanying swirling litter.

A technical survey of the site will need to be undertaken to ascertain its load-bearing qualities, the soil type and the likelihood of subsidence, this being a major consideration in mining areas. (A special legal search can be done with British Coal, for example in Wales to establish the whereabouts of old tunnels and shafts, although even they have somewhat limited records.) A wary eye should be kept on nearby spoil tips. where imperceptible solifluction (soil creep) can threaten a development. For example, the Welsh Development Agency has done a wonderful job of greening the valleys and covering dereliction and slag heaps, but much of this land is unstable for construction purposes. In industrial locations, possible noise and smells from adjacent sites should be considered. The location of cables, drainage pipes and sewers should be established in consultation with the relevant statutory undertakers. A site's development potential may be limited by the absence of adequate sewerage and storm drainage facilities, all of which cost money to install. As stated earlier, the developer will normally contribute substantially towards these services but, even so, if a site is miles from the next phase of proposed main sewer extension it is unlikely to be built up. Likewise water does not flow uphill unless it is pumped, and the cost of developing a site may be prohibitive simply because of the lack of services. Some aggrieved owners on new housing estates would also point out that adequate television reception is equally important to them and that houses should not be built in 'shadow' areas or where reception is poor (which does affect house sales once word gets around, although cable television may provide an answer).

Access and circulation within the site need to be considered, in respect of existing road and other transport connections. There are some sites which look ideal on a map but on closer investigation are found to be completely 'landlocked', surrounded by other houses. Sometimes there will be just one possible access point through a strip of land which, because of the exorbitant price the owner is likely to ask, is called the ransom strip. Nowadays more attention is required to the provision of adequate footpaths, and bicycle path access, something which was often accorded secondary importance in the past when it was assumed everyone would have a car. Also, Section 76 of the Town and Country Planning Act, 1990, requires local authorities to pay attention to the question of accessibility for the disabled when determining a planning application. This relates particularly to access to individual buildings, especially offices, shops and other public buildings, under the Code of

Practice for Access of the Disabled to Buildings (BS 5810: 1979) and Design Note 18, 'Access for disabled people to educational buildings', published in 1979 by the Department of the Environment. Increasingly local authorities are writing into their plans and design guides wider controls on the unnecessary use of steps and changes of level, and the need for dropped kerbs in all layouts, to help the disabled, the elderly and also mothers with prams. All these people may find steps an insurmountable barrier even in getting in and out of their own front door. Related to this, it is now considered good practice to ensure adequate lighting and visibility on public footpaths.

The visual qualities of the site and its surroundings need to be investigated. The vegetation should be recorded. Many local authorities require the retention of trees and hedges on new housing developments, and buyers are often thrilled at the idea of real country hedges in their back garden, with so much greenfield site development on the edge of town being on erstwhile farmland. Of course, it may be that on principle the planners are against such suburban invasion of the countryside, but the Department of the Environment often favours such developments on appeal nowadays. Some trees may have preservation orders on them, meaning that they cannot be destroyed or, if they are, trees of a similar species must be put in their place. As to new planting, fashions vary, but there is still some applicability in the traditional principles found in books such as Keeble (1969). Ash, beech, blackthorn and spruce used to be recommended as windbreaks (but take ages to grow); ash, elm, oak, yew, poplar and willow are good for open spaces (requiring a wide radius for their roots); cedar, chestnut, lime and walnut are good for squares but hardly 'instant' trees. Acacia, birch, horse chestnut, plane and laburnum are suitable for wide roads, and almond, cypress, holly, Lombardy poplar or rowan for narrower roads. But trees with flowers and berries, especially flowering cherry, are often seen as rather kitsch or suburban in taste. Trees that are likely to drop leaves over cars and pavements should not be used. Developers prefer 'instant', fast-growing, maintenance-free trees, whilst local authorities want vandal-proof trees or prickly bushes that keep people on the footpaths and off the gardens, with dense plant cover that discourages weeds and dogs. However, women's groups and crime prevention groups advise against putting tree cover, high walls or screening near footpaths, as they may obscure visibility and act as a haven for muggers. Railings or walls of spaced bricks or blocks that can be seen through are preferred where possible, provided they do not reduce privacy in gardens.

There are wider issues of the protection of wildlife, wild

flowers, etc., which may come into play in some out-of-town locations. There have been several well-publicised incidences of science parks having to shift sideways to allow rare species of frogs and newts to keep their ponds. Drainage of development sites without a preliminary ecological analysis is seen as a somewhat crude approach to development. As stated in the last chapter, environmental assessment is required on larger schemes by the EC. Also, planners are unwilling to allow development on high-grade agricultural land (shown blue on MAFF maps) although it is often inevitable nowadays. There are five grades of agricultural land classification, running basically from very good to very poor, with grades I and II seen as the most in need of protection from development. The characteristics of the local building materials, style and colour should also be investigated to ensure that the new scheme blends with the surrounding area, especially in urban infill sites and rural locations. In many incidences the use of materials will be controlled by the planners in any case, especially in Conservation Areas. Also existing gates, fences, walls and other townscape features may be incorporated in the design to good effect.

There are many other odds and ends of some importance which need to be taken into account in the design process, indeed any one of these 'little' issues may put the developers off altogether. The legal rights over the land must be checked, and normally a local search will be undertaken by the purchaser's or the developer's solicitor at the local authority before the land is bought to reveal any existing charges on the land such as planning permissions, listed building designations, etc. An 'additional enquiries' form would also show up wider planning issues as related to the Structure Plan, sewer alterations, road widenings, etc., affecting the site. In addition various people (and their animals or vehicles!) may have private legal rights over the land. So a site is likely to be criss-crossed by a range of public and private rights, footpaths and easements which give people, cables, even herds of cows a right of way. Of course the tenure situation must be established as to who owns what and whether there are any restrictive covenants over and above any zoning controls the planners may have placed on it. For example, some Victorian houses with large back gardens which look ideal for infill development are still governed by covenants which prevent an increase in density, a condition imposed when they were built, to preserve the quality of the area. In passing it is of interest that in the United States the planning and zoning law is as much related to density as to land use, thus ensuring the separation of income groups and the preservation of property values – and this is in a so-called classless society.

Once all these factors have been mapped on the site plan a possible design solution to the layout may already be suggesting itself because of the constraints of the site (such as the retention of vegetation) and the demands of the sort of housing which is required by the developer and the planners. Indeed, to save time, preliminary discussion with the planners is advisable, with the presentation of a draft brief of what is in mind, in the case of larger-scale developments. Some say the design process should start with sketching in the roads (taking into account any existing sewers, etc.) and then arrange the houses around them. Others block in the main areas of housing first, subdivide them to the density required, then add the roads. Some designers go for the creative intuitive leap and cannot explain quite how they arrived at the final design. For example, if there are twelve houses per acre one is going to have plots about 40 ft wide with a total depth of around 120 ft composed of, say, a 50 ft back garden, a 35 ft depth house, a 20 ft front garden, 5 ft of pavement and, say, 10 ft to the white line in the middle of the road. Housing plots are usually measured to include half the estate road's width with pavement. However, having discussed these guidelines, the design process should not be mechanical. Seldom are plots likely to be identical all over a housing estate, because of topographical factors and other constraints.

Densities

Residential densities measure the number of dwellings, that is, the number of habitable units, not just the number of buildings. The two may coincide on a new housing suburban housing estate, but it does not work like that if one is measuring say a Conservation Area of older houses where the properties have been subdivided into flats, where the number of dwellings may be several times the number of buildings. In fact crude density is not always a good measure of plot coverage, which may need to be measured by other criteria for design purposes. For example, the planners may stipulate that no more than 50 per cent of the site is to be developed. One has to be particularly aware of these factors with tall residential buildings, where there may be an apparently high net density but low plot coverage because all the dwellings are piled on top of each other. Nor is density in itself a measure of the quality of the area; some Conservation Areas consisting of Georgian town houses and mews may have a high density.

Controls on commercial development are, relatively speaking, more concerned with the intensity of development on a particular site than with overall density. In commercial development the floor space index gives the relationship between the size of the plot (usually including half the width of the surrounding roads) and the total floor space. The floor space index has been used in central London, particularly in relation to office building development in the past. Plot ratio is also used for both commercial and residential development to determine how much of the site can be built over. Note that the same floor space index can be achieved in a variety of ways – building one tall block on a small part of the site, spreading the building over the whole site, or stepping the building back (like a staircase, in tiers) as in New York. There are height restrictions in many areas, for example many enterprise zones have a height limit of 200 ft, except Dudley, where there are proposals to build the tallest building in Europe. Meanwhile an enormous skyscraper has been developed at Canary Wharf in the London docklands. Tall residential buildings (unlike commercial buildings in Britain) are required to receive a certain amount of natural daylight, so they cannot be built too closely together, this being controlled by the Sunlight and Daylight Regulations (DOE, 1971).

There are two main types of residential density, net and gross. Net density is based on the dimensions given above, that is, the width of the house plot times the length of the total plot made up of the house standing within its front and back garden plus the distance up to half way across the estate road. If all such blocks were put together they would cover the whole area of the housing estate. Gross density includes all the above, plus the land taken up by shops, schools, amenity space, distributor roads, that is, it is a neighbourhood density, and therefore is likely to appear lower than the net density. (Make very sure which type of density the planners require in respect of a particular site.)

There are a variety of other types of density which one might come across, ranging from measurements of the town density of the urban area as a whole – i.e. it is not solely a residential density – down to the very detailed accommodation densities which involve the number of rooms or even bed spaces in an area, the latter being used by housing management officers working out how many council tenants they can fit into an area. Density can be based on the number of dwellings or the number of people. On average it is assumed that there are three persons per household (although there may be one person in one house and six in the next), so obviously person densities are usually three times greater than dwelling densities. The word 'dwellings' is normally used rather than 'houses', as it includes flats, bedsitters, etc. The distinction is important from the perspective of the planners if they are trying to estimate the number of people who will be living in an area and for whom they will need to provide a certain level of shopping or school provision. This is particularly important where there are large Edwardian houses. They may be only about four per acre, but if one counts all the flats they have been subdivided into the number of dwellings may run into five times that figure. Some planning authorities operate density controls, to stop an area becoming too built-up, and for example may therefore refuse an extension or the subdivision of a house into more than two units. This can seem most insensitive to the occupiers who may want a granny flat for a relative, but the planners have to take into account the fact that, once granted, the permission 'runs with the land': it attaches to the property rather than the family in question, who may well move on later (and cannot take the extension with them). In practice the answer may be to make sure the flat is linked to the house, without a separate entrance, so that it does not count as a new dwelling (i.e. development) – fire regulations permitting.

Here are some illustrations of the sort of densities one would find in connection with different types of housing area. (An acre is 0·405 ha and a hectare is 2·471 acres.) Both the persons per acre/hectare and the dwellings per acre/hectare are given, but for simplicity's sake after the first few examples only the d.p.a. will be given. Persons per acre (p.p.a.) or per hectare (p.p.h.) is normally three times density per acre (d.p.a) or per hectare (d.p.h.). Large detached houses in big gardens on the edge of town are likely to be built at 1–4 d.p.a. (2·5–10 d.p.h.), which is the same as 3–12 p.p.a. (or 7–13 p.p.h.). Typical inter-war detached houses come out more like 8 d.p.a. (20 d.p.h.), whereas semi-detached suburbia itself was normally built to around 10–12 d.p.a. (30 d.p.h.). Council housing also used to be built around this figure, but the densities became higher on new schemes as the years went by. Moving further into the city, terraced housing averages around 15 d.p.a., as does patio housing, which was much used in some New Towns and inner locations where there is little garden space, the house forming an L shape around an internal courtyard. Three-storey terraces and maisonettes (one house on top of another but, unlike flats, with their own separate entrances; known as duplexes or even triplexes in the United States) come out around 20–30 d.p.a. Six storeys or over, at around 40 d.p.a., falls into the medium-rise category, some would say the beginnings of high-rise. Levels of 80 d.p.a., around ten to fifteen storeys in a set of blocks, can be achieved in high-rise development so long as not much ancillary space is allowed around the base of the blocks. However, in Britain, unlike, say, Hong Kong, where densities go far beyond this, it is impossible to achieve really high densities by going high-rise because of the Sunlight and Daylight Regulations, which require that space must be left around the block, so little is gained by building higher. Very high densities are achieved in older districts where there has been a great deal of subdivision into bedsits or studio flats of moderate medium-rise buildings such as six-storey converted Victorian town mansions. Indeed, using linked and clustered forms of low-rise dwelling forms, such as town housing, quite high densities can be attained without going high-rise: the two should not be confused.

Estate layout

In the past developers used to build along roads, creating ribbon development, as we saw in earlier chapters. It is unusual nowadays to find a through road going through a new housing estate because of safety considerations. Nor do planners and highway engineers want cars coming out of lots of little access roads, or individual driveways, all giving on to a main road and slowing down the through traffic. Nowadays one is more likely to find layouts which emphasise the use of culs-de-sac and the safety of pedestrians, the roots of which go back to the Radburn concept.

In the 1920s the US town of Radburn was based on a series of neighbourhoods, each ringed by an external peripheral road from which a series of culs-de-sac penetrated into the neighbourhoods, providing access for residents but preventing through traffic finding a short cut through. The idea is very similar to Buchanan's environmental areas in the 1960s in respect of reconfiguring road systems in existing urban areas in Britain. Within the Radburn neighbourhoods the pedestrian footpath system was designed to be completely separate from the road system. People coming home by car would arrive at the 'back' of the house, park in a garage or garage court and approach the house through the 'back' door. But pedestrians would walk along the landscaped footpaths which ran between the houses to the 'front' of the house. The inverted commas remind us that once one gets away from the idea of pavements running alongside roads and houses facing the street the concept of front and back becomes almost irrelevant. Indeed, these departures from convention in the external access did involve a rethink of how the inside of the houses should be planned.

The Radburn principle was adopted in many of the post-war British New Towns in combination with the neighbourhood unit concept. Such schemes often proved unpopular, for whilst they were meant to increase safety by separating the footpaths from the traffic on the roads, many residents were unhappy with the remote, cut-off nature of some of the paths, especially lone women walking home in the evenings, particularly in subways under the peripheral roads. Contrary to the scheme at Radburn, pedestrians' needs had become secondary to those of the motor car. It was often expected, too, that bicycles should share the footpaths with the pedestrians, an arrangement which was unsatisfactory for both groups. People were also confused and unhappy about their houses not having a clear front and back, and housewives got fed up with people tramping up the back garden and then leaving muddy footprints across the kitchen floor. It was not even safe, as children often used the garage court areas to play football and inevitably accidents happened as motorists reversed into the parking spaces. Cars were often vandalised, too. Purists would say that if the true Radburn design had been adopted, rather than cheap and nasty versions, known as pseudo-Radburns, many of the problems could have been avoided. However, most local authorities now accept 'Radburnisation' in some form or other as a basis of their design principles, with particular emphasis on the use of culs-de-sac to provide car access to the houses, and also the inclusion of footpath systems. However, there are usually pavements alongside the roads as well. The whole idea of separate front and back access for pedestrians and car drivers died a natural, but slow, death.

The concept of the Radburn peripheral road can still be seen in some larger-scale developments. However, it is common on smaller schemes to see the reverse, a branching tree type of layout, with a spine road giving access to the centre of the estate and a series of distributor roads branching off it. They, in turn, subdivide into smaller roads in the form of culs-de-sac which serve clumps of houses, each driveway giving access on to a cul-de-sac. In the immediate post-war period the turning arrangements at the end of culs-de-sac used to resemble lollipops – the road went round a little circular traffic island with a touch of greenery in the middle (these can still be seen in other countries). Nowadays culs-de-sac normally end in a hammerhead or T-shaped turning space which leaves room to reverse in. In some cases the planners have tried to soften this arrangement by creating a courtyard effect in which the change from road to private driveway is marked by a change in the type of paving stone. Whilst this might look impressive, and create an urban mews atmosphere on inner urban infill sites, many pedestrians find the arrangement ambiguous and therefore potentially dangerous.

Once one gets away from the fixed layout of houses fronting on to the garden, pavement and road one can develop a range of layouts setting the houses in different arrangements. For example, garage courts, play spaces and communal gardens were often incorporated into local authority schemes at the expense of traditional gardens, pavements and garages. Some architects believed that this freeing up of the estate layout created a greater sense of space, and also got away from what they saw as the restrictive nature of individual house plots. Such experiments were often combined with the open-plan formats for front gardens and separate 'no man's land' landscaped areas. However, most people prefer a private exterior zone for each house. Indeed, as has been said earlier, people want a sense of what Oscar Newman (1973) calls 'defensible space'. It has been found that vandalism and graffiti are reduced by such measures, since people apparently think twice about stepping on to a garden. In the Essex design guide it is suggested that everyone should also have a minimum 100 m^2 (about 30 ft^2) of back garden with walls around each plot, which gives residents a sense of private external space (but can be intimidating for pedestrians, especially women, walking along footpaths between the gardens).

Roads and parking

The principles of residential layout are all determined by the question of how you want to live. However, this branch of planning, which is meant to make people's homes and lives better, has, sadly, developed a false, mechanical, technological image, no doubt because of its association with site engineering and road planning. Of course, there do have to be practical standards to ensure, for example, that the fire engine can get to every house, or to enable the dustcart to get through (without the dustmen having to walk more than a certain distance as laid down by their union). By way of guidance it is normal for local authorities to specify varying widths of road according to capacity, desired speed and function. For example, local distributor and residential spine roads will be in the region of 24 ft wide (3 ft 3 in. = 1 m), with a maximum intended speed of 30 mph, whereas smaller access roads and culs-de-sac may be down to 18 ft, and individual driveways to houses are likely to be around 8 ft single, 15 ft shared. Footpaths and pavements are usually around 6 ft plus, this dimension being based originally on the idea that it enables two prams to pass. Highway engineers also set standards as to the radius of curves on all roads, and the dimensions of junctions, turning spaces and hammerheads, which again vary from area to area, but 20 ft to 30 ft radii on the inner turning bends of hammerheads are common.

Visibility splays work like this. Imagine a Pythagorean triangle of 30 ft by 40 ft by 50 ft laid on a junction between a side road and a main road so that the 30 ft side runs along the white line in the centre of the side road to where it meets the white line of the main road, creating a right angle with the 40 ft side, which runs from this point along the white line of the main road to the right (so drivers have an unobstructed view of the traffic coming along from the right; the opposite for Europe). If the end of the triangle in the main road is joined with where the other side starts in the side road one will get a hypotenuse (the side opposite the right angle on the white line where the centres of the road meet) of 50 ft which slices off part of the right corner plot. This slice is the visibility splay. In reality, dimensions vary considerably, with a longer lead side on major roads and shorter sides on minor estate roads (see Department of Transport, 1990).

Car parking is always a problem and the subject of potential negotiation. Normally, for residential development, at least one off-road parking space per new dwelling is required (on the road does *not* count), with at least one other per two dwellings, or more, depending on the size of the dwellings and households. In social housing, e.g. housing association housing for the single person, the elderly or the disabled, a minimum of one per dwelling is often permitted. A car parking space is usually 2·4 m by 4·8 m and 3·4 m by 4·8 m for disabled parking. The question of how much parking space is allowed on non-residential developments, such as offices, industry and retail, depends on what the aim is. For example, where there are no space restrictions one parking space per 200 ft^2 of office space may apply, e.g. on a purpose-built business park. In a central area location where the planners want to discourage more congestion, and land is limited, figures of one parking space per 3000 or even 5000 ft^2 of office space apply. This may appear as a disincentive to developers, but they themselves do not want to use up valuable site space on parking and are only too happy to leave the office workers to park on someone else's land or side roads elsewhere. In an ideal world if there are restrictions on parking there should also be good public transport but such is seldom the case. After all, the planners allowed, even encouraged, suburban development in the past, so why should they punish suburban commuters today? When calculating for complete urban car parks it is necessary to allow for aisles between the rows and for access roads, so the figure usually given is around 200 ft^2 (1 m is approximately 3 ft 3 in.). This means that, in schemes where one parking space per 200 ft^2 of office space is allowed, the total space devoted to parking will be equal to the office space itself, based on the space taken up by the office worker's desk and chair plus 'gross' space made up of his/her proportion of corridor, circulation, storage, amenity space of the building as a whole.

New directions

Newcomers to the subject are always keen to learn the standards and rules of estate layout, and some of these have been outlined above. However, this form of layout is just one aspect of the wider subject of urban design, which is concerned with the appearance and function of all types of areas both existing and newly developed. Whilst above some of the key considerations highlighted have been density, road layout, and layout, there are at least three other overarching issues which nowadays are increasingly being taken into account, namely environmental factors, social aspects, and aesthetic considerations, none of which can be reduced to technical standards but require professional judgement. Firstly, the influence of the green movement and the desire to create sustainable cities is inevitably reshaping traditional assumptions about layout principles (see Barton *et al.*, 1995 entitled, *Sustainable Settlements: A Guide for Planners, Designers and Developers*). Policies to control levels of motor car circulation and penetration within an area, including traffic calming, are nowadays an integral aspect of street design (Hass-Klau *et al.*, 1992).

Secondly, as to social aspects of design, many of the traditional assumptions embodied in foundational texts such as the Essex Design Guide have been challenged by those who are concerned about reducing crime, and increasing safety and convenience on housing layouts. Meandering paths across open ground away from buildings, high fences alongside paths, and close planting, might according to some designers create an element of 'surprise' and 'excitement' but many ordinary people are more concerned about lack of visibility and the dangers of being mugged. A whole new design industry has developed around the topic of 'crime and design' (for example see Circular 9/94 Designing out Crime). Likewise other users, such as women, children, the disabled, and other pedestrian groups have long campaigned for more practical, and accessible layouts and nowadays some of their ideas are gradually beginning to penetrate the psyche of the designers themselves (see WDS, 1995 publications for a range of alternative design solutions).

Thirdly, as to the aesthetic aspects of design, as a result of these various new influences urban design itself is beginning to change its image. Whereas in the past the 'great achitect' often seemed more concerned about creating an aesthetically impressive layout, as he saw it looking down from above at his drawing board, nowadays there is more thought given to the plight of the likely user actually battling through urban space at ground level in all weathers, and probably in the dark coming home in the evenings. Therefore the emphasis in urban design, relatively speaking, is moving more towards more consideration of functionality for the user, than mere form. This new socially and environmentally conscious mood is reflected in books such as Bentley *et al.*, 1985, revised 1996) appropriately entitled, *Responsive Environments: a Manual for Designers.* These alternative themes are also present in Volume IV of the present series which deals with urban design.

PART IV

The social aspects of planning

Chapter 11

Urban social perspectives on planning

Political and historical perspectives

Political context

This chapter looks at some of the main social theories which have affected town planning policy in order to provide a background understanding of the social aspects of town planning. In the next chapter some of the issues will be pursued further from an alternative perspective. Many of the social theories which have informed town planning reflect the political ideology and perspective of their creators: for example, some of the critics of planning are of the left, and many of the proponents of the use of planning to improve society and create a more stable sense of community come from the more liberal or reformist centre of politics; and some of the opponents of town planning are to be found on the right – but one hesitates to generalise. As stated in the preface, it is not the intention of an introductory book like this to pursue the political context of planning *per se* in any depth (as has been done from various perspectives in Simmie, 1974; Kirk, 1980; Healey *et al.*, 1988; Montgomery and Thornley, 1990).

However, three urban political components are reflected in the evolution of urban sociology, and should be borne in mind whilst reading this chapter in order to form links across to the wider political context of the social aspects of planning, namely the role of theory, processes and people in urban politics. Firstly, at the overall level, planning is inevitably political because it is concerned with land and property, and has therefore been the subject of scrutiny by those concerned with political *theory*, for example in respect of capitalism, class and other such components of society. This theoretical perspective is particularly prominent in Marxist urban analysis (and neo-Marxist theory) but may be seen in the other nineteenth-century foundational theories described in the first part of this chapter. Linked to it is concern with the role of planning as regulator of the market or successor to market forces, this being the subject of much debate and political activity, particularly over the last twenty years.

Secondly, at the implementation level, the planning *process* is a political activity because it is concerned with the allocation of scarce resources, the planner being seen to act as urban manager or social policy-maker (Pahl, 1977: Simmie, 1974). This is played out in the on-going politics of the town hall, and in the activities of urban community and pressure groups seeking to influence the nature of town planning policy and decision-making. Competition and conflict among such groups are significant related political themes. This is reflected widely in urban sociological studies which seek to make sense of how the system works, this having been a particularly popular theme in urban sociology in the 1960s and 1970s.

Thirdly, there is the political issue of the *people* involved in the planning process, firstly the professional planners themselves and secondly the planned – that is, the public on the receiving end. Urban politics is not just a matter of theories, processes and policies, it is shaped by the nature of the people involved. In particular, in recent years, women working in the community have drawn attention to the fact that 'the personal is political' but there is a long history of urban sociological study, especially in North America, concerned with the role, power and personal characteristics of elite professional and political groups. As Gibbs (1987) puts it in relation to the British situation, 'Who designs the designers?' As stated in Part I, planners seem to plan best for people like themselves, that is, male middle-class white car owners, thus drastically affecting the fairness of policy-making. But the planned, the consumers of urban goods and services (Saunders, 1979), may consist of a range of types of human beings, none of whom has much in common with the above stereotype. The phenomenon of a great diversity of groups contesting planning decisions in recent years cannot be explained away by a minimalist class-based view of urban theory and politics. Gender, disability, ethnic origin and a range of other individual characteristics come into play, such as regional location and environmental setting, and this complexity is increasingly reflected in urban sociological literature.

Pre- and post-industrial perspectives

The industrial revolution was a major turning point in the development of modern society and town planning. It called forth a new academic discipline, sociology, which sought to explain what was occurring. Comte (1798–1857), a French academic, is generally credited with inventing the word (Brown, 1979). Many of the early sociological theories were based on the differences between the pre-industrial city (usually seen as good) and the industrial city (usually seen as bad). Tönnies (1855–1936), a German sociologist (other European countries were experiencing a similar process of industrialisation) wrote about the differences between what he called *Gemeinschaft* and *Gesellschaft*. He defined *Gemeinschaft* as community, based on traditional rural village life where everyone knew everyone else, social relations were based on kith and kin ties and traditional values and duties. *Gesellschaft* (the German word for 'business') community is where everything is based on formal and impersonal relations, bureaucracy, law and order. Nobody knows anyone else, and people deal with complete strangers in their daily life and work.

Durkheim, a French sociologist (1858–1917), identified the new urbanised society as characterised by a sense of 'normlessness' and 'namelessness', *anomie* (literally, 'without a name'), because, in coming to the city from the villages, many had lost their individual identity and sense of belonging. Note that *anomie* is a societal state, people do not catch it like chickenpox! Durkheim observed that it led to increased levels of suicide and social unrest. Fascination with the study of the contrasts between the pre- and post-industrial ways of life continued well into the twentieth century. One of the more famous, often cited, writings is Wirth's article 'Urbanism as a way of life', published in 1938 (reprinted in Hatt and Reiss, 1963). The work of Sjoberg (1965) on the pre-industrial city is also relevant.

Many of the theories expressed the view that something had been lost as a result of industrialisation, especially the stability and security which had apparently existed in close-knit traditional villages. It was argued that traditional controls over deviance (crime and social unrest) were lost (such as the role of the village elders in seeing what was going on). One of the factors behind the popularity of the Garden City movement was the desire to recreate the village community of the past, in order to re-establish the social structures which were destroyed as a result of the industrial revolution. Many of the ideas of the early town planners reflect a somewhat negative anti-urban attitude; a yearning to get back to an (imagined) idyllic rural past, and may be seen as 'conservative' or even reactionary politically. Town planning could be used as one of the means of helping to re-establish a sense of order in new urban areas, through well-planned districts and zoning controls, which, it was believed, would reduce crime, disease and overcrowding.

Even today town planners are sometimes seen as the 'soft police' of society because they have tried to stabilise people's behaviour in new towns by social engineering, and in the inner city by means of environmental controls. Whether planners really intended this is another matter. Town planners have often been criticised by those who adopt a more radical, or even revolutionary, perspective who are of the opinion that it is not possible to contribute to the creation of a better society through redesigning towns and cities. Such critics argue that more drastic political and economic measures are needed to remove the inequalities which, it is alleged, create the conflict, crime and disease in the first place. The idea that you can achieve social change, 'salvation by bricks', through the replanning of the built environment is still with us and will be discussed below in relation to the planning of the New Towns, before we continue with the evolution of urban sociological theory. Town planning has a specific role in dealing with some societal problems through physical changes in the built environment, but that does not preclude the need for other social, economic and political measures as well.

Social aspects of new towns

Community and neighbourhood

The effect of these ideas on new town development in the twentieth century will now be discussed. Following this, the account of the historical development of urban social theory will be resumed. Many of the New Towns were planned on the basis of being divided into neighbourhoods, or neighbourhood units as they were called. This enabled the development to be phased logically and enabled the physical provision of shops and schools with ready-made catchment areas. Forty years ago fewer people had cars, so it all worked realistically. But the neighbourhoods had a second, more mystical objective of trying to create community spirit and to solve a range of social problems. Clarence Perry (1872–1944) devised the concept as a way of effectively planning new neighbourhoods in New York in the 1920s and 1930s. Perry's ideas were copied in England by Parker at the garden suburb of Wythenshawe in Manchester, and were incorporated in the Dudley Report (1944) on New Towns.

Perry proposed that if around 5000–6000 people were located in a neighbourhood at 37·5 persons per acre, that is, at approximately twelve houses per acre, allowing for three people on average per house, the result would be a neighbourhood unit of 160 acres, that is, an area half a mile by half a mile, or a quarter of a square mile. In this way everything could be based on walking distances of a quarter to half a mile, with a community centre in the middle of each neighbourhood and shops on the fringe, at the four corners, so they could be shared by up to four different neighbourhoods (Hall, 1989). A junior school was to be located in the centre, 5000 being considered adequate population to generate the number of children to make it viable. Perry's work was linked with the work of two architects, Stein and Wright, who further developed the neighbourhood idea in relation to restricting traffic circulation to a peripheral road around each neighbourhood unit in Radburn, New Jersey, in the 1930s (the neighbourhood unit being conterminous with the Radburn 'superblock', as the traffic unit was called).

The neighbourhood unit concept had many practical aspects to it, but it was more questionably associated with a mystical desire to recreate a sense of community by influencing people's behaviour and making them mix by virtue of the constraints of the layout, e.g. designing footpaths so that they ran past everyone else's front doors, and putting the community centre alongside the school. Many of these ideas were mirrored in the British New Towns. Various studies were carried out on both sides of the Atlantic, monitoring people's behaviour in new housing estates (Carey and Mapes, 1972; Bell and Newby, 1978). Not suprisingly it was found that people who lived nearer the centre of a cul-de-sac, or by a lift shaft in a block of flats, were likely to have a higher level of contact with their neighbours than those who were further away from their comings and goings.

Not only was there a lack of a natural community at the beginning but the planners were concerned about the imbalanced nature of the community population, which consisted predominantly of young families with children, all of a similar social class. The lack of age balance meant tremendous pressure on facilities as all the children grew up and went through the successive stages of school, work and eventually retirement together. Once the wave had passed, the facilities provided for such large numbers proved uneconomic for subsequent smaller cohorts. Later British New Towns attempted to encourage a wider age range and family mix among applicants. Socially it was seen as dangerous politically for so many working-class people to be all together, and there were attempts to attract more middle-class people, and to get employers to live in the New Towns, to provide more leaders for the community. At the neighbourhood level there were attempts to achieve a social mix of classes by mixing house types and tenures which did not work well.

Many other factors are involved in community formation. It may not be the shared locality (the fact that everyone lives in the same neighbourhood) but the extent to which people have other interests in common which determines the level of identity and sense of community. In the case of the New Towns, the fact that most of the population consisted of young families with school-age children who played together inevitably drew the families together. Sociologists have pointed out the importance of community of interest, i.e. non-place-related as against place-related concepts of community, with communities based, for example, on the work, hobbies and sporting interests of individuals rather than on where they live. Some people are loners and do not wish to be part of a community with others. Many residents felt that their community developed in spite of the planners. They found a sense of solidarity in adversity, in fighting the planners to get better facilities and amenities, or in seeking to rid themselves of some of the worst aspects of the plan and get what they really wanted instead.

Environmental determinism

The planners of the New Towns were frequently criticised for going much further than seeking to provide adequate practical facilities in the neighbourhood, indulging in social engineering by means of environmental determinism, that is, seeking to control people's behaviour (for their own good) through the nature of the layout (the built environment). Environmental determinism (also known as architectural or physical deter-minism) has been an enduring theme in justifying planning *if* the layout of plans can really help solve the problems of society and bring about 'salvation by bricks'. Critics of the theory argue that many of the problems of society derive from the nature of the economic system that underpins it: typically the development of modern industrial capitalism is cited as the root of all evil (Bailey, 1975; Simmie, 1974). There has been much criticism from the left, particularly as a result of the popularity of neo-Marxism in recent times to the effect, that planners are only the lackeys of the bourgeoisie who spend their time tinkering with the superstructure (which basically translates as 'rearranging the deckchairs on the *Titanic*') when, it is argued, more radical economic measures are required, such as the abolition of capitalism. Would these critics produce a better built environ-ment? Many of the problems which are related to physical land use, design practicalities, and the need for different types of facilities and developments, always exist in society and have to be dealt with, whether one is planning within a capitalist or a socialist society. For example, road widths are not going to change substantially just because one moves from, say, a Marxian to a market economy. One still needs sewers and drains. Likewise it does not follow that, if one went over to a more radical or neo-Marxian government which had all the answers for running the economy and abolishing inequality in society, the new masters would be sensitive to and conscious of all the little design issues which affect the quality of people's lives in urban areas, particularly if the people in charge had no training in or understanding of the built environment professions.

Maurice Broady, a sociologist disquieted by the apparently magical powers attributed to such theories, has said, 'architectural design, like music to a film, is complementary to human activity, it does not shape it' (1968). But this does not invalidate the importance of design. Often all that is needed is quite small improvements, rather than high-flown theories and complicated ideas. Most would agree that practical improvements such as more lighting, less planting and hence more visibility around buildings, plus reorientation of pedestrian routes, would make them safer and reduce crime. Others would go much further, such as Alice Coleman, who in her book *Utopia on Trial* (1985) makes much of the ways in which modifications in the design of the environment can alter the behaviour of the residents. Oscar Newman, (1973) stressed the importance of quite simple strategies like ensuring that there is a distinct demarcation between public and private space around buildings on large housing estates, so that people think twice before crossing such boundaries and indulging in graffiti or vandalism. Des Wilson, one of the founders of Shelter, the housing pressure group, wrote a book entitled *I know it was the place's fault* (1970) showing the effect a poor-quality environment and sub-standard housing could have on people's lives and misfortunes. There is undoubtedly some truth in the theory, but many other factors have to be taken into account.

Consensus or conflict?

The context

Returning to the account of the historical development of sociological theory, the two main schools of thought as to the nature of society will now be discussed, namely the consensus and the conflict viewpoints. It is important to appreciate these theories, as how one perceives the nature of society and the cause of urban social problems will determine one's actions in trying to improve the situation. If one sees social problems as the result of oppression, then it may seem meaningless to play around with town planning: a revolution might be more realistic. If, on the other hand, one sees social problems as a temporary and resoluble result of unexpected social change, then a gradual policy of reform in which town planning can play a part would be the chosen solution. Even if many of the town planners themselves have little interest in social policy or sociological theory, paradoxically their actions and plans have been blamed for the increase in urban social problems such as crime, racial tension and the decline of the inner city.

Functionalism

To return to Comte, he was basically what is known as a functionalist: he took the view that society was like a big machine which operated mechanically, and in which different processes and groups of people had different functions, ensuring its smooth running and the maintenance of the *status quo* of authority and social order. The industrial revolution was seen as a major upset in the natural order of things which had all sorts of economic and social effects, which temporarily put the system out of sync. But it was believed that this could be righted. Society would pull itself back together again, provided its various institutions and value systems were reconstituted to re-inspire people's trust in the system, so that business confidence, stability, law and order could be maintained. Consensus people tend to favour bringing the system back into line and re-establishing equilibrium, by means of gradual reforms, improvements and adjustments, in which town planning as a form of social policy may form a part, for example by recreating a sense of community (which was apparently lost in the industrial revolution) in the model Garden Cities and New Towns. Functionalists therefore see social problems as temporary occurrences, with the subtext that there exists a natural consensus of what society ought to be like which could be nursed back again.

Other functionalists who, broadly speaking, favoured a consensus view of society include such famous sociologists as Spencer (1820–1903) and in the twentieth century Talcott Parsons (1902–79) and Merton (1910 onwards). Durkheim was also part of this movement, as was Max Weber (1864–1920) (Weber, 1964) to some extent. The main rival to the consensus view of society was the view that society was in a constant state of conflict, and that it held together not because of agreement but because of one group actively oppressing the others. The classic example is expressed in Marxist theory, which centres on a perceived clash between the interests of capitalists (employers) and the proletariat (workers). As discussed in this chapter, there are a range of other non-Marxist, conflict viewpoints too. Marxist theory will be discussed later when the resurgence of neo-Marxist ideas in the 1970s is considered, because it has had an influence on urban sociological theory for many years and thus a major impact on some branches of town planning.

The functionalists showed an element of cynicism in their writings on the nature of society, fully realising that although an ordered, consensus-based society was meant to be natural, in fact there was a strong element of conflict within the elite groups at the top of society as to who ran it, and a fair amount of social engineering and pulling of strings behind the scenes to make the *status quo* appear normal. The new urban entrepreneurial (business) classes had replaced the old feudal landowners as lords and masters of the working people. These new leaders of society needed to grasp the reins of society and take control. Both Durkheim and Weber (separately) talked of the need to legitimate the new power structures which emerged, legitimation being defined as 'the process of transforming naked power into rightful authority'. Such notions should not necessarily be seen as oppressive, since it was considered that a return to stability would be good for society, as well as good for those in authority. Note, one also hears the word 'legitimation' used in relation to town planners who seek to legitimate their somewhat questionable policies on the basis that they are planning for the good of society or for the working class.

The functionalists accepted the need for a limited amount of conflict and unrest among the masses as being functionally necessary (a safety valve) to ensure the well-being of society. What Merton was later to term dysfunctions were simply seen as healthy signs that change was occurring which required adjustment and solution on the part of society. But, unlike the Marxists, the functionalists did not see society as divided into two camps, but saw healthy competition existing between a plurality (range) of power groups at different levels of society; that is, they took a pluralist viewpoint (cf. Bottomore, 1973). Parallels may be seen in the theories which were developing in the natural sciences in the nineteenth century, for example in Darwin's theory of evolution. In this, natural selection, as a result of continuous competition, was seen as 'normal' and 'functional' in the sense that it led to progress and further evolution. These ideas were to have a profound effect on the development of urban sociological understanding.

Social ecology

In North America the early twentieth-century development of sociology was influenced more by functionalist conservative views of society than by socialist conflict models, as was the case in Europe. Sociology reflected ideas from scientific theory which could be used to justify the *status quo*, in particular the ideas of Darwinism and evolution theory. The inequalities between man, and even the class system itself, and the competitive and aggressive nature of the American market economy (and related political system) could be justified by the application of scientific theories to human society. In fact Darwinism and the theories of evolution which developed in the nineteenth century were not value-free but reflected the changing political, philosophical and religious attitudes of the time: it is a chicken-and-egg question as to what caused what first. Social Darwinists were not against change or competition, which they saw as inevitable and as progress, reflecting the principles of freedom and the market. Social Darwinism legitimated the power of the ruling classes, justifying it as a result of the natural process of the survival of the fittest.

The Chicago school of sociology (Bulmer, 1984; Hatt and Reiss, 1963; Strauss, 1968) and its theories of urban social ecology were strongly influenced by Social Darwinist thought. Such theories were originally part of what is known as social ecology. Ecology is the study of plants and animals in relation to their environmental setting, and is concerned in particular with the process of competition for living space and territory. After the initial fight a state of equilibrium is apparently reached, with each plant or animal securing its own little patch (applied to the urban human situation, each different group of people getting their own locality or neighbourhood within the city). Social ecology has been widely adopted and modified by geographers and town planners, and much of the original background of the theories has been discarded over the years. Studies were first undertaken in Chicago in the 1920s because of public alarm at the high levels of gang warfare in the inner city (as in the movies and Al Capone). The aim of the original study was to consider the relationship between the crime wave and the high levels of immigrant groups (mainly white southern and central European) moving into the poorer areas looking for housing, creating intense competition for space. The research team included Robert Park and Ernest Burgess, both of whom were functional-ists. Deviance and crime were analysed as symptoms of the process of the city trying to regain equilibrium after the influx of large numbers of immigrants, not because of underlying class conflict. It was assumed that in time the groups would assimilate and move 'up and out' to the suburbs, fulfilling the great American dream of success.

The model is not static but dynamic because the concentric zones should be seen as like ripples on a pond, continuously moving outwards, as in Fig. 11.1(a) (Chapin, 1965: 12–25). The city was growing outwards and expanding as each of the zones within it were growing owing to immigrant pressure in the centre causing the inner area to expand and thus putting pressure on the next zone out. Burgess described the outward movement of the zones of residents into the previous territory of another zone as 'invasion and succession', and believed the process was one of the reasons for urban unrest. Chapin describes the processes of 'sub-dominance' and 'dominance', in which the incoming colonising group gradually takes over from the previous resident group. This process may be described by the residents in phrases such as 'the area is going downhill' or 'the area has got a lot better in recent years'.

The concentric zones model *is* only diagrammatic, as Chicago is situated on the shores of a large lake! It is not intended to be a land use plan of how cities should be, but rather a diagram to illustrate a theory of what cities have been observed to be like. The zone of transition around the Central Business District is of particular interest. This is the area where the older, run-down, cheaper housing is found, but it is also the area where the CBD is expanding, leading to rapid changes in land values and types of development. Many British cities possess an historical central area and inner ring of housing, some of which has declined and may fit the description of the zone of transition, but other areas may consist of higher-class housing and nowadays be designated Conservation Areas. The zone of transition has become virtually synonymous with the inner city and is often associated nowadays with high concentrations of ethnic minority populations. Many European cities are quite different from British or North American ones, and have much higher concentrations of people of all classes living in the centre (and less suburban development) but different districts still have very distinct class connotations. Meanwhile in North America's large cities, particularly in New York, one can still observe the on-going conflict for space between competing groups, nowadays made more visible by the use of graffiti to mark territories between street gangs, many of whom are black or Hispanic ethnic groups, rather than European, as in the days of Burgess in Chicago.

The other zones on the diagram are fairly self-explanatory and broadly applicable to the British situation. The zone of working men's homes might consist of small terraces around older factory areas, but in Britain because of state intervention in housing and town planning one might also find working-class council estates on the edge of the city where the land is cheaper,

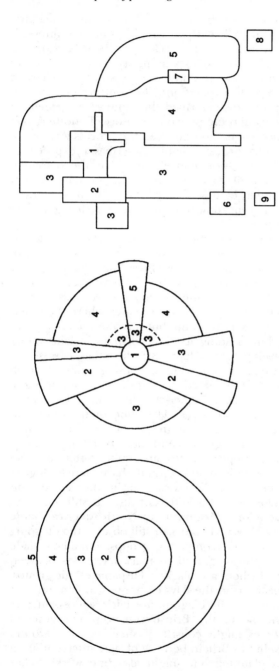

Figure 11.1   Three social ecology models: generalised explanations of the land use patterns of cities. (a) *Concentric zone concept*: 1 Central Business District, 2 zone of transition, 3 zone of working-men's homes, 4 zone of better residences, 5 commuters' zone. (b) *Sector concept*: 1 Central Business District, 2 wholesale light manufacturing, 3 low-class residential, 4 medium-class residential, 5 high-class residential. (c) *Multiple nuclei concept*: 6 heavy manufacturing, 7 outlying business district, 8 residential suburb, 9 industrial suburb. *From Chauncy D. Harris and Edward L. Ullman, 'The nature of cities',* Annals of the American Academy of Political and Social Science, *November 1945*

or where industry has been decentralised and re-zoned. The zone of better residences is where the average family is meant to live, in a deviance-free area. In reality the suburbs have proved to be the source of many problems, especially for people without cars, as they are separated from the rest of the city by land use zoning and poor transport. Further, the suburbs and zoning generate traffic, commuting and parking problems back in the centre of the city. The next circle, the commuter zone, is meant to be the best area in the model, and is entirely dependent on the motor car (note that it has no outer boundary). In Britain one often finds a planned Green Belt around the edge of the city, and so the suburbs leapfrog the Green Belt and form a secondary ring.

The ideas of Burgess and Park were modified by a series of subsequent models. The sector concept (Fig. 11.1(b)) developed by Homer Hoyt in the 1930s laid emphasis on the importance of transport routes in creating linear wedges of development, superimposed on the concentric structure. Also sectors of better development can develop on one side of the city because of the direction of the prevailing wind (from the east in this American diagram, from the west in Britain) as more affluent people prefer to live in less polluted areas. The working classes are seen as being more likely to live downwind from the industry and the smoke drifts over them. Many cities have a distinct East End and West End, but nowadays all areas are probably equally polluted by gases and sediments in the atmosphere. Other geographical factors such as the existence of an attractive hillside ideal for the development of better housing, or the presence of a river or valley, will also create natural sectors. Roads and railways can also act as barriers: in North America working-class people are often said to come from 'the wrong side of the tracks'. Lastly, the multiple nuclei concept (Fig. 11.1(c)) was developed by Harris and Ullman in the 1950s. This theory reflects many of the realities of contemporary metropolitan land use, allowing for decentralisation, zoning and state intervention. There have been a variety of further developments of these theories over the years, by sociologists such as Mann in Britain, and the alternatives are endless.

Urban problem areas in Britain

Empirical studies and social reform

Whilst in Europe there was an emphasis on grand theory in the development of urban sociology, there were two other strands which were particularly strong in British urban sociology in the nineteenth century. Firstly there were a range of empirical social studies of the poor based on statistical evidence and extensive fieldwork such as that of Lady Bell, a social reformer who made a study of factory workers' lives in Middlesbrough (1911). Rowntree (factory owner, town planner and builder of New Earswick) was a pioneer in social research and wrote *Poverty: a study of town life* based on York (1901). He was a key figure on government committees set up to deal with the social problems of the time. Charles Booth, philanthropic businessman and amateur social researcher, undertook extensive studies of inner London (1903). He is not to be confused with General William Booth, founder of the Salvation Army, who also wrote widely on urban problems (1890). Secondly, there was a flourishing social policy and reform movement, supported by figures such as Octavia Hill and the Webbs in respect of housing and town planning reform. Quite apart from the work of the famous social reformers there had for over 100 years been considerable political pressure from the people themselves for social change in the form of chartism, early trade unionism and, in Europe, actual revolutions. The working classes were not passive recipients of theory or reform but were themselves active in pressing for change.

Community studies

In the first half of the twentieth century British urban problems and urban sociological studies often appear overshadowed by the wealth of American studies both at local and city level. These run across the full spectrum of urban communities, from inner area studies, and studies of deviant groups such as the gangs described by Whyte in *Street Corner Society* (1943), to studies of middle-class suburbs such as Gans's study (1967) of Levittown, a speculative private housing development (a classic, and readable). Generally the problems of the inner city appeared worse and more violent in American cities, an image still projected via television. Likewise the suburbs always seem more claustrophobic, monotonous and more distant from the rest of the city in American studies than in Britain, where the scale is less spread out.

In Britain, until the late 1950s, the emphasis continued to be on demolishing problem areas rather than studying them, with few exceptions. However, there were on-going studies of poverty, often carried out in conjunction with housing, education and health authorities (not town planning, note). Post-war reconstruction planning in Britain had no real concept of the inner city as a major issue of the future, and the concerns of mainstream sociology itself were somewhat different. It was assumed that when the slums could eventually be cleared the social problems would go away, and this was expressed in the town planning of the time (see Chapter 6). The Greater London Development Plan of 1944 already identified and named certain areas as 'inner urban' and recommended demolition. The problems of the zone of transition were still seen as essentially American and connected with racial tension. The question of ethnic issues (or race relations, as they were called in the 1960s) did not surface in Britain until immigration began from the West Indies in the 1950s and from the Indian subcontinent in the 1960s. In the immediate post-war period planners were spellbound by the idea of creating new communities in New Towns, rather than seeking to preserve existing working-class communities. As mentioned, a series of studies were undertaken of how people were relating to their new housing estates, linked with empirical work on the question of environmental determinism and the creation of 'community spirit' (Carey and Mapes, 1972; Bell and Newby, 1978).

A few sociological studies of inner areas were emerging in the 1950s. Under the growing influence of the American social ecology theory with its emphasis on deviance it became fashionable to identify the 'criminal area', as in Morris's study of that name (1958), based on a study of an inner-city area in south London. However, most urban social studies of the time were related to studying the effects of slum clearance and the decentralisation of population to new housing estates and the New Towns. Vast amounts of demolition were undertaken in the name of slum clearance, although many saw it as a convenient way of justifying the removal of housing in the way of new roads or the expansion of central area schemes. In the process many valuable working-class communities were destroyed (Ravetz, 1980). Young and Willmott (1957) highlighted this in their study of Bethnal Green in the East End. They studied the residents before and after they had been moved out to a new council estate on the fringes of London. Before the clearance the sociologists observed a close-knit community based on strong networks of kith and kin which were demolished along with the buildings. When the people were rehoused no attempt was made to keep them together, and they were mixed up among complete strangers from other areas. As a result greater attention was paid to the nature of working-class communities. Frankenberg (1970) gives an interesting account of a range of studies from the period. He includes urban and rural studies as yet again people sought to analyse the ingredients of community that made village life so different from the modern urban situation. (See also Lambert and Weir, 1975; and Rees and Lambert, 1985, for further accounts of community studies.) Many sociologists would question the whole idea of defining problems in relation to areas rather than in relation to specific groups of people (as victims or aggressors), whilst others would argue that society itself, rather than space, i.e. the built environment, should be taken as the starting point of change.

Ethnic issues

By the 1960s the inner city had become more newsworthy and visible because many of the people suffering from poverty and unemployment were of ethnic minority origin, i.e. 'black', adding an urban dimension to the problem of racial discrimination. Although the term 'ethnic' and 'ethnic minority' is commonly applied by white sociologists to black groups, arguably everyone belongs to an ethnic group, and British Anglo-Saxons, from a global perspective, are also an ethnic minority. It is common to see the black ethnic minority groups themselves as 'the problem', but many of them would comment that they find it is the white majority which is the problem for them because of discrimination. As the saying goes, 'We are here because you were there,' that is, over the centuries Britain built up an overseas empire and many of the ethnic groups originate from former colonies. The film title *The empire strikes back* takes on a new meaning in respect of racial unrest (Birmingham University, 1987).

Over the centuries Britain and other European countries had promoted the idea of the need for their 'excess population' to settle in their overseas territories. The writings of the economist Malthus (1798) had legitimated the need for such measures. It was believed that the population of Britain was growing at such a rate that there would always be poor people, as the land could not support them all. This idea resulted in a punitive approach to poor law relief, deterrent workhouse regimes (because it was thought that charity only 'encouraged' them) and emphasis on migration to the colonies (even compulsory transportation). Between 1871 and 1931 outward migration from Britain was, on average, at the rate of 0·5 million per year. After the First World War the level dropped, but gradually inward migration became more pronounced. Between 1931 and 1951 there was a net gain of 60 000 people per year. Many migrants were European coming for a variety of economic and political reasons. Needless to say, most of them were white and therefore less visible, although there was still a certain amount of racial tension in some areas of London.

Between 1951 and 1961 immigration continued to grow, with around 30 000–50 000 people coming in per year; outward movement was also high, with a net outflow of 5000 people, but three-fifths of incoming people were 'ethnic dark-skinned' (as the *Telegraph* newspaper put it in the 1960s). It should be pointed out that many migrants arrived from the West Indies because they were invited to Britain owing to labour shortages in the post-war period. For example, London Transport ran a bus driver training programme in Trinidad to prepare people for the move, and guaranteed them jobs. Likewise various hospitals and other public institutions sought to attract skilled staff from the West Indies, and from India and Pakistan. Others simply exercised their right of British citizenship and decided to make the move, mainly because of economic necessity, often sending money back home. Later there were migrations of relatively affluent Asian business people displaced from Uganda and other parts of the Commonwealth. 'Black people' are not a unitary group, they are made up of many different nationalities, language groups and religious bodies. They are also varied in terms of social class, ranging from urban professional people to peasants from underdeveloped rural areas. They cannot be categorised as working-class as is sometimes the case in inner-city planning studies (S. Smith, 1989).

Town planners began to get more involved in ethnic issues, because minority groups tended to be strongly concentrated in certain urban areas. Seventy per cent of ethnic minority groups are concentrated in 10 per cent of urban areas, with inner-city locations in London and metropolitan areas of the Midlands being the main centres, for example over 25 per cent of Leicester's population is of Asian origin. One needs to be cautious in talking about ethnic 'minorities' because in some London boroughs people of ethnic origin constitute over 50 per cent of the population. Also, over half the people in Britain of Afro-Caribbean origin were born in Britain, some describing themselves as 'Black-British'. It is estimated that around 5 per cent of the population of the British Isles is of black ethnic minority origin. Immigration has now declined as a result of a growing restrictive trend in immigration legislation, expressed in the Commonwealth Immigrants Act, 1962, the Race Relations Act, 1965, the Immigration Act, 1971, the Nationality Acts of the 1980s and further controls in the 1990s. The trend seems to be away from encouraging people to come and live in Britain as citizens with a right to bring their dependants, and towards a European model in which ethnic minority groups are seen as migrant workers or 'guest workers'. Indeed, harmonisation with the rest of the EC in 1992 is seen by many black groups as creating a Fortress Europe (European Castle (EC)) mentality towards outsiders, including British Commonwealth citizens.

There are very few black town planners, male or female, and it is argued by the RTPI itself that this may affect the nature of town planning policy (RTPI, 1983 written in conjunction with the Commission for Racial Equality. It is a fundamental 'social aspects' question whether white male middle-class town planners possess sufficent professional neutrality and understanding to plan equally well for the needs of the rest of the population who are not like themselves; this being a particularly sensitive issue in inner-city ethnic areas. In fact there has been much criticism suggesting that the town planners cannot. It came out particularly strongly in the inquiry following the 'race riots' in Brixton, in south London, in 1982, when Lord Scarman (1982) attributed much of the blame to the planners! The area had become run-down and subject to planning blight as a result of indecision and insensitivity on the part of the planners as to its future development. Planners are an easy target, and many would argue that other public bodies, such as the education authority, the police, and the social services also contributed to the situation.

One of the problems is that many black people feel restricted as regards where they can move to and the jobs available to them. The Commission for Racial Equality (1989) identified the problem of 'red-lining' whereby estate agents discourage black applicants ('Sorry, it's gone') from buying houses in white areas because they perceive it as leading to a drop in property values. Likewise, local authority housing officers may encourage black tenants towards 'residual sink estates' (as in the case of Broadwater Farm in London) and seek to keep them out of 'nice' areas. In the early 1980s a series of riots flared up, including St Paul's in Bristol; Brick Lane, Notting Hill, Brixton and Southall in London; Toxteth in Liverpool; and Handsworth in Birmingham. Since then a race relations 'industry' has grown up, and planners and other public bodies have tried to be more aware of the issues. In spite of this, there are still very few black town planners, surveyors or architects (excluding overseas professionals), and many ethnic areas are as run-down and deprived as ever.

Subsequent development of urban theory

Urban conflict theory

Ethnic issues cannot be separated from the wider economic and social context of inner-city society, and are an important dimension of urban politics. Both black and white groups suffer high levels of unemployment and environmental deprivation, with run-down services and public amenities. Further, they are the ones who have to suffer all the commuter traffic coming through from the suburbs, and who are likely to find their streets filled with parked cars belonging to office workers from the central area. Inevitably conflict emerges between deprived groups, the 'poor whites' blaming the newcomers for taking 'their' houses, and the newcomer groups feeling unwanted and discriminated against by the white population. Other deprived groups such as elderly people and single-parent families on low incomes are concentrated in the inner districts but are composed of both black and white (race criss-crosses gender, age, class and income – it is never straightforward). Increasingly, urban sociology became concerned with answering the question of who gets what, where and why, that is, with the allocation of scarce resources in the urban context and the role of the controlling power elites in society in this process (Pinch, 1985).

The theme of conflict between groups for scarce resources was first incorporated in urban social analysis in Britain in the 1960s, by Rex and Moore (1967), who made a study of Sparkbrook in Birmingham, an area with a high concentration of ethnic minority groups. In the context of Weberian theory Rex and Moore identified a process of conflict over the allocation of the scarce resource of housing, which they saw as leading to the development of distinct housing classes, and social unrest. Weber made much of the concept of 'life chances', the idea (simplifying it, for clarity's sake) that different types of people had access to different levels of resources, opportunities and 'chances' according to the level of power and status they had in society, and obviously ethnic groups came low in the pecking order (Dahrendorf, 1980).

Rex and Moore (1967) identified seven housing classes which may be seen as 'class positions' or indications of the level of life chances and therefore the relative power which each group enjoyed. It is significant that they concentrated on housing rather than on race itself as the subject of conflict. Different groups found their access barred to different types of housing, because, for example, building societies would not give them a mortgage or local authorities decided they had not enough points to merit a council house. Ethnic groups could be disqualified on several grounds, including low income, inadequate residence qualifications and lack of a conventional breadwinner or a respectable family structure, none of which was technically racial discrimination, of course.

Increasingly attention shifted in urban sociology from looking at the groups on the receiving end to investigating the political role of the urban professionals who decided the fate of the inner-city residents. There was already a substantial body of theory in America on the role of power elites in shaping society, such as the work of C. Wright Mills (Mills, 1959). In Britain, Ray Pahl (1977) developed the idea of 'urban managerialism', by which, he suggested, urban managers such as public council housing managers and local authority planners acted as political 'gatekeepers' and influenced the distribution and allocation of scarce resources, thus affecting people's life chances (Dahrendorf, 1980). Rather than seeing the planners and other professionals as benevolent beings working for the good of the people, urban sociological research increasingly cast them as biased conspirators working in collaboration with other business, governmental and professional elites actively keeping the people down and under control. This may not have been intentional, as studies have shown that some members of the land use professions have a very limited view of social issues, and generally do not think in terms of the social implications of their actions (Joseph, 1988: chapter on chartered surveyors; Howe, 1980 on town planners; Greed, 1991).

Town planning policy was not seen as impartial or value-free but highly biased (re-read Keeble's (1969) definition of planning in Chapter 1 in the light of this criticism). Although many urban sociologists at this time broadly subscribed to a consensus 'liberal' pluralistic view of society, inevitably there was movement towards a more conflict-oriented perspective. Already in the late 1960s students, community activists and aggrieved groups were turning to radical politics and socialist theory for explanations of what was wrong with cities, and with town planning itself. There is a lot more to all the theories and changes which occurred in the late 1960s and 1970s. Therefore it is suggested that Simmie (1974) and Bailey (1975) are perused to get a better idea of the debates and atmosphere of the time, and Cockburn (1977) and Aldous (1972) to appreciate the nature of urban politics at the grass roots.

Neo-Marxist urban theory

The subsequent development of urban sociology in the 1970s and 1980s was strongly influenced by Marxist theory (see McLellan, 1973, for an explanation of Marxist ideas). Marxism is more than an academic theory intended to increase understanding, it has also been seen as a programme of political action to intervene in history and bring about the ideal new society of the future, and in this respect it is unlike most other sociological theories. Academic

Marxist theory (of which there are many versions) should not be confused with what is sometimes called 'pub Marxism'; even Marx said of himself, 'I am not a Marxist.' Marxists argue that many of the problems and inequalities of society derive from the nature of the economic system underpinning it. In particular the development of modern industrial capitalism as had emerged in the nineteenth century is often cited as the root of all evil. Basically Marx saw only two classes – the capitalists (bourgeoisie), i.e. the owners of production and the factories, and the workers (proletariat), the producers – which he saw as having a fundamental conflict of interest. Until it was resolved by revolution there would always be problems in society. Simply seeking to change the nature of the built environment was seen as superficial. As mentioned, the planners are thus seen by Marx's followers as 'lackeys of the bourgeoisie' tinkering with the superstructure. Marx described the economic base of society as the substructure, and above it is the superstructure, which consists of the social and cultural institutions, the built environment and everything else which makes up our civilisation.

Marxian theory is strongly determinist in that it says that the superstructure takes the form it does in order to facilitate the continuance and maintenance of the 'social relations' and 'means of production' which enable the capitalist class to get the most work out of their workers at the lowest wages possible. Therefore, for example, it was argued there was little point in carrying out improvements to the built environment if people could not afford to benefit from them. If their wages were too low (because of the structure of society) they would simply move elsewhere rather than pay higher rents for improved property. As Engels, Marx's colleague, said, 'You don't solve the housing problem, you only move it,' alluding to the fact that there would always be slums until people had the means to afford better housing. The solution was therefore to deal with the cause rather than the effect: to change society rather than the built environment. Marx believed that society could be transformed only by adopting a socialist mode of production in which the private ownership of capital and indeed of all private property was abolished. If the people owned the system and were running it themselves (on the principle 'from each according to his ability and to each according to his need') no one would be poor again: indeed, there would ultimately be no need for money or profit in a truly socialist state. *But,* as we have now seen in Eastern Europe, it is easier said than done, because of human nature. Followers of Marx believed that the revolution was too important to be left to the workers. There had to be an elite cadre, the party leaders, who would take the initiative in creating the new society.

(Parallels with some British town planners?) Like any elite group, in time they lost touch with the people and pursued their own interests at their expense, without even the measure of account-ability that democracy gives.

Postmodernist developments

Urban sociology went through a neo-Marxist revival in Britain, being strongly influenced by French urban sociological thought in the 1970s (see Pickvance, 1977; Castells, 1977; Harvey, 1975; Dunleavy, 1980). There were attempts to apply neo-Marxian explanations to real urban situations, as in the work of Saunders (1979, 1985) on the London borough of Croydon, and Bassett and Short on Bristol (1980). Many of the ideas seemed to work better in the abstract. Indeed as Harvey himself pointed out, in dismissing the built environment as merely part of the superstruc-ture, and attributing extreme importance to underlying economic forces, it was as if people were living in a spaceless vacuum. The urban sociologists had dug themselves into an *impasse.* Also there was much criticism of the idea that economics determined everything – for example, it did not explain adequately why black people and women were more disadvan-taged than white male workers if all were equal units of labour. If women workers complained about their needs being mar-ginalised they were likely to be told to wait until 'after the revolution' or to go and make the tea. Neo-Marxism was good at explaining (from its perspective) what was wrong but had little to offer as a basis for solving practical planning problems.

The emphasis in Marxism on the importance of industrialisa-tion, and production, as the path to societal transformation seemed more and more out of date in the light of modern social and technological change. It did not fit well with the post-industrial emphasis on green environmental issues and Third World and other global issues (as described at the end of Chapter 9). Also the overemphasis on production in Marxist theory as against distribution and consumption, gave only a partial view of urban economic systems. Indeed, Saunders (1985) and others subsequently adopted a more rounded sociological viewpoint in which urban issues were looked at from the perspective of the urban resident who 'consumes' goods and services such as housing, infrastructural services, schools and shops provision within the community, rather than concentrating on the world of the worker and capitalist involved in production in the workplace and away from the home.

Many community groups felt that Marxist and other 'grand

theory' socialist ideas could not help them, seeing the whole movement, like traditional town planning itself, as another elitist top-down attempt to help the working classes. As will be seen in the next chapter, many disadvantaged urban groups started thinking and working for themselves in order to press for the sort of cities and society they wanted, rather than accepting the views of academics and professionals about how they should live. Indeed, the importance of their activities as pressure groups within urban politics eventually registered with urban sociologists, who sought to acknowledge it in their academic theories. Neo-Marxism eventually went out of fashion, and the whole paradigm (conceptual framework, way of looking at the issues) shifted again, into what is known as the post-Marxian, postmodernist phase (this phrase is also used in respect of architecture, reflecting a similar return to more traditional values). Weber's ideas are now coming back into favour, and people describe themselves as neo-Weberian. The current resurgence of interest in the study of the professions and other decision-making groups reflects a neo-Weberian interest in the nature of power in society. This also reflects a longer sociological tradition of studying the culture of different occupational and professional groups, which had become somewhat obscured in neo-Marxian times because of this sociological tradition's emphasis on 'softer' participatory empirical observation and 'people issues' rather than on 'hard', aggressive grand theory (Greed, 1991: Chapter 1).

There has been a retreat from the emphasis on heavy deterministic theories, and a greater acceptance of the variety and complexity of factors, over and above economics and class, which can influence people's life experiences (cf. Hall and Jacques, 1989; Hamnett *et al.*, 1989). Indeed, nowadays one constantly finds words like 'culture', 'discourse' and 'diversity' being used by sociologists, as the pendulum has swung from emphasising large-scale, and often generalised, divisions within society, towards studying the minutiae of individual difference and variation among groups within society. Likewise there has been greater acceptance of the diversity of individuals' experience of the urban situation, and the effects of their own personal characteristics (such as race, gender and home locality) on their status and power in society. New Right values have come in under the influence of the enterprise culture created by the Conservative government of the 1980s, and there is a greater emphasis on self-help and private-sector solutions to urban problems.

Coexisting uneasily with this ethos, there has been an ongoing commitment in many local authority areas to more equal opportunities for ethnic minority groups, women and the disabled, rather than a demand for radical social change based on class-bound analysis as was the case with the erstwhile New Left of the 1970s. In the next chapter the effect of the demands on town planning, of one such 'minority' group – women – is discussed. One might ask 'why women?' In response, it should firstly be noted that women comprise 52 per cent of the population, and since 'planning is for people', over half the attention of the planners should, reasonably, be focused on the needs of women. In the past 'planning for people' has 'meant' by default 'planning for men', for gender considerations were not consciously taken into account in the days when the vast majority of town planners were men. But, the reader might ask, is it really necessary to plan 'specially' or 'differently' for women than for men? It is argued that women's urban needs, and the way they use the city, are different from men's. This is because they are more likely to be the ones responsible for childcare, shopping, and a range of other caring roles, all of which generate different usage of urban space. Also, as stated in earlier chapters, less women than men have access to the use of a car, and they comprise the majority of public transport users in many areas. Also, as will be illustrated further in the next chapter, women's daily activities and travel patterns are likely to be different and more complex than men's, as many will be combining work with childcare, and other commitments. Therefore the classic 'male' commuter, monodimensional 'journey to work' upon which so much transportation planning policy has been based in the past, does not fit well with women's lives and needs. Women also comprise the majority (variously) of the elderly, disabled, low paid, carers, urban poor, and total ethnic minority population (check current edition of *Social Trends*).

The second reason for choosing to discuss 'women and planning' in the final chapter, is that, in recent years the topic has become more 'visible' as more women themselves have become town planners and pressed for change (see membership figures in Chapter 3) resulting in policy documents produced by the profession (such as RTPI, 1989), and the inclusion of policy statements on women in development plans. Linked to this there has been a growth in the influence of the wider 'feminist movement' in society as a whole, and of 'urban feminism' within the built environment professions. It is not appropriate in this short book to define 'feminism' in depth, and readers are referred to other work by the author (Greed, 1994) in which both the sociological and urban planning aspects are discussed in depth (see Appendix II of Greed, 1994, for a list of key texts). However, a brief summary is given below, centred around two of the most used, and misunderstood sociological words, found in feminist jargon, namely 'gender' and 'patriarchy'. Regarding gender, while it is not denied that women and men are different sexually, in particular because most women can give birth and men cannot, it is held by those who subscribe to feminism, that such biological differences should not necessarily determine cultural differences, as to how people live their lives, to the disadvantage of women. Therefore the word 'gender' is used to describe this package of cultural differences and roles that are given, respectively, to women and men in society, whereas 'sex' denotes the biological differences between them. (Therefore all those official forms which ask for an applicant's 'gender' rather than 'sex' are strictly speaking incorrect.) Feminists argue that sexual differences should not determine gender differences, such as, for example, who should be responsible for childcare, who should go out to work, and which sex should receive higher wages. Nor should they be used to justify social inequality, and differences in power within society, between men and women.

Gender roles are seen by feminists as being cultural inventions which are imposed on women because of 'patriarchy'. This is seen as a social system created by powerful men to serve male interests alone, at the expense of women. This does not preclude the fact that some individual men might be more egalitarian towards women than others, or that men can be oppressive to other men (as detailed in traditional class theory as described in this chapter). Nor can it be denied that some women are anti-women too, because patriarchal cultural attitudes – because they are so powerful – may be held by women as well as men. But structurally, as individuals, men are more likely to benefit from the present organisation of society and cities than women. Also, the above, simplified explanation does not exclude the reality that there are several different versions of feminism, with different groups stressing different aspects, and disagreeing on various points, for women (like men) are not a unitary group (discussed more fully in Greed, 1994). Also, there are many 'ordinary' women who do not particularly subscribe to any form of feminism, and may accept their role in society. But they are still likely to complain about practical problems, such as the design of the built environment, as they try to carry out traditional homemaking tasks, and they try to get around the 'city of man', particularly if they have babies and small children. Therefore there has been a great deal of enthusiasm and support across society (from women at least) for attempts by women town planners to implement change, as described in the next chapter. This topic is by no means 'solved' or 'done', but is likely to remain actively on the planning agenda into the twenty-first century.

Chapter 12

An alternative viewpoint and unresolved issues

In order to highlight the fact that there is no one right answer in town planning, and that it all depends on 'who you are and what you want to achieve', this chapter first reconsiders the social aspects presented in the last chapter, and secondly re-evaluates the nature of cities, as already outlined in the book, from the 'women and planning' viewpoint which has arisen as a major challenge to conventional town planning in recent years. In the final section other unresolved, outstanding issues in planning, which are likely to prove significant for the future, are raised. Similar coverage of planning policy in relation to 'race' and 'disability' is given in Volume II.

Women and planning

Reappraisal of the social aspects literature

Women are scarcely visible in much of the nineteenth-century literature. If working-class women are mentioned they are likely to be seen as those who caused the problem of overpopulation because of their low morals and poor hygiene (Richardson, 1876). If upper- or middle-class women are mentioned they are presented either as angels on a pedestal or, paradoxically, as neurotic and contributing to the breakdown of society (Durkheim, 1970). Women and their needs are presented as a supporting cast to the main actors, not as people with problems and needs of their own in the new industrial society. It should be remembered that women were not entitled to own property for much of the nineteenth century, and so they had limited access to the world of property and planning, although many were active in the early housing reform movements (Atkins and Hoggett, 1984).

In defining his two models of society, the old and the new, as either *Gemeinschaft* or *Gesellschaft* Tönnies left women in the awkward position of not quite fitting into either category (Bernard, 1981: 520). Women's lives and work do not divide into public and private realms in quite the way men's do, particularly if they are full-time housewives. Marx appears to have ignored women altogether, or perhaps he included them as 'workers' (Hartman, 1981). Marx's world view was founded on an arguably sexist emphasis on male work and production, with little regard to women's role in production, reproduction and consumption, as home-makers, mothers, shoppers and carers (Kirk, 1980; Markusen, 1981), all of which are forms of work necessary to the creation and sustaining of life itself. Such attitudes had planning implications, for in the more socialist areas of planning in the past women's needs were often not seen as related to production and therefore not as a worthy subject for urban policy-making.

The first wave of feminism at the end of the last century had a strong emphasis on the built environment (Gilman, 1915; Boyd, 1982; Greed, 1991) which was reflected in model communities and in co-operative housing ventures pioneered by women (Hayden, 1981; Pearson, 1988). 'Material feminism' existed in a form quite different from that of today, often tied in with Utopianism, evangelical reformism and the public health and housing movements. Ironically, notable individuals from this first wave such as Octavia Hill (Hill, 1956; Darley, 1990) are often seen disparagingly nowadays as (in Hill's case) 'only a housing manager'. Her ideas were influential over a wide range of land management issues, including rural planning and regional economic policy (Cherry, 1981: 53), and she played a major part in the setting up of the National Trust (Gaze, 1988).

Some of the early urban social studies were by women (Bell, 1911), but later as urban sociology became formalised women were more likely to be mere assistants (as in Moore's study of Sparkbrook, 1977) with some notable exceptions (Stacey, 1960; Aldridge, 1979). Women's influence on the subject might be seen as stronger in North America. It is notable that some of the Chicago sociologists did allow of the possibility of women being workers as well as mothers, as is reflected in the questionnaires used by Zorbaugh, one of the main researchers (Bulmer, 1984: 103). In Britain women appear in studies of working-class communities as a variety of oversimplified stereotypes, based on observing them as mono-dimensional residents tied to the area rather than as people with jobs, interests and aspirations beyond its boundaries. Young and Willmott gave some emphasis to women in their study, but their fondness for seeing them in the role of 'Mum', as virtually tea machines, and almost as wallpaper to the main action of life, is open to question. Their later work on the symmetrical family (1978) is seen as nothing more than wishful thinking by urban feminists (Little *et al.*, 1988: 86).

The studies of deviants in the 'criminal areas' of cities, in the genre of the Chicago school in Britain (e.g. Morris, 1958), were extremely moralistic towards young women, and tended to blame juvenile delinquency on the mothers' influence and perceived lack of responsibility. In contrast North American studies of the suburbs presented women as bastions of respectability, but as apparently idle, reinforcing the popular male image of the 'stupid housewife' (Gans, 1967; cf. Betty Friedan's early feminist book, 1963, one of the early foundational texts of the second wave of feminism, in which she talks about women in the American suburbs who were profoundly dissatisfied with their lives and environment). Of course poorer women living in the inner city on social security find it difficult to understand why middle-class women living in large houses appear to have so many problems. Women are not a unitary group and, as with men, there are many class and cultural differences among them.

Identifying it as a place of danger and conflict (Lawless, 1989) created a threatening 'macho' image of the inner city, although over 52 per cent of inner urban dwellers are women. Studies of race tended to concentrate on black 'men', whilst studies of crime and deviance often seemed to have more interest in, even admiration for, the aggressors (usually young males) than in the victims (usually women, children and the elderly). The emphasis on impersonal macro sociological forces in neo-Marxian sociology, combined with occasional references to an abstract 'working class', often gave the impression that there was no place in the new urban theories for real people as individuals and families. In his writings the urban sociologist Manuel Castells gave the impression that he saw the city as nothing more than 'a unit of labour power' (1977); not as encompassing the homes and lives of the inhabitants. In these debates the place of women was somewhat ambiguous, as they represented neither land nor society. Sometimes, one feels, they are 'land' as the suburban housewife seems to be plumbed-in along with the washing machine in much neo-Marxian theory on housing classes (as in Bassett and Short, 1980).

It was considered bourgeois and trivial to raise community issues in this setting, let alone to mention women, the prevailing emphasis being on political issues and urban structures rather than on individual people. There was considerable animosity from the male left towards feminism in the 1960s, and women were likely to be told that they were selfish and should be concerned with more serious issues, such as the trade union movement. Indeed, pioneers who went into town planning in the 1960s and 1970s reported high levels of hostility, sexual harassment and open aggression. They were certainly not made welcome or seen as having any insight into women's experience of the built environment. Ethnic minority planners (some of them women) encountered similar problems. However, greater sympathy was gradually extended to the needs of so-called minorities and Equal Opportunities policies were beginning to take effect – even in town planning departments, although such attitudinal problems are by no means solved yet. Later, neo-Marxism laid greater emphasis on consumption (albeit defined in male terms) (Saunders, 1985: 85). This opened the way for women to redirect attention within urban politics to the significance of the domestic realm and the residential area, and to redefine production and consumption and their relationship from a feminist perspective (Little *et al.*, 1988: Chapter 2).

One could argue that men were only catching up with women urban sociologists such as Cockburn (1977), who had already produced a key book on the importance of community politics. However, some (men) would suggest that the second wave of urban feminism had grown as an offshoot of the radical politics of the 1960s and early 1970s, urban feminist theory being seen as a sub-set of post-Marxian theory. There may be an element of truth in this. But much more of the impetus for change came from ordinary women who had been involved in various grass-roots community groups fighting the planners; some being concerned with design issues related to their traditional role as carers of children (Leach, 1979). Also, as more women students entered higher education in the 1960s and onwards they could not help but question much of what they were being taught in planning schools. In addition, there was a strong influence from both Europe and America. North American women architects and sociologists had not entirely lost the heritage of first wave of urban feminism (Jacobs, 1964). Elaine Morgan's book (1974) may be seen as one of the first attempts in Britain to look at urban issues from the 'new' feminist perspective. A series of valuable books from North America dealing with a wide range of urban feminist issues past and present were appearing (Torre, 1977; Wekerle *et al.*, 1980; Hayden, 1981, 1984; Keller, 1981; Stimpson *et al*, 1981).

Urban feminist studies were developing internationally (Hadjimichalis, 1983), the ideas and current literature of British feminist geography being encapsulated in the work of the Women and Geography study group (McDowell, 1983; WGSG, 1984). A Canadian periodical entitled *Women and Environments* (published by the Centre for Urban and Community Studies, Toronto) was established in the 1970s and is still going strong. Feminist academics were producing their own community studies of the inner city to rival some of the earlier male classics, for example Campbell's study of working-class girls (1985) made the link strongly between class, location and gender. Meanwhile women planners and architects were developing their own policies, and seeking actively to change the urban situation, rather than just studying it or developing theories about it. It is one thing to come up with policies; it is quite another to implement them through the planning system.

It would seem that ethnicity (and disability, to some extent) was initially stronger than gender as a factor which legitimated the need for the development of special urban policies for groups who are 'different'. The issue of Equal Opportunities was gaining prominence among local authorities, affecting their role as employers and policy-makers, especially in London. In spite of this apparent progress, black women urban feminists have pointed out that they are often squeezed out of the debate, commenting that many white people still assume that (as the saying goes) 'all black people are men, and all women are white' (SBP, 1987). Access for disabled people is now a material consideration in determining a planning application, and it is illegal to discriminate against people in the provision of public services on the basis of race (Section 20 of the Race Relations Act, 1976). Also there are various provisions which provide additional incentives or funding to recruit and train more black people, such as 'Section 11' programmes. In contrast it took longer for gender to be taken seriously, partly because women were 'already there' as 'part of the scenery' in the typical planning office, but in clerical rather than professional roles.

By the early 1980s, the 'women and planning' movement was emerging more visibly (Foulsham, 1990). This trend was greeted with complete misunderstanding by many men planners and surveyors, who made comments like 'Women? That's not a land use issue,' and therefore took the view that women's issues were *ultra vires*, outside the scope of planning law. Meanwhile the GLC women's committee was producing a series of 'women and planning' reports, including the most comprehensive, *Changing places* (GLC, 1986). Women's committees were beginning to have a major influence in several cities in getting things done (B. Taylor, 1988; J. Taylor, 1990). 'Women and the built environment' became a fashionable topic and several main journals devoted a special issue to the topic (*IJURR*, 1978; *Built Environment*, 1984; *Ekistics*, 1985; TCPA, 1987). By the late 1980s a series of conferences had been held, and working parties established, by the various built environment professional bodies, looking at women's needs as fellow professionals, as clients and as members of urban society. Many women set up in practice on their own or in groups, for example Matrix (1984), an all-women collective of architects.

Implementation of the social aspects of planning

Whether one is concerned with gender, race, homelessness, or any other social issue, one cannot use planning legislation directly to implement social policy. For example, one cannot control the tenure or characteristics of the occupants of new housing (except in some special cases, as in rural areas where there is a need for cheaper housing for local residents: circular 7/91). Any conditions attached to planning permission must be for a 'genuine planning reason' (Morgan and Nott, 1988: 139). Legally, town planning is strictly to do with physical, not social issues. However, there have been instances of planning authorities putting conditions on planning permission to achieve provision for women. Such instances, although relatively minor, are precedents which further confirm the argument that women's issues are a material consideration in granting the planning permission, and are valid within the guidance of circular 1985/1, 'The use of conditions in planning permissions'.

Many would see the distinction between what counts as social and what counts as physical under planning law as gender-biased. The need for sporting facilities used predominantly (by men) for leisure is often accepted without question as within the ambit of physical land use planning, whereas the provision of creches used by working women is frequently seen as a social matter, although the issue may have major implications for central area office development. Planners happily accept the National Playing Fields Association standard of providing six acres of open space per thousand population in urban areas as one of the goals of their development plans, but few would accept the idea of providing one crèche space per 500 ft^2 of office space as part of normal planning. Also, many women want decent public conveniences, nappy-changing areas and sitting areas in shopping centres, and would argue that this is a material planning matter, as it affects their access to and use of retail development. Women's needs do not fit into the existing classifications of land use and development as embodied in planning law and development plans; although creches, for example, now fall into Use D2 (significantly, within the class which covers 'non-residential institutions' and includes day nurseries and day centres but also museums and libraries). Some would see creches as a potential element in the mixed B1 (business) use class of the 1987 Use Classes Order (LPAS, 1986a, b). Permission is not normally needed for the use by a householder of a room in a domestic house for child minding unless the use becomes 'dominant' or 'intrusive' (DOE advice,

1992). The requirements of the Children Act, 1989, have to be met as to child care ratios and standards, over and above planning law.

However, the local authority or other relevant statutory authority is required by law to take gender issues into account in the provision of public facilities under the Sex Discrimination Act, 1975. It is illegal to refuse or deliberately omit to provide goods and services because of the recipients' sex, and this may be construed as applying to town planning matters. There is no circular or White Paper which specifically gives guidance on gender issues in town planning, although circular 22/84 (updated by PPG 12) states that the unitary development plan system will 'provide authorities with positive opportunities to reassess the needs of their areas, resolve conflicting demands, and consider new ideas and bring forward appropriate solutions'. It also mentions minority groups, albeit not women. Many argue that women *are* a material consideration in planning, because women and men use space in different ways (J. Taylor, 1990: 98). The Royal Town Planning Institute's Code of Professional Conduct (1986) makes it illegal to discriminate on the basis of race, sex, creed or religion, and this alone should govern individual planners' conduct, and it should be their duty to enlighten the local authority on these matters. This is another evolving, constantly changing area of planning law and policy. In 1995 the RTPI produced a PAN (Practice Advice Note) on 'Planning for Women', (RTPI, 1995) which was circulated to all members, and which gives advice on policies and procedures.

As stated in Part I, planners have sought to get developers to provide or contribute to these needs by making it a requirement of the planning permission that they enter into a planning agreement. Planning gain agreements must be used only for the purpose of 'restricting or regulating the development or use of land' and must be 'reasonable' (circulars 22/83, 16/91). An additional problem is that, even if the developers are willing to build social facilities, someone has to pay for their maintenance and management. Local authorities themselves cannot afford to at a time of government cut-backs. A good example of how to solve this problem was a Section 52 agreement (under the previous Town and Country Planning Act, 1971; now Section 106) on the Ropemaker Street site in the London borough of Islington in 1985, where a creche for thirty children under the age of five was provided to go with a new office block on the site, plus funding for ten years. Such agreements must be directly linked with the planning permission or they will fall foul of the Local Government and Housing Act, 1989, which requires 50 per cent of capital receipts (such as inducements from developers not specifically related to the development site) to be set aside to repay current debts, a complex rate-capping issue which can limit the provision of social facilities (Ainsbett, 1990). It is important to be aware of these snags, as planning does not operate in a vacuum.

Provided clear policy statements as to what is expected on a site are written into the statutory plan, developers can reasonably be expected to provide related social facilities in order to obtain planning permission without the need for complex planning agreements. Indeed, the Department of the Environment appears to prefer this approach to leaving it to the *ad hoc* imposition of complicated conditions of permission at the planning permission stage, or to complex planning agreements. Many of the new London borough Unitary Development Plans contain 'women's policies' either as a separate chapter in their written statement (taking as the model Chapter 6, 'Planning for equality: women in London', of the GLDP draft of 1984; GLC, 1984) or threaded through the UDP document in relation to the various policy issues. As accepted and approved policy these 'women and planning' statements have the force of law when determining the planning application, but they have to be sound enough to stand up in a planning appeal; that they are 'good' is not enough.

Subsequently by 1995, many of the UDPs had gone through the approval stage, and it was found, in several instances, that planning inspectors required that some of the 'women and planning' policies be removed, a fate which several other more socially orientated policies suffered, such as those related to the needs of ethnic minority groups, disability, and social deprivation. It was alarming that there appeared to be some inconsistency between the decisions of different planning inspectors, indicating lack of gender-awareness, and training on these matters (WDS, 1994). Generally, the reason for disapproval was that the policies in question were seen as *ultra vires* in that they were seen as seeking to impose requirements which were seen as unreasonable and not land-use matters. Requirements for the provision of creches, toilets, babychanging facilities, and other such social facilities were likely to be seen as 'imposing quotas' and setting detailed space standard requirements which were not seen as being appropriate at the development plan level. Such decisions are seen as somewhat biased, from a gender-perspective, as many development plans include car parking standards, and these have never been seen as inappropriate. Also it may be argued that the provision of such facilities *is* a 'land use' matter, as it affects the way people 'use land', affecting accessibility in the first place, and affecting the nature of development itself (Cullingworth and Nadin, 1994: 251).

This whole issue is pursued further and more fully in Volume II, as this is a 'continuing story' that must eventually be resolved by Department of the Environment intervention. Significantly, at present, there is no PPG on any of the policy areas which have come under fire, namely planning for women, disability, and ethnic minority needs. Although there has been a spread of good policy statements in development plan documents (as surveyed and detailed by Little, 1994) there is not, as yet, a commensurate level of approval and implementation.

However, the situation is very variable between different areas, and, at the 'coal face' of development control, in some local authorities 'women and planning' conditions on a planning permission go through without question, whereas in others they are overturned. This again reflects an ad hoc approach brought about by lack of stong central government guidance. Also much depends upon the political 'will' of the members (local councillors) and 'spirit' of the local planning authority in question. However, this is also an area 'to which' for the future in terms of likely EC intervention at a pan-European directive level, owing to pressure from women across Europe (OECD, 1994). A European Charter for Women in the City has already been produced by DG V, Equal Opportunities Unit (EC, 1994) (qv page 25 Chapter 2) although its status is only advisory at present. The Commission's approach to town planning, has not only been more environmental in outlook, but also more orientated towards 'social planning' and related to concepts of 'equal treatment' and 'social justice'. There are many other issues, which women's demands for better facilities and design provision have brought to the surface, as alluded to earlier in the book. In particular the barriers to effective policy implementation that the division of powers between the planners and other controllers of the built environment presents is still unresolved, particularly when trying to implement provision inside buildings or shopping malls, which fall outside the jurisdiction of traditional planning law, but which affect people's access to and use of urban space. (These include those responsible for building control, environmental health, British standards, public transport provision, and security, all of whom appear to work on quite different agendas from the planners). This issue is also pursued further in Volumes II and III as a continuing theme in the series 'Exploring Town Planning'.

This section has been included to demonstrate the complexities of implementing social planning policy. The situation is constantly evolving as the lawyers define the parameters of the current legislation through the planning appeal system and the resulting case law. It is important to read the professional journals to keep up with the current state of play. In the final analysis what happens in a particular local authority depends on whether the local planners are co-operative or negative towards such issues. There is a need to train professional planning staff to be aware of the issues. The existence of senior women officers, or at least sympathetic male officers, is essential, as is support from the councillors themselves (RTPI, 1988).

Women and land use patterns

The context

The purpose of this section is to reconsider the development of the main land uses in cities from a 'women and planning' perspective and to suggest future trends and alternatives. Whilst at present much of 'women's planning' seems to be preoccupied with traditional women's issues such as child care facilities, or with the problems of safety and local design principles, to plan effectively for women would in the long run require the restructuring of our cities at the macro city-wide development plan level in order to realign the relationships between the different land uses and introduce major changes in transportation systems.

Planning theorists such as Geddes, Abercrombie and Le Corbusier saw the main components of the city as consisting of home areas, work areas, and leisure areas, and this tradition still influences attitudes today. In contrast, many women would argue such a viewpoint makes the fundamental mistake of equating work with what is done outside the home, ignoring all the home-making and child care work which goes on in the home and the local neighbourhood. From this attitude flows a whole series of flawed approaches to town planning. It seemed logical to planners to encourage the separation of work and home by land use zoning, which was meant to lead to greater efficiency and less pollution from a public health viewpoint. But it disregarded the fact that increasingly women were adopting two roles: that of home maker but also that of worker; nowadays over 60 per cent of married women work outside the home. The separation of work and home, and the associated separation of business-related land uses and facilities from domestic work-related land uses such as food shops, schools and community facilities, increased the travel burden of women, the very people who are much less likely to have access to a car during the daytime. To compound the problem, much transportation planning was based on the assumption that the journey to work by car in the rush hour was the main category of journey in urban areas. In reality the majority of journeys in some areas are undertaken by women, at times which are spread throughout the day, and chiefly by public transport or (of necessity) on foot, as is shown in a survey undertaken by the GLC in London, *On the move* (1985). The three categories of home (residential), work (employment) and leisure will now be discussed from a women and planning perspective.

Residential areas

The inter-war period was characterised by the growth of single-land-use suburban housing estates at relatively low density, consisting of speculative private estates for the new middle classes and also decentralised estates of council housing. There was a preference for greenfield sites, where land was cheaper. There was still quite an extensive system of public transport, and urban life was not yet geared to the assumption that everyone had a car. Transport was mainly by bus, tram, bicycle, or suburban railway, and people without cars were better served than they are nowadays. Many food supplies were still delivered to the home by the butcher, baker and greengrocer, whereas nowadays only deliveries of milk and dairy goods remain. There were also more shopping parades and community buildings on the new housing estates; often built by the developer to attract buyers.

In the immediate post-war reconstruction period local authorities continued building traditional low-rise houses in the form of dispersed council estates often miles from anywhere. Many housewives preferred the pre-fabs built on a temporary basis near existing centres on bombed sites. They had all mod. cons such as fitted cupboards and modern kitchen equipment. By the 1950s private house building was back in business and many people aspired to own their own house. The building societies played a major role in offering finance and also in perpetuating the image of a home of one's own, with publicity aimed at the breadwinner encouraging the idea that an Englishman's home is his castle. Few wives, however, really owned their own house jointly, as was to become painfully evident when the more liberal matrimonial laws of the 1960s led to a rise in the divorce rate and more homeless wives and single-parent families. The housing stock and planning policy were not suited to providing for such groups, nor for the post-war growth of young single people seeking a house, (Hoggett and Pearl, 1983).

Whilst people in both the public and the private sector

undoubtedly had better houses than in the past – indeed, some middle-class women lived in very affluent owner-occupied houses – the quality and accessibility of transport to suburban areas, and within cities, declined for those without cars in the 1960s because of the planners' overemphasis on the motor car. There were cuts in urban and rural branch railway lines at a time when outer suburban residential estates were growing. The growth of large supermarket chains was putting small shops out of business and making it more difficult for people without cars to shop locally (Bowlby, 1989). There were other insidious trends towards greater 'efficiency' (for whom?) in the siting and concentration of new health facilities, schools and social services. The era of the out-of-town comprehensive school campus and hospital complex miles from anywhere had arrived. Car drivers may prefer towns to be spread out, with lots of roads, car parks and out-of-town centres, but pedestrians and those dependent on public transport might prefer them as they were, close-knit, with everything within walking distance. Again, it comes back to the question 'How do you want to live?' (DOE, 1972a)

As public transport became worse and essential social facilities became more decentralised, more people acquired cars, until it was no longer considered economic to provide services or shops at the local community level. There was much criticism from consumer and women's groups (even before the rise of feminism) in the 1960s about the fact that planning permission would be given for new developments with little consideration of how people would get to and from them. Many propose that nowadays because many land uses are less noxious and more compatible than they used to be, the arguments behind zoning land uses are out of date. Office development in particular could easily be decentralised back into the residential environment. The decentralisation of shopping and other community facilities to out-of-town locations reflects outdated land use ideas about 'thinning out' cities and reducing congestion. It is not surprising that many women planners now press for strong policy statements on the provision of local shops at the local residential area level, greater controls on out-of-town shopping centres, and revitalisation of the food shopping component of Central Business Area retail units for women office workers who can shop only in the lunch hour.

Changes in architectural design and housing provision affected women badly as they spent more of their time living with the results, trying to carry on with household chores and child care. The 1960s were marked by the relatively short but disastrous phase of high-rise building, which was worse than traditional housing although some estates were more central. Women, especially those with children, do not like high-rise blocks or the small size of rooms in such schemes. If their flat is much above the ground floor all sorts of problems as to the supervision of children, disposal of rubbish and drying of washing arise. However, as Marion Roberts (1991) explains in her book on London County Council blocks, one should not merely see women's needs as being linked with child care and home making, which are likely to take up only a limited number of years until the children have left home. Many women combine work and home duties and find that blocks of flats are located far from centres of employment. An address on an estate with a bad name can reduce the chances of employment, even for those who are not the perpetrators of the activities that gave it a reputation in the first place (and of course this applies to men too). It is often suggested that families with children should be taken out of high-rise flats, which it is said, are more suitable for single people. But women living on their own may feel vulnerable in blocks of flats where there is no escape from an assailant except on to a corridor or a dangerous lift shaft.

There have in recent years been some fairly drastic suggestions and moves to 'solve' the high-rise problem, including the demolition of some estates, and 'beheading' blocks to reduce them to a more human scale. A whole industry of environmental sociology, community architecture and high-powered designers has grown up to deal with 'problem areas'. Many women architects and planners, in contrast, would suggest that simpler solutions, such as increasing the level of lighting, improving visibility, etc., would help a great deal. Most important of all, actually listening to the people who live in the flats and encounter all the 'little' problems daily, and acting on their advice, would solve some of the problems without the need for major upheavals. As with horizontal housing estates, women are still concerned about the mono-use of the blocks, as well as their condition.

To his credit, Le Corbusier originally designed into his *Unité d'Habitation* block an integral play area, community and nursery rooms. It is not uncommon in other countries to find communal lounges, hobby rooms and laundrettes integrated within the scheme. In North America quite up-market residential high-rise blocks often incorporate restaurants, sports facilities and child care facilities, particularly in private-sector condominiums. There really is no point in piling people up together if there are no practical community facilities and nowhere for them to meet. There is much to be said for employing more caretakers and security staff, and for a *concierge* system such as exists in France, with someone who can take in parcels, keep an eye on the place and 'screen' visitors. Some women would like to see more communal facilities in low-rise housing estates, too. For example, the designation of, say, one house in every twenty as a community area, with a built-in creche and community centre, would be very useful. In her book *Redesigning the American dream* (1984) Dolores Hayden shows ways of converting existing estates in this way. Again the emphasis on detail, the importance of multiple use of individual buildings, and the question of internal house design, are seen as directly related to effective town planning.

The development of the New Towns has been much commented upon from a 'women and planning' perspective (Attfield, 1989; Morris, 1986). There are many problems associated with the concept of the neighbourhood. First of all, it is based on the assumption that it is chiefly a women's zone, separated from the 'real' world of work into a world of community and children, in which men presumably, have little involvement in the daytime. In fact many of the women in New Towns work – indeed, cheap female labour was one of the factors which attracted light engineering and assembly industries. Whilst the planners might put shops and schools in close proximity within the neighbourhood, they were likely to put the factories outside it, creating transport problems, and much rushing to and fro between the different land uses (as Attfield describes). The 'safety' of the neighbourhood concept and the separation of pedestrian footpaths from main roads has also been much criticised. For example, in Milton Keynes it was found that women were unwilling to use the footpaths and cycle paths in the evening (Deem, 1986). Many of the footpaths were designed in such a meandering manner that people took their own short cuts or risked straying on to busy main roads. Many women prefer straight footpaths, with good visibility on all sides, preferably in full view of houses and other buildings. This sort of problem is not a characteristic of the New Towns only but a feature of many design guides, such as the famous Essex one. In their desire to create interesting townscape architects and planners unitention-ally created a threatening environment for women, with blind corners, narrow alleyways, footpaths away from the houses, pedestrian underpasses, ill lit back routes, and textured paved surfaces which ruin women's shoes and make the manoeuvring of pushchairs and wheelchairs hard going.

From the late 1970s there has been a swing to conservation and historic development, with the related phenonemon of gentrification. One might imagine there is little mileage in discussing the gender aspects of all this. Indeed, in this field, class may be a more important factor, as working-class areas have been colonised and house prices have gone beyond the reach of the former occupants. However, many women see the emphasis on urban renewal as gender-biased. The fondness for marinas and concern for the needs of the boat-owning fraternity in revitalising dockland areas have not passed unnoticed, especially when the price has been sterilising water frontage which might otherwise have been used for public benefit. This is not to deny that women participate in water-based activities, and revitalisation schemes do attract tourists, around half of whom are women. Docks naturally lend themselves to water-based leisure development. But many women would welcome the re-use of redundant buildings in central areas as creches or as useful food shops rather than as yet more trendy shops and pubs.

Employment areas

It is in discussing the issues of employment, in respect of both industry and office development, that one senses most strongly the illogicality for women of the separation of work and home, as reinforced through zoning and a whole range of other public health, building, office and factory legislation. Large numbers of women work in the retail trades, although they are often marginalised in the debate, or their work is relegated to the realms of leisure for 'pin money' (although it may involve standing eight hours a day and working very hard). Vast numbers of women work in factories, but they have frequently been excluded from the official figures and from the image of the working class in sociological literature. The post-war trend in town planning, towards both re-zoning and decentralisation of industry on to greenfield sites, created severe problems for working women. The trend continues today as industry seeks to locate near motorway intersections on the edges of urban areas, and affects both up-market high-tech science parks and more mundane light engineering and warehousing facilities. As stated, women office workers now constitute the largest single employment group in Britain (Crompton and Mann, 1986). The demand for office development is related to the changes in the economy as Britain moved from being the industrial centre of the world to the financial centre. At the beginning of the century most office workers, including clerks and, perhaps suprisingly, typists, were men. Increasingly, however, office jobs became 'feminised' and the men were more likely to be found at a managerial or professional level. In the post-war period office development really took off, although there was already a highly developed office sector in other countries (as epitomised by the skyscrapers of New York).

Demand for new office accommodation increased following the lifting of the building licence controls in the 1950s, this growth peaking in the property boom of the 1960s, as we have already seen in an earlier chapter. Restrictions were increasingly imposed on office development through the regional planning system of outline development plans. Regional planning concentrated on the needs of the traditional male working-class Labour voter employed in highly unionised industries. Indeed, for many years women's employment was not even counted, in respect of either the depressed regions or the growing south-east (WGSG, 1984). Many men did not see office work, or indeed shop work, as real work, and were against office development itself. But women planners were in favour of policies which encouraged office development, as it was the main source of women's employment. One of the reasons why male planners saw them as bad was the traffic which they generated. But most of it came from male car drivers, whereas women office workers tended to travel by public transport, or were more likely to live in the surrounding inner residential areas. (For example, black women are likely to find jobs in city centre shops and offices whereas their male counterparts may experience much higher levels of unemployment.)

Another controversial aspect of offices is their architecture. Women, and indeed most men who actually work in them, have never been too keen on high-rise office blocks. High-tech designs such as the Lloyd's building designed by Richard Rogers, have given rise to great dissatisfaction among the people who work in them. The new postmodernist, neo-classical and neo-vernacular buildings (so beloved of Prince Charles) are often portrayed as having a more human scale and therefore being more attractive to women. Many women would find this argument academic, because, as with all buildings, when working or living in them, it is what they look like and how they function internally that are of greater importance. Whatever the building looks like outside, many women are concerned about the changes which are occurring in the nature of office work, and about the lack of concern for their needs in office buildings. Many commentators see office work being 'proletarianised' because of the coming of high-speed word processors, making women office workers more like factory operatives than traditional secretaries and typists, who had some control and discretion over the pace and sequence of their work. There has been an increase in work-related illness and disability associated with the incessant speed of the new office machinery. Men as well as women have suffered the effects of what has come to be known as 'sick building syndrome'. Women in particular are more at risk in terms of miscarriages and ophthalmic or physiological disorders brought on by radiation from VDUs when typing on PCs, office chemicals and the poor design of equipment and facilities.

The separation of work and home creates major problems for women with children, indeed the whole ethos of the business world is unwelcoming to them. When women go to work, particularly in offices, it is as if they have to pretend they have no children; it is considered unprofessional, even unglamorous to admit to domestic duties and pressures. Yet, many women go through immense problems because of lack of child care, or simply in juggling office hours with school hours and food shopping trips. For some reason shops in Britain close early in the evening. If the intention is to protect shop workers, their hours of employment rather than the hours of opening should be controlled. Although on average 60 per cent of all workers in offices, and 80 per cent of all workers in the central area, including shop workers, are women, there is very little provision of child care either in the office buildings themselves or out in the Central Business District. Few women are in managerial or decision-making positions with the power to change these factors and reshape the built environment (Avis and Gibson, 1987; Gale, 1989; Law Society, 1988).

Many women planners would add that the biggest need is for more child care rather than more car parks, which, as we have seen, are used by less than 30 per cent of those coming into central areas. If vast sums can be spent on roads to bring the cars in, and on car parks to leave them in (at an average of 200 ft^2 per car gross, when the office workers themselves only take up 200 ft^2 gross on average), why cannot space be provided on a similar basis and level of public investment for good-quality childcare? This would be a start, and a whole series of other policies would flow from it, further integrating work and home, and other land uses and facilities would gradually shift and realign in relation to this.

But the Central Business District may be doomed as offices decentralise and city centres become more congested. If the traditional argument applies that there has to be face-to-face contact in business, it holds true only for more senior people. In future the trend may be to retain central area headquarters but to decentralise office accommodation elsewhere, and this would be an ideal moment to suggest that it should be moved into the suburbs rather than into the greenfield out-of-town sites which are difficult to reach for those without transport and far from shops, schools and other facilities (Herrington, 1984).

Retail development areas are both work areas to large numbers of women and also essential areas for shopping. Men planners bring to their professional work all sorts of stereotypes and false assumptions at the personal level. Many regard shopping as 'fun' and 'leisure' and have little idea of the difficulties and time pressures which women do it under. The great Lewis Mumford, in his epic work (1965) on the development of the city in history (a book that is still referred to on many planning courses), made much of the importance of man the noble hunter and food gatherer at the dawn of history. In another context the same author remarked (1930) of women doing the same job of food hunting and gathering in modern towns, 'the daily marketing [shopping] is all part of the fun'. It is now becoming popular to put leisure facilities beside out-of-town shopping centres such as Wonderworld at Merry Hill in Dudley. Most women are more concerned about getting the shopping home before it spoils and then arriving at work on time. As mentioned earlier, shopping policy has been bedevilled by the emphasis on retail gravity models which assume that most people travel by car, that the whole family travels and that the journey is a straightforward one from home to shops rather than from work to shops. Some developers are at last becoming more aware of practical shopping needs (Fitch, 1985) because it makes financial sense.

Leisure and play

There has been relatively little specific consideration of women's leisure needs in contrast to the immense amount of land, money and effort which has been devoted to playing fields and sports centres used primarily by men. Women's needs tend to get subsumed under the need of their children for play areas. Provision specifically designed by men for 'women and children' have also come in for much criticism from women planners. The fixation with providing generalised grassed open space and 'playing' fields, apparently for the needs of all age groups and types of people, in both old as well as new neighbourhoods has been questioned for many years (Jacobs, 1964). The problems of 'open space as unpaid childminder' reflect deeper problems in society itself, in that Britain has one of the lowest levels of child care provision in Europe.

Town and country planning has always been imbued with reverence for the importance of lots of grass and trees (one even hears of local authorities painting the walls of flats in problem estates green, presumably because of its associations with the countryside). It is often assumed that streets are wrong and open space is right for children's play. In fact unless open space areas are adequately supervised they can rapidly become vandalised, and the potential location, or 'turf', of gangs of youths (and dogs) terrorising the smaller children. However, the provision of children's play areas, or even play streets on housing estates, can also give rise to problems. It assumes that the mothers and other residents have little to do but keep an eye on the children. Indeed, some planning guides suggest that kitchen windows should overlook the street or play area for this purpose. It takes no account of the noise and disruption that children make, which may be disturbing to people on night shift or seeking to work at home. It is still assumed that child care is a woman's job although men who are parents and fathers too do not appear to see it as their problem.

To solve some of these problems many women planners suggest that what is needed is clearer definitions of different types of open space, with different uses, and more supervision. Traditional parks with keepers and a range of activities are more useful than bleak windswept unsupervised areas. Many would also like to see better back-up facilities such as public conveniences, distinct supervised safe play areas (Leach, 1979; WDS, 1990), with safe surfaces instead of hard asphalt or muddy grass (around the play equipment). To digress, the issue of public conveniences is another national problem. As explained in *At women's convenience* (WDS, 1990), lavatory facilities for women and children are underprovided, in fact men have three times more provision, according to an official survey of London (WDS, 1990). Many men planners do not see it as a problem, as they can always use a pub or club and are unlikely to have child care responsibilities. Also, of course, greater provision of purpose-built creches and child care facilities (including indoor and outdoor areas) is needed nationally, integral to residential and employment zones.

What are the open space needs of women themselves, assuming only some of them want six acres of playing field per thousand population? Most women, most of the time, are not accompanied by children, and indeed those with dependent children are a relatively small proportion of the female population. Women on their own tend to be wary of public open space but still welcome the existence of parks and green areas. However, in any landscaping or park scheme attention should be paid to security and surveillance. For example, the use of open railings rather than hedges around inner-city park areas helps women to see what they are walking (or jogging) into. Public conveniences and seating areas should be positioned prominently, not hidden behind bushes. Sports facilities should provide creches, and playing fields should be equipped with changing rooms for women as well as men; the sports pavilion is usually seen as male territory. Many women feel intimidated by the 'body beautiful' image of leisure centres, or may have religious or ethnic objections to mixed facilities. It is not enough to say the facilities are there for everyone who wants to use them; careful programming and organisation are needed to cater for women as well as men.

Younger women, and for that matter ethnic minorities, are less likely to use open space in the countryside for leisure as compared with men. There exists a rather macho youth culture in the world of rural planning (and rural estate management) in which the emphasis on rock climbing, adventure sports and fell walking rather marginalises women, and is often accompanied by contempt and disparagement of people in cars and the provision of tourist facilities for the urban masses. In fact many women who do visit the countryside do so in the family car, bringing child care responsibilities with them in the back seat! Many of the people in cars and coaches are older (as is the population as a whole), and may want to see the countryside but have no inclination to twenty-mile walks. The needs of all groups ought to be respected. Several UDP policy documents now have an emphasis on provision for women, ethnic groups and minorities in their leisure and recreation section.

Conclusion

Unresolved issues

'Women and planning' is one of a range of outstanding issues still not solved in modern town planning. Another of the unresolved problems is that of transportation policy (which overlaps with women and planning and with green issues). The way transport has been dealt with reflects the fact that planners have tended to base policies on readily quantifiable factors and standards (such as traffic flows or road widths) rather than looking at the alternatives and the causal context. This approach has tended to underplay the need for radical urban change and sought to tackle short-term, manageable problems, thus reinforcing the *status quo*: it has dealt with effects rather than causes. In transportation planning there is a need to go beyond purely negative policy (such as road pricing and parking control) and introduce more fundamental changes, such as better public transport and rearranging the land uses which generate traffic congestion in the first place.

Planners have often ignored the qualitative, social and cultural changes in society (which cannot be mechanically quantified) that generate demand for new land use patterns; for example the demand from women for less segregational zoning in order to reunite work and home. Ironically, if more attention were paid to this, it would reduce and change the nature of traffic flows in cities, as everything really does seem to be linked to everything else in urban planning (as was suggested by the systems approach to planning in the 1960s: McLoughlin, 1969). In fairness, the scope for using planning policy for social ends is somewhat limited by the legal parameters of town and country planning in Britain, which requires planners to deal, strictly speaking, only with physical land use matters. This does create a somewhat artificial division. As has been seen, planners have sought to extend their powers into social policy at the city-wide level by utilising the development plan system (as in the way UDP policy statements are framed) and, in site-specific cases, by the use of planning gain agreements. Further, there is a related tension and unresolved dualism within the subject area of town planning: between the strategic policy level and the detailed development control level – between planning for the future of whole cities and dealing with Mr and Mrs Bloggs's house extension. In theory the latter is meant to be the detailed implemention of the former, but in practice development control can take on a counter-productive life of its own as a bureaucratic function of local government. It has done much to alienate the general public from town planning and, arguably, has not generally resulted in a better designed or more convenient built environment.

In respect of broader environmental issues, the planners' preoccupation with the needs of industry and employment, whilst reasonable, has diverted attention from the ecological implications of such development. Likewise in rural planning the perceived need to protect the countryside has been seen as over-restrictive and counterproductive by some, based on a romanticised and outdated view of agriculture and a negative view of urbanisation. (Indeed, some think we might all be better off living in a New Age self-sufficient quasi-rural environment, each dwelling with its own computerised work station *and* smallholding.) The agenda of planning is changing within the wider context of the EC environmental planning directives and the effects of the green movement, in which a concern for global ecology overarches the traditional fields of town and country planning, making the division seem increasingly irrelevant. Of course those living in the inner city may see the emphasis on both urban and rural conservation as a middle-class luxury. Indeed, it might be argued that social differences, poverty and homelessness are on the increase, and that planning has done little to mitigate the situation, despite its professed concern for the working class.

Still believing in planning?

As has been seen in this book, there has been much cricitism of town planning, in relation to both theory and practice. Indeed, planners sometimes solve one problem and create ten worse ones in the process! If we had left the land uses unzoned, kept the trams and railway lines, kept the working-class slums and communities intact, not redeveloped central areas, and not interfered with the regional distribution of industry – who can say, would we be any worse off? Of course, it is easy to be wise after the event; at the time, no doubt, many of the policies we see as wrong made perfect sense (Buchanan, 1972).

Whilst the planners have undoubtedly made mistakes, planners continue to justify their existence by stressing that towns and cities are in a state of potential chaos, likely to grind to a halt altogether were it not for their efforts, and it is true to a degree. Although the general public notice and remember when things go wrong – and, admittedly, planners do sometimes make mistakes on an enormous scale (Hall, 1977) – there is also much that the public take for granted in British cities which is good and exists because of the work of the planners in holding unwanted development at bay and keeping cities running relatively smoothly. But there are terrible dilemmas in planning in that some people do get hurt by the bureaucratic machinery. Middle-class groups may be only too quick to cry wolf – or, rather, NIMBY, 'Not in my back yard', or even NOPE, 'Not on planet earth' – if a development proposed for the general good affects their property; less articulate people have little defence against the planning system. Ideally citizens should always receive adequate compensation and be fully consulted as to the alternative solutions; something which has not always happened in the past. Also it should be constantly borne in mind that the way for the planners to fulfil their role as managers and resolvers of competing demands on the urban environment may be to plan for the needs not of some sort of average amalgam man but of different groups of people in the same urban area. This requires greater sensitivity and sophistication than is often manifested in the present British planning system.

In conclusion, it would require a considerable change of attitude in society, and in the property world itself, to alter current policies. Town planners do not operate in a vacuum and can achieve very little unless policies are supported by their political masters at central and local government level. Nevertheless many people within planning, especially women planners and others who have come fresh to the situation, unfettered by traditional assumptions, believe that as a governmental agency town and country planning can still be used to achieve a better urban society. For example, far from being negative and restrictive, many of the new Unitary Development Plan policy statements are extremely positive in outlook, and their creators see the potential for a more pro-active, constructive form of planning in the future. Many such planners are both less condemnatory towards the private property sector – welcoming negotiation and discussion – and at the same time more in touch with the needs of people at the grass roots. Rather than abolishing planning, the need is for a more sensitive, intelligent type of planning to emerge in the future.

One of the greatest challenges in recent years to the scope, spirit, and nature of traditional British town planning has been the demands of the green movement for environmentally directed policy to create 'sustainable cities'. This new agenda rests somewhat uneasily with existing urban location priorities in relation to industrial, retail and office development, whose location is generally still dependent upon motor car access, and orientated towards dispersed and decentralised sites. Restriction of existing car usage without commensurate increase in the levels of provision, coverage, and reliability of public transport, plus a reconceptualisation of location policy to create more compact cities, will create both economic and social problems, which are likely to most affect those least likely to have the financial means to relocate. It is as important that green policies should have a gender pespective, as vice versa. In practice town planners cannot plan for one policy in isolation from others, and therefore the future demands on the profession are likely to be great as planners seek to reconcile the demands of the different town planning agendas, past and present (as identified in this book, namely physical, economic, social, aesthetic and environmental) and to create workable policy directives and development control systems out of this complexity.

Guidance for students

How to approach planning as a subject

Preconceptions

These notes are written in a more direct, interactive style for you, the student. They provide advice on how to approach and study the subject, how to use the book references, comments for you to think about and discuss (as would be the case in a live tutorial), and tasks to undertake.

Many students entering professional courses have studied some urban issues in school geography or urban sociology. Everyone has watched persuasive television documentaries by journalists who are wise after the event on what is wrong with modern town planning and architecture – so much so that students may believe they already know what town planning is about. You may mistakenly believe that planning is easy because it is common sense and 'obvious'.

Whilst geography is linked with town planning, academic urban geographers (many of whom belong to the Institute of British Geographers) are more concerned with studying and understanding spatial (physical) issues than primarily with seeking to change the urban situation by policy-making (Hall, 1994). In contrast, the job of the planner is not 'just' to study or criticise the nature of urban development but to seek to bring about change and improvement and to ensure that new development occurs in an acceptable manner which fits in with current policies. This calls for negotiating and management skills in dealing with conflicting interest groups, all of whom think their solution is the only reasonable one. Therefore although some of the 'facts' may be the same there is a great difference between the academic field of geography and the professional area of town planning, each requires a different approach and way of thinking, as will have been seen from the book.

The nature of the subject

The dual element of 'facts and waffle' in town planning, as described in Chapter 1, often confuses people, particularly if they are inclined towards a developers' view of planning and do not realise the importance of the policy-making levels. Town planning is not a bookish subject, which you learn about in libraries alone, because the results of town planning are happening all around us, 'out there in the urban laboratory'; policies are being implemented as actual land use patterns and development changes. It is important to relate what you read in this book to what is going on in your own area, which you can find out by getting 'out and about' and looking at the built environment, by talking to people, by reading the planning items in the local newspapers, and by watching television programmes which deal with controversial town planning issues (if in a somewhat unbalanced manner). It is hoped that by the end of this book you will have developed your own informed views and judgement on town planning matters, both as a future urban professional and as a citizen of our highly urbanised society.

In town planning there is often no one right answer to a particular problem but several different answers, depending on one's priorities. Town planning laws and policies may appear very solid and unchangeable but, as developers often find to their advantage, they can be successfully challenged through the appeal system, provided equally valid counter-arguments can be put forward. This is because planning law is not based on some fixed code of moral absolutes defining what is right or wrong (as in certain branches of criminal law, for example), nor are planning policies necessarily based on objective, quantitative, unchangeable 'facts', for example in negotiating over parking standards, making up bills of quantities or basic property valuation. Likewise, in planning projects and examination questions, there is not going to be one right solution, but the good student is the one who brings in all the relevant aspects and the main points related to the question. Your views on the subject do not have to be identical to the lecturer's – they can be quite different – *but* you are a good student if you can justify and substantiate your views on each issue by means of sound reasoning and examples.

Always aim at covering a range of points in an essay or examination answer. Most answers are marked on the basis of a marking scheme in which there are likely to be about ten to twelve main issues or points the student is expected to cover (building each one of them up into a few sentences or a paragraph to create a complete essay). Just going on and on about one aspect whilst ignoring others is unlikely to lead to good marks. It is important not merely to remember the facts but to understand why they are important and the reasons behind them. Out in planning practice where the same facts can be used – in a planning inquiry, for example – to justify quite different conclusions and arguments, 'it's not so much what you say as why you say it that's important'. The same applies to what you write and why you write it in projects and essays. Town planning, both in college and in practice, is very much a 'discursive' (discussion-based) subject, in which you muster facts to justify a particular viewpoint. This can be seen clearly in local government, where Labour and Conservative councillors may be using quite different facts to justify their differing proposals for particular policies within the area's Development Plan.

In the 'real world' of planning practice decisions are not made purely on the basis of logic or good sense; the choice of policies reflects complex power relationships. Planning is a very political area, both at local and at national level. It is not easy to implement planning policy because of financial constraints, private land ownership rights, a whole range of other bargaining points and legal issues, and the activities of opposing interest groups. Many times students have said, 'If only we could take the politics out of town planning, it would be so much more straightforward!' Negotiating, politicking, legal strategies and management ploys are therefore all aspects and means of implementing town planning on a day-to-day basis.

Individual examples

You may not agree with all the material presented, for example the order of events presented in Chapter 2 on the process of property development. In reality, in some situations, the various processes may be going on in parallel, or in a slightly different order, because of the particular development situation in question. It is up to you to use your judgement if this situation rises, because in an examination you may achieve higher marks if you can provide updated or more detailed material on such issues. On the other hand, if your knowledge and experience of the planning system are limited you should be cautious before disagreeing, and check the facts in books and planning reports. Likewise, if you are unhappy about aspects of the book, and it goes against your own experience, it is quite justifiable to question it, provided you can give reasons and substantiate your views. Everyone's experience of urban issues is likely to be different, depending on age, gender, ethnic origin, where they live, and their socio-economic class.

Books

Throughout the text the name of the author and date of key reference books are given in brackets, often with the specific page following the colon, e.g. '(Healey, 1988: 27)'. Full details are to be found in the bibliography. The aim of these references is to direct you to more detailed reading. If you want to read further on the question of 'what is town planning' look at Chapter 1 of Hall (1994) and Chapter 1 of Ratcliffe. Find where the planning books are in your library (usually classified by the Dewey system under 711.00).

Planning law guidance

At the introductory level of studying town planning, as in this book, only a small amount of law is normally included, with specific attention being given to the main landmarks of planning legislation upon which the present system is based; detailed planning law is normally taught later on. Again one needs to understand the reasons behind the policies and the laws, as they cannot be operated mechanically without some awareness of the wider goals and objectives of town planning. Those of you whose future career will put you on the other side from the planners (in the capacity of surveyor or estate manager advising private-sector clients) need to understand how and why planners think the way they do in order to argue against them. Those who intend to become housing managers should be aware that housing departments cannot automatically grant themselves planning permission but are subject to the decisions of the planning department in their local authority just like anyone else. However, the procedure is more expeditious for in-house applications, although there are moves to increase controls on contentious applications, and the regulations have been amended somewhat under Section 20 of the Town and Country Planning Act, 1991 (see *The Planner*, 77, 29–31, for the main aspects of the 1991 legislation).

The two aspects of land law – 'public' town planning law, and 'private' real property law – are not separate subjects but frequently interrelate in the real world. For example, in lawyers' language planning obligations (such as covenants) 'run with the land', limiting what can be done on it and how it can be developed (Chapter 2). Sometimes public health, highway or licensing laws may interact with planning law too. Most important of all is to realise that planning law is not fixed but constantly being revised and updated, and therefore it is most important always to check for the most recent edition of any publication or piece of legislation, and to look at current government circulars, White Papers and guidance material (as found in the loose-leaf *Encyclopaedia of planning law*). For example, the Planning Policy Guidance notes are frequently revised, so that one should not assume that one with a particular number in 1988 is going to be on quite the same topic in 1995.

Historical guidance

There are many books on the history of town planning and architecture which you may wish to consult if you are doing a project or tutorial on a particular aspect, including Bacon, Bell, Betjeman, Bor, Burke, Cherry, Dyos, J. Hall, Morris, Mumford, Pevsner, Prizeman, Ravetz and Summerson, all to be found in the bibliography. To avoid peppering the text with distracting references individual books are mentioned only occasionally in the historical chapter, but it is strongly recommended that you go and look at what is to be found in the History of Planning section of your own library (around 711.4). You are also advised to check the dates in chronology of architectural styles (Table 8.1). You are also strongly recommended to get hold of one of those 'world history of architecture' coffee-table books full of pictures of buildings from different civilisations and the pocket guide book *The observer's book of architecture.*

It is important to look at the differences before and after conservation. When looking at the architecture of an area, always look at the subsequent fate of the area and the nature of the current inhabitants, because they will help you see how cities 'work' and how people adapt to the conditions and opportunities offered by their home-built environment. Do not divorce 'architecture' from the rest of your planning studies.

Sociological guidance

Don't worry if the names of the people and theories mean nothing to you yet; it is more important to grasp the general themes. Many physical town planning policies were strongly influenced by sociological theory. If you wish to pursue it all further look at the introductory sociology books such as the long-standing series of Penguin paperbacks, edited by Peter Worsley, with titles such as *Introducing sociology* and books such as Brown; Joseph, who is also a surveyor; Haralambos or Abbott and Wallace and Giddens. New introductory sociology books are coming out all the time; have a browse in your local bookshop, as they come in varying levels of difficulty.

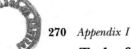

Tasks for each chapter

In each chapter you are encouraged to do further work, such as finding out more from other planning books or government publications, writing essays and going out into and seeing for yourself actual examples of the build environment such as the chapter has been describing. Reading this book should not be seen as substitute for personal research and further study, rather it is intended to draw you deeper into the subject and motivate you to go off and find out more for yourself.

Chapter 1

1. Go out and find out what the main town planning issues and problems are in your area, before you go any further. Visit your local library, read the local newspapers, and find out whether any local plans affect where you live. Write a short essay on what you find out, and start a file on your area. (Give yourself two weeks to achieve this task.)

2. Go to the library, find the *Encyclopaedia of planning law* and see what you make of it. Look at the journal section and find *Planning Bulletin*, *Planning* and *The Planner*, the main sources of up-to-date information. Also look at some of the property journals, such as *Estates Gazette*, *Estates Times*, *Chartered Surveyor Weekly*, and find the planning items in them. Choose one topic, look through the month's journals, and write a short essay on what you find and the differing emphasis of the above journals.

Chapter 2

1. What are the names of the present Secretary of State for the Environment and the junior ministers who assist him, and what aspects of the environment are they responsible for?

2. Find out what type of planning authority exists in your area, e.g. is it a Metropolitan District Council, a London borough, or a shire county and district system? Find out what stage the authority is at in the production of the main Development Plan.

3. Get a copy of a planning application form and the accompanying guidance notes from your local planning office, read it and see what you think of it. (But do *not* submit it, or you will have to pay.)

Chapter 3

Write an essay of about four A4 sides setting out whether or not you consider town planning and town planners are necessary, basing your answer on material which you have gleaned from the first three chapters of this book, plus examples to substantiate your views from your own area.

Chapter 4

1. Do you consider that people's town planning needs differ on the basis of their gender or class? Make notes on this, and add to them as you read the rest of the book.

2. Check the current figures on the average size of households in *Social Trends* (OPCS, annual): it may surprise you.

3. What do you see as the main urban changes which are occurring at the end of the twentieth century and what are the implications for town planning? Write a short essay relating your views to examples both of changes and instances of land use and development which reflect these on-going changes.

Chapter 5

1. Find out whether there are any model communities, Garden Cities (or, perhaps more likely, garden suburbs) in your home area. Examine the layout and design and write a short essay on their origins, characteristics and objectives. Get out your camera and start a file of examples of housing architecture which interest you.

2. Write a short examination-type essay describing the ideas of Ebenezer Howard and discussing what you consider to be his influence on twentieth-century town planning. To do this you will need to read further in this book, and to consult books such as those by Hall, Mumford, Ravetz and Burke.

Chapter 6

1. Compare and contrast the ideas of Howard and Le Corbusier. Who do you consider had the greater influence on the development of British town planning in the twentieth century? (A useful examination question.)

2. Write a short essay on the following: 'What were the aims and objectives of post-war reconstruction?' Illustrate your answer

by reference to relevant legislation, policy and committee reports. (Note that this question is asking you to discuss the aims and objectives, *not* to give a list of facts for their own sake, although you must bring in the details to illustrate the answer.)

Chapter 7

What do you consider is the role of the town planner in dealing with inner-city problems? Write down your views, with examples to substantiate your opinions.

Chapter 8

Look at the history of your own local town. Write a short essay describing its historical development, relating each stage to specific examples of streets or buildings that are still there.

Chapter 9

1. By means of a map and explanatory essay show the location and describe the nature of the urban Conservation Areas in your local town or a city with which you are familiar.

2. Write a short essay describing the main pressures on the countryside and discuss the implications for town planning policy.

3. Discuss the extent to which you consider the green movement has shifted British town planning more towards being concerned with environmental issues. Relate your answer to examples, legislation and policies as relevant.

Chapter 10

1. Get hold of some planning application forms with guidance notes and study them.

2. Obtain the local version of the *Design guide* or *Planning standards for developers* publication from your local planning authority. Read the Essex design guide also, and look at *Roads in urban areas*. Write a short report, with diagrams and plans where appropriate, setting out the nature of the planning layout standards which apply in your area. Standards are subject to variation on the basis of locality and indeed with time itself; it is suggested that you find out what standards apply in your area as

to road widths, parking and other factors involved in estate road layout.

3. Measure the size of the plot of your home or digs. If you live in a flat or over a shop you can still get a general idea of the density of the area, although it will not, strictly speaking, be the same as a pure net density, as above.

Chapter 11

Do you consider that the concentric zone theory is of relevance to British cities? Write an essay, relating your answer to examples of the characteristics of different areas which correspond to the zones in the model in respect of one city with which you are familiar.

Chapter 12

1. Name ten issues which you consider are unresolved planning issues.

2. Write a report on the future of cities (2000 words), covering the main physical, social, economic, political and ecological factors that are likely to be significant in the next twenty years. Suggest, where appropriate, alternative urban forms and structures at both the city-wide and individual Local Plan level, using diagrams and plans to illustrate your ideas.

Traditional vernacular architectural styles

This appendix should be consulted in conjunction with Chapter 5 on the Garden City movement, and in relation to Part III on the visual aspects of town planning.

Before the mass production of bricks, and their nation-wide distribution by rail in the nineteenth century, each region of Britain had its own distinctive style of building, reflecting the availability of local materials and climatic factors, e.g. houses in areas of heavy rainfall such as west Wales had a steeply pitched roof, built of local slate rather than thatch. Note that most of these natural materials were once cheap. But many of the cottages were literally hovels until they were done up in the twentieth century, given 'mod. cons' and transformed beyond recognition. One of the most common styles in the south-east and Midlands was half-timbering, originally introduced by the Anglo-Saxons, who originated from areas of Central Europe where there was an ample supply of timber. The areas between the wood were filled in with wattle and daub and with other materials which were locally available, e.g. flints. In areas where stone was easily quarried it became the main material. Different qualities were given to the buildings by different building materials, e.g. hard stone and granite in the Pennines (which weathered to black), as against soft, golden stone in parts of the south-west. The colour and texture of the materials were important factors in creating the townscape and atmosphere. This is why some areas look warm and cosy, others bleak and cold. Cob – a mixture of clay, sand and mud – much used in areas such as Devon where neither stone nor wood was plentiful. Walls were built up about 2 ft thick to create a flexible load-bearing material which stood by its own weight, as is found in Dorset. Gable ends of the cob and half-timbering were sometimes decorated by pargetting, with folk-art patterns and mouldings raised in stucco.

Clunch was sometimes used in the chalk areas but is generally rarer. It consists of blocks of chalk used like stone. Chalk is porous, so a damp course of hard stone or brick was often laid first (or even tar from the local boatbuilding industry was used in some seaside areas). Weatherboarding is an attractive form of exterior cladding often found in seaside areas, and apparently copied from the design of ships' hulls. In England it normally consists of horizontal slats of wood used to clad wattle walls. But in North America wood boarding and wooden shingles are frequently used on their own as the main structural material, particularly in New England. In Britain tile-hanging was often used on walls as a form of weather protection at the windward end of the building, often in conjunction with weatherboarding. Bricks, suprisingly, are not a native material but were originally imported from Holland, although there are earlier examples left by the Romans. However, they were used for expensive public and royal buildings, Hampton Court in Kingston upon Thames being a classic example from Tudor times (parts of which were recently burnt down and restored). During the industrial revolution there was a boom in factory-made bricks which eventually replaced most of the traditional building materials.

Likewise mass-produced roof tiles replaced traditional materials such as thatch and slate. Strange variations of factory-produced tiles such as 'foreign' Roman tiles, and even green tiles, became popular with some speculative house builders (and development control battles still continue on such issues today, Spanish tiles being particularly popular with people who have been abroad on their holidays). Indeed, some of the more controversial residential buildings from the past are now listed as being of architectural importance. In the twentieth century materials such as concrete, glass and steel-frame buildings as popularised by the modern movement in architecture have created an international Westernised style throughout the world. As we saw in Chapter 6, flat-roof houses built of concrete became the fashion in some areas in the 1930s under the influence of Continental architectural trends. Nowadays natural materials are used only by the very poor or the very rich! (See Prizeman, 1975; Munro, 1979.) Whilst it is seen as ecological to use natural materials, it is not considered 'green' to use endangered species of timber such as tropical hardwoods, e.g. mahogany. Global policies are needed to ensure the future supply of the natural materials which make vernacular construction possible.

Bibliography

Government publications

These are constantly being changed and updated, with later publications replacing earlier ones (as shown in brackets in the list) but this list provides a basic picture of the situation. It is *very* important to check the most recent versions for policy changes. You should also check the planning press, for example, see *Planning*, 18 August 1995, pp.1132–3 for changes to PPG 1.

Circulars and Policy Guidance notes

Minerals Planning Guidance

1995 (was 1988) MPG 1 General Conditions and the Development Plan System

There are also MPGs 2–9 covering a range of mineral policy topics.

Regional Planning Guidance

1995 RPG3 Strategic Guidance for London Planning Authorities

There are also other RPGs (1–10 some of which are being updated) and which cover different regions.

Important PPGs (Planning Policy Guidance notes) include:

1 General policy and principles
2 Green belts
3 Housing
4 Industrial and commercial development
5 Simplified Planning Zones
6 Town Centre and Retail Development
7 Countryside and the Rural Economy
8 Telecommunications
9 Nature Conservation
10 being replaced (previously regional guidance)
11 being replaced (previously regional guidance)
12 Development Plans and Regional Planning Guidance
13 Transport
14 Development of unstable land
15 Planning and the Historic Environment

16 Archaeology and Planning
17 Sport and Recreation
18 Enforcing planning control
19 Outdoor advertisement control
20 Coastal Planning
21 Tourism
22 Renewable Energy
23 Planning and Pollution Control
24 Planning and Noise

N.B. These are constantly being changed, renamed and updated, with
later editions replacing earlier ones. It is very important to check
the most recent versions for policy changes. Frequently, consultative
drafts are produced by the Department of the Environment in an
on-going process of updating existing PPGs and creating new ones
reflecting current policy issues. For list of available publications see
The Building, Housing and Planning Catalogue, HMSO, (Annual).
Consult Encyclopaedia of Planning Law for reference purposes
(loose leaf tome which is updated frequently).

Circulars

Please note this is a small selective list, based mainly on circulars
mentioned in individual chapters. Nowadays key policies statements are
more likely to appear in PPGs than Circulars or Command Papers (white
Papers). For fuller lists and description consult most recent editions of
planning law books such as Heap, Telling, Moore, and also refer to
Cullingworth and Nadin. However, it is more important to understand
the policies and principles reflected in the circulars than to know the full
lists.

22/83 Planning Gain
14/84 Green Belts
15/84 Land for Housing (cancelled by PPG3)
 8/87 Historic buildings and Conservation Areas (replaced by PPG15)
16/87 Development involving agricultural land (cancelled by PPG7)
 3/88 Unitary Development Plans (cancelled by PPG3)
15/88 Town and Country Planning (Assessment of Environmental
       Effects) Regulations
 9/90 Crime Prevention: the success of the partnership approach
       (replaced by 5/94)
 7/91 Planning and Affordable Housing (cancelled by PPG3)
12/91 Redundant hospital sites in the green belts
 7/94 Environmental Assessment: Amendment of Regulations
 9/94 Planning out Crime

Command Papers

This only includes those mentioned in this particular volume. There are
also many more specifically on town planning, although over the last ten
years the trend has been to put key policy statements in PPG's rather
than Department of the Environment Command Papers, but other

departments and ministries also produce relevant white papers. A full list is to be found in Cullingworth, 1994; and in the HMSO *Building, Housing and Planning* annual catalogue.

1966   Leisure in the Countryside Cmnd 2928
1977   Policy for Inner Cities Cmnd 6845
1985   Lifting the Burden Cmnd 9517
1990   This Common Inheritance Britain's Environmental Strategy Cmnd 1200
1992   (and annually) This Common Inheritance: The First Year Report
1994   Sustainable Development: The UK Strategy Cmnd 2426

British Standards Institute

Although not listed, please note there are a number of BSI documents covering a wide range of standards applicable to the built environment such as BS 6465 Sanitary Installations Part I: Revision 1995, which relates to public toilet provision.

Building Regulations and Fire Regulations

Although not listed, please note there are many other regulations controlling building design and development some of which contradict town planning principles as discussed more fully in Volume II.

Main twentieth-century acts of parliament relevant to town planning

1909   Housing and Town Planning Act
1919   Sex Disqualification (Removal) Act
1919   Housing and Town Planning Act
1935   Restriction of Ribbon Development Act
1945   Distribution of Industry Act
1946   New Towns Act
1947   Town and Country Planning Act
1949   National Parks and Access to the Countryside Act
1952   Town Development Act
1953   Historic Buildings and Ancient Monuments Act
1957   Housing Act (slum clearance)
1960   Local Employment Act
1965   Transport Act
1967   Civic Amenities Act
1968   Countryside Act
1969   Housing Act (General Improvement Areas)
1970   Community Land Act
1971   Town and Country Planning Act
1972   Industry Act
1972   Local Government Act
1974   Town and Country Amenities Act
1974   Housing Act (Housing Action Areas)

1975 Community Land Act
1978 Inner Urban Areas Act
1980 Highway Acts
1980 Local Government, Planning and Land Act
1981 Minerals Act
1982 Local Government (Miscellaneous Provisions) Act
1982 Derelict Land Act
1985 Housing Act
1986 Housing and Town Planning Act
1988 Housing Act
1988 Local Government Act
1989 Local Government and Housing Act
1990 Town and Country Planning Act
1990 Planning (Listed Buildings and Conservation Areas) Act
1990 Environmental Protection Act
1990 Planning (Hazardous Substances) Act
1991 New Roads and Street Works Act
1991 Planning and Compensation Act
1992 Local Government Act
1993 Housing and Urban Development Act
1994 Local Government (Wales) Act
1995 Environment Act

Note ·
Planning legislation is constantly being updated and amended.

In addition to the Acts there are a series of Regulations and Orders which enable the legislation to be implemented, such as the General Development Order, described in the chapter on development control. For example the full name of the GDO is actually contained within two linked documents.

1995 Town and Country Planning (General Development Procedure) Order
1995 Town and Country Planning (General Permitted Development) Order

Note that planning legislation is constantly being updated, amended and consolidated. The above list does not include all Acts, but the main ones of relevance to this book. It is more important for examination purposes to understand the reasons behind the development of planning legislation than to learn the list for its own sake. You will soon become familiar with the most commonly quoted Acts, and remember the most used sections (such as S106 on planning gain, 1991 Act) by second nature.

European planning controls

Article 119 of the Treaty of Rome 1957 established principle of equal opportunities, and the Equal Treatment Directive 76/207.

1987 Single Europe Act

EC Directive 85/337 on Environmental Assessment 'The Assessment of the Effect of Certain Public and Private Projects on the Environment' is applied in Britain under 'Assessment of Environmental Effects Regulation' No. 119 of the 1988 Town and Country Planning Regulations. (All EU legislation must be embodied in relevant domestic state legislation, and in case of dispute takes precedence.)

Books and papers

Abbott Pamela, Wallace Claire 1990 *An introduction to sociology*. London: Routledge.

Abercrombie Patrick 1945 *Greater London Development Plan*. London: HMSO.

Ahmed Yunus 1989 Planning and racial equality. *Planner* **75** (32): 18–20.

Ainsbett Alan 1990 Public/private-sector joint ventures: Local Government and Housing Act 1989 effects. *Estates Times* 24 February 24–9.

Aldous Tony 1972 *Battle for the environment*. Glasgow: Collins.

Aldridge Meryl 1979 *The British new towns*. London: Routledge.

Ambrose Peter 1986 *Whatever happened to planning?* London: Methuen.

Ambrose P 1994 *Urban Processes and Power*. London: Routledge.

Ambrose Peter, Colenutt Barry 1979 *The property machine*. Harmondsworth: Penguin.

Arber Sara, Dale Angela, Gilbert Nigel 1986 The limitations of existing social class classifications for women, in A. Jaccoby (ed.) *The measurement of social class*, Guildford: SRA, Department of Sociology, University of Surrey.

Arvill Robert 1969 *Man and environment: crisis and the strategy of choice*. Harmondsworth: Penguin.

Ashworth William 1968 *The genesis of modern British town planning*. London: Routledge.

Atkins Susan, Hoggett Brenda 1984 *Women and the law*. Oxford: Blackwell.

Atkinson R and Moon G 1993 *Urban Policy in Britain: The City, the State and the Market*. London: Macmillan.

Attfield Judy 1989 Inside Pram Town: a case study of Harlow house interiors, 1951–61, in Judy Attfield, Pat Kirkham (eds) *A view from the interior: feminism, women, and design*. London: Women's Press.

Avis Martin, Gibson Virginia 1987 *The management of general practice surveying firms*. Reading: Faculty of Urban and Regional Studies, University of Reading.

Bacon Edmund 1978 *Design of cities*. London: Thames & Hudson.

Bailey Joe 1975 *Social theory for planning*. London: Routledge.

Balchin Paul, Bull Gregory 1987 *Regional and urban economics*. London: Harper & Row.

Ball Michael 1988 *Rebuilding construction: economic change in the British construction industry*. London: Routledge.

Ball Simon, Ball Stuart 1995 *Environmental Law*. London: Blackstone.

Banks Olive 1981 *Faces of feminism: a study of feminism as a social movement.* Oxford: Martin Robertson.

Barlow J, Cocks R and Parker M 1994 *Planning For Affordable Housing.* London: HMSO.

Barlow Report 1940 *Report of the Royal Commission on the Distribution of the Industrial Population,* Cmd 6153. London: HMSO.

Barrow Jacqueline, Crawley Gerald, Wood Tony 1988 *Married to the council?: The private costs of public service.* Bristol: Bristol Polytechnic, Department of Economics and Social Science.

Barton H, Davis G and Guise R 1995 *Sustainable Settlements: A Guide for Planners, Designers, and Developers.* Bristol: University of the West of England and Luton: Local Government Management Board.

Bassett Keith, Short John 1980 *Housing and residential structure: alternative approaches.* London: Routledge.

Bell Colin, Bell Rose 1972 *City fathers: the early history of town planning in Britain.* Harmondsworth: Penguin.

Bell Colin, Newby Howard 1978 *Community studies.* London: Allen Unwin.

Bell Florence 1911 *At the works.* London: Nelson.

Benevelo Leonardo 1976 *The origins of modern town planning.* London: Routledge.

Bentley I, Alcock A, Murrain P, McGlynn S and Smith G (1985, new edition forthcoming) *Responsive Environments: A Manual for Designers.* London: Architectural Press.

Bernard Jessie 1981 *The female world.* New York: Free Press.

Betjeman John 1974 *A pictorial history of English architecture.* Harmondsworth: Penguin.

Birmingham University 1987 *The empire strikes back.* Centre for Continuing Cultural Studies.

Blowers A (ed.) 1993 *Planning for a Sustainable Environment.* London: Town and Country Planning Association and Earthscan.

Boardman Philip 1978 *The world of Patrick Geddes.* London: Routledge.

Bolsterli Margaret 1977 *The early community at Bedford Park: the pursuit of corporate happiness in the first garden suburb.* London: Routledge.

Booth Charles 1968 *Life and labour of the people of London,* published in series 1889–1906. Chicago: University of Chicago Press.

Booth William 1890 *In darkest England and the way out.* London: Salvation Army.

Bor Walter 1972 *The making of cities.* London: Hill.

Bottomore T 1973 *Elites and society.* Harmondsworth: Penguin.

Bowlby Sophie 1989 Gender issues and retail geography, in Sarah Whatmore, Jo Little (eds) *Geography and gender.* London: Association for Curriculum Development in Geography.

Boyd Nancy 1982 *Josephine Butler, Octavia Hill, Florence Nightingale: three Victorian women who changed the world.* London: Macmillan.

Briggs Asa 1968 *Victorian cities.* Harmondsworth: Penguin.

Brion Marion, Tinker Anthea 1980 *Women in housing: access and influence.* London: Housing Centre Trust.

Broady Maurice 1968 *Planning for people.* London: NCSS/Bedford Square Press.

Brown C 1979 *Understanding society: an introduction to sociological theory.* London: Murray.

Brundtland Report 1987 *Our Common Future.* World Commission on Environment and Development, Oxford: Oxford University Press.

Bruton Michael 1975 *Introduction to transportation planning.* London: Hutchinson.

Buchanan Colin 1963 *Traffic in towns.* Harmondsworth: Penguin.

Buchanan Colin 1972 *The state of Britain.* London: Faber.

Built Environment 1984 Special issue on 'Women and the built environment' *Built Environment* 10 (1).

Bulmer Martin 1984 *The Chicago school of sociology.* London: University of Chicago Press.

Burke Gerald 1976 *Townscapes.* Harmondsworth: Penguin.

Burke Gerald 1977 *Towns in the making.* London: Arnold.

Burke Gerald, Taylor Tony 1990 *Town planning and the surveyor.* Reading: College of Estate Management.

Burnett John 1977 *Useful toil: autobiographies of working people from the 1820s to the 1920s.* Harmondsworth: Penguin.

Burton, Rosemary 1990 *Travel Geography,* London: Pitman, Longman.

Cadman D, Austin-Crowe L, Avis M 1983 *Property development.* London: Spons, 1990 edition.

Campbell Beatrix 1985 *Wigan Pier revisited: poverty and politics in the eighties.* London: Virago.

Carey Lynette, Mapes Roy 1972 *The sociology of planning: a study of social activity on new housing estates.* London: Batsford.

Carson Rachel 1962 *Silent spring.* Harmondsworth: Penguin.

Carter Ruth, Kirkup Gill 1989 *Women in engineering.* London: Macmillan.

Castells Manuel 1977 *The urban question.* London: Arnold.

Chadwick Edwin 1842 *Report on the sanitary condition of the labouring population of Great Britain.* London.

Chapin Francis Stuart 1965 *Urban land use planning,* 1979 edition with J. Kaiser, Urbana, Ill.: University of Illinois Press, pp. 12–25.

Cherry Gordon (ed.) 1981 *Pioneers in British town planning.* London: Architectural Press.

Cherry Gordon 1988 *Cities and plans.* London: Arnold.

Chinoy Ely 1967 *Society: an introduction to sociology.* New York: Random House.

CISC 1994 *Occupational Standards for Professional, Managerial, and Technical Occupations in the Construction Industry in Planning, Construction, Property and Related Engineering Services.* London: Construction Industry Standing Conference, Building Centre, London.

Cockburn Cynthia 1977 *The local state: management of people and cities.* London: Pluto Press.

Coleman Alice 1985 *Utopia on trial.* London: Shipman.

Collard Andrée, Contrucci Joyce 1988 *Rape of the wild: man's violence against animals and the earth.* London: Women's Press.

Community Network 1989 Special issue on race relations, autumn.

Countryside Commission 1990 *Planning for a greener countryside.* Manchester: Countryside Commission.

CRE (Commission for Racial Equality) 1989 *A guide for estate agents and vendors.* London: CRE.

Crompton Rosemary, Jones Gareth 1984 *White-collar proletariat; deskilling and gender in clerical work.* London: Macmillan.

Crompton Rosemary, Mann Michael 1986 *Gender and stratification.* Cambridge: Polity Press.

Crompton Rosemary, Sanderson Kay 1990 *Gendered jobs and social change.* London: Unwin Hyman.

Cullen Gordon 1971 *Concise townscape.* London: Architectural Press.

Cullingworth J B 1993 *The Political Culture of Planning: American Land Use Planning in Comparative Perspective.* New York: Routledge.

Cullingworth J B and Nadin V 1994 *Town and Country Planning in Britain.* London: Routledge.

Dahrendorf Ralf 1980 *Life chances: approaches to social and political theory.* London: Weidenfeld & Nicolson.

Darley Gillian 1978 *Villages of vision.* London: Granada.

Darley Gillian 1990 *Octavia Hill.* London: Constable.

Davies Lyn 1992 *Planning in Europe.* London: RTPI.

Deem Rosemary 1986 *All work and no play? The sociology of women and leisure reconsidered.* Milton Keynes: Open University Press.

Denington Report 1966 *Our older homes: a call to action.* London: HMSO.

Denyer-Green Barry 1987 *Development and planning law.* London: Estates Gazette.

Department of Transport 1990 *Roads in urban areas.* HMSO: London.

Dixon Roger, Muthesius Stephan 1978 *Victorian architecture.* London: Thames & Hudson.

DOE (Department of the Environment) 1971 *Sunlight and daylight: planning criteria and design of buildings.* London: HMSO.

DOE 1972a *How do you want to live? A report on human habitat.* London: HMSO.

DOE 1972b *Development plan manual.* London: HMSO.

DOE 1995 *Housing and construction statistics,* annual. London: HMSO.

DOE 1992 *Development Plans: Good Practice Guide,* London: HMSO.

DOE 1995 *A Householder's Planning Guide for the Installation of Satellite Television Dishes.* London: HMSO.

DOE 1993 *Good Practice Guide on the Environmental Appraisal of Development Plans.* London: HMSO.

DOE 1994 *Sustainable Development: The UK Strategy,* Cmnd 2426. London: HMSO.

DOE 1995 *Your Permitted Development Rights and Environmental Assessment.* London: HMSO.

Donnison David, Eversley David 1974 *London: urban patterns, problems and policies.* London: Heinemann.

Donnison David, Ungerson Claire 1982 *Housing policy.* Harmondsworth: Penguin.

Dower Report 1945 *National Parks in England and Wales.* London: HMSO.

Dresser Madge 1978 Review essay on Leonore Davidoff, Jean L'Esperance, Howard Newby 1976 Landscape with figures: home and community in English society. *International Journal of Urban and Regional Research* **2** (3), special issue on 'Women and the city'.

Dudley Report 1944 *Design of dwellings.* Central Housing Advisory Committee of the Ministry of Health. London: HMSO.

Dunleavy Patrick 1980 *Urban political analysis.* London: Macmillan.

Durkheim Emile 1970 *Suicide: a study in sociology.* London: Routledge.

Dyos H (ed.) 1976 *The study of urban form.* London: Arnold.

EC (European Commission) 1990 *Green Paper on the urban environment.* Brussels: EC Fourth Environmental Action Programme 1987–92.

EC (European Commission) 1994 *European Charter for Women in the City,* EC, Directorate-General V (five). Employment, Industrial Relations and Social Affairs, Brussels (No. V/2336/94-EN).

Ekistics 1985 Woman and space in human settlements. *Ekistics* **52** (310).

Elson M 1986 *Green Belts.* London: Heinemann.

Esher Lionel 1983 *A broken wave: the rebuilding of England, 1940–80.* Harmondsworth: Penguin.

Essex 1980 *Essex design guide.* Chelmsford: Essex County Council.

Eversley David 1973 *The planner in society.* London: Faber.

Fitch 1985 *Women.* London: Fitch & Co. Shopping Consortium (Shopping centre report 8).

Fitch Rodney, Knobel Lance 1990 *Fitch on retail design.* Oxford: Phaidon.

Foley Donald 1964 An approach to urban metropolitan structure, in Melvin Webber, John Dyckman, Donald Foley, Albert Guttenberg, William Wheaton, Catherine Bower Wurster 1964 *Explorations into urban structure.* Philadelphia: University of Pennsylvania Press.

Fortlage Catherine 1990 *Environmental assessment: a practical guide.* Aldershot: Gower.

Foulsham Jane 1990 Women's needs and planning: a critical evaluation of recent local authority practice, in John Montgomery, Andy Thornley (eds) 1990 *Radical planning initiatives.* Aldershot: Gower.

Frankenberg R 1970 *Communities in Britain.* Harmondsworth: Penguin.

Friedan Betty 1963 *The feminine mystique,* Harmondsworth: Penguin, 1982.

Gale Andrew 1989 Attracting women to construction. *Chartered Builder* September/October.

Gans Herbert 1967 *The Levittowners.* London: Allen Lane.

Gardiner A 1923 *The life of George Cadbury.* London: Cassell.

Gardner Godfrey 1976 *Social surveys for social planners.* Milton Keynes: Open University.

Gaze John 1988 *Figures in a landscape: a history of the National Trust.* London: Barry & Jenkins.

Geddes Patrick 1915 *Cities in evolution: an introduction to the town planning movement and to the study of civics.* London: Ernest Benn, 1968.

Gibbs Lesley 1987 Who designs the designers? *WEB: Newsletter of Women in the Built Environment* **6** (4): 2–3.

Giddens Anthony 1993 *Sociology.* London: Polity Press.

Gilligan Carol 1982 *In a different voice: psychological theory and women's development.* Cambridge, Mass.: Harvard University Press.

Gilman Charlotte Perkins 1915 *Herland.* London: Women's Press, 1979.

GLC (Greater London Council) 1985 *On the move.* London: GLC, now London Residuary Body.

GLC 1984 Planning for equality: women in London, chapter VI of *Greater London Development Plan,* Draft Plan, London: GLC, now London Residuary Body.

GLC 1986 *Changing places.* London: GLC, now London Residuary Body.

Goldsmith Michael 1980 *Politics, planning and the city.* London: Hutchinson.

Goldthorpe John 1980 *Social mobility and class structure in modern Britain.* Oxford: Oxford University Press.

Grant Malcolm 1982 with 1990 supplement *Urban planning law.* London: Sweet & Maxwell.

Greed Clara 1991 *Surveying sisters: women in a traditional male profession,* London: Routledge.

Greed Clara 1992 The reproduction of gender relations over space: a model applied to the case of chartered surveyors. *Antipode* **24** (1): 16–28.

Greed C 1994 *Women and Planning: Creating Gendered Realities.* London: Routledge.

Greed C (ed.) 1995 *Implementing Town Planning.* Harlow: Longman (Vol. II of this series).

Greed C (ed.) 1996 *Investigating Town Planning.* Harlow: Longman (Vol. III of this series).

Greed C and Roberts M (forthcoming) *Urban Design.* Harlow: Longman (Vol. IV of this series).

Grieco Margaret, Pickup Laurie, Whipp Richard 1989 *Gender, transport and employment.* Aldershot: Avebury.

Griffin Susan 1978 *Woman and nature: the roaring inside her.* London: Women's Press.

Grover Richard (ed.) 1989 *Land and property development: new directions,* London: Spon.

Hadjimichalis Vaiou Dina 1983 Space–gender relations in the production of the built environment, in Bartlett International Summer School *The production of the built environment,* London: Bartlett School of Architecture (Proceedings of the Bartlett International Summer School 5). Geneva.

Hall Peter 1977 *Containment of urban England.* London: Allen & Unwin.

Hall Peter 1980 *Great planning disasters.* London: Weidenfeld & Nicolson.

Hall P 1994 *Urban and Regional Planning.* London: Routledge.

Hall Stuart, Jacques Martin 1989 *New times: the changing face of politics in the 1990s.* London: Lawrence & Wishart.

Hall S and Jacques S (ed.) 1989 *New Times: The Changing Face of Politics in the 1990s.* London: Lawrence and Wishart.

Hamnett Chris, McDowell Linda, Sarre Philip (eds) 1989 *Restructuring Britain: The changing social structure.* London: Sage.

Haralambos Michael 1990 *Sociology: themes and perspectives.* London: Unwin Hyman.

Hartman Heidi 1981 The unhappy marriage of Marxism and feminism, in Lydia Sargent (ed.) 1981 *Women and revolution.* London: Pluto Press.

Harvey David 1975 *Social justice and the city.* London: Arnold.

Hass-Klau C, Nold I, Böcker G, Crampton G 1992 *Civilised Streets: A Guide to Traffic Calming.* Brighton: Environmental and Transport Planning.

Hatje Gerd 1965 *Encyclopaedia of modern architecture.* London: Thames & Hudson.

Hatt P, Reiss A 1963 *Cities in society.* New York: Free Press.

Hayden Dolores 1976 *Seven American utopias: the architecture of communitarian socialism, 1790–1975.* London: MIT Press.

Hayden Dolores 1981 *The grand domestic revolution: feminist designs for homes, neighbourhoods and cities.* Cambridge, Mass.: MIT Press.

Hayden Dolores 1984 *Redesigning the American dream.* London: Norton.

Healey Patsy, McNamara Paul, Elson Martin, Doak Andrew 1988 *Land use planning and the mediation of urban change: the British planning system in practice.* Cambridge: Cambridge University Press.

Heap Desmond 1995 *Outline of planning law.* London: Sweet and Maxwell.

Herrington John 1984 *The outer city.* London: Harper & Row.

Hill William Thomson 1956 *Octavia Hill: pioneer of the National Trust and housing reformer.* London: Hutchinson.

Hobhouse Report 1947 *Report of the National Parks Committee (England and Wales).* London: HMSO.

Hoggett Brenda, Pearl David 1983 *The family, law and society.* London: Butterworth.

Hoskins John 1990 *The making of the English landscape.* Harmondsworth: Penguin.

Howard Ebenezer 1898 *Garden cities of tomorrow,* London: Faber, 1960.

Howatt Hilary 1987 Women in planning – a programme for positive action. *Planner* **73** (8): 11–12.

Howe Elizabeth 1980 Role choices of urban planners. *Journal of the American Planning Association* October: 398–401.

Hudson Mike 1978 *The bicycle planning book.* London: Open Books.

Hurd Geoffrey (ed.) 1990 *Human societies: introduction to sociology.* London: Routledge.

Hutchinson Max 1989 *The Prince of Wales: Right or Wrong?* London: Faber and Faber.

IJURR (International Journal of Urban and Regional Research) 1978 *Women and the City,* special issue, **2** (3).

Jackson Alan 1992 *Semi-detached London: suburban development, life and transport.* Oxford: Wild Swan.

Jacobs Jane 1964 *The death and life of great American cities: the failure of town planning.* Harmondsworth: Penguin.

Jacobs Jane 1970 *The economy of cities.* Harmondsworth: Penguin.

JFCCI (Joint Forecasting Committee for the Construction Industries) 1991 *Construction forecasts.* London: National Economic Development Office.

Joseph Martin 1978 Professional values: a case study of professional students in a polytechnic. *Research in Education* 19: 49–65.

Joseph Martin 1988 *Sociology for everyone.* Cambridge: Polity Press.

Keeble Lewis 1969 *Principles and practice of town and country planning.* London: Estates Gazette.

Keeble Lewis 1983 *Town planning made plain.* London: Longman.

Keller Susan 1981 *Building for women.* Lexington, Mass.: Lexington Books.

Kirk Gwyneth 1980 *Urban planning in a capitalist society.* London: Croom Helm.

Knox Paul (ed.) 1988 *The design professions and the built environment.* London: Croom Helm.

Kunstler James 1993 The geography of nowhere: The rise and decline of America's man-made landscape. Cambridge, Mass: MIT Press.

Lambert Camille, Weir David 1975 *Cities in Britain.* London: Collins.

Lane Peter, Peto Monica 1995 *Blackstone's Guide to the Environment Act 1995.* London: Blackstone.

Lavender Stephen 1990 *Economics for builders and surveyors.* London: Longman.

Lawless Paul 1989 *Britain's inner cities.* London: Paul Chapman.

Law Society 1988 *Equal in the law: report of the Working Party on Women's Careers.* London: Law Society.

Leach Penelope 1979 *Who cares? A new deal for mothers and their small children.* Harmondsworth: Penguin.

Le Corbusier 1929 *The city of tomorrow.* London: Architectural Press, 1971, and also *The radiant city.*

Leevers Kate 1986 *Women at work in housing.* London: HERA.

Legrand Jacques 1988 *Chronicle of the twentieth century.* London: Chronicle.

Levison Debra, Atkins Julia 1987 *The key to equality: the Women in Housing survey.* London: Institute of Housing.

Lewis Jane 1984 *Women in England, 1870–1950.* Brighton: Wheatsheaf.

Lewis Richard, Talbot-Ponsonby Andrew 1986 *The people, the land and the Church.* Hereford: Hereford Diocesan Board of Finance.

Lichfield Nathaniel 1975 *Evaluation in the planning process.* London: Pergamon.

Little Jo, Peake Linda, Richardson Pat 1988 *Women and cities: gender and the urban environment.* London: Macmillan.

Little J 1994 *Gender, Planning and the Policy Process.* London: Elsevier.

LPAS (London Planning Aid Service) 1986a *Planning for women: an evaluation of local plan consultation by three London boroughs.* London: TCPA Research Report 2.

LPAS 1986b *Planning advice for women's groups.* London: Town and Country Planning Association (Community Manual 6).

Lynch Kevin 1960 *The image of the city.* Cambridge, Mass., and London: MIT Press.

McDowell Linda 1983 Towards an understanding of the gender division of urban space. *Environment and Planning D: Society and Space* **1**: 59–72.

McLellan David 1973 *Karl Marx: his life and thought.* London: Macmillan.

McLoughlin J 1969 *Urban and regional planning: a systems view.* London: Faber.

Macey John, Baker Charles 1983 *Housing management.* London: Estates Gazette.

Maguire D, Goodchild M, Rhind D 1992 *Geographical information systems: principles and applications.* London: Longman.

Malpass Peter, Murie Alan 1990 *Housing management.* London: Estates Gazette.

Malthus Thomas 1798 *Essay on the principles of population.* London: Dent, 1973.

Marcus Susanna 1971 Planners – who are you? *Journal of the Royal Town Planning Institute* **57**: 54–9.

Markusen Anne 1981 City spatial structure, women's household work and national urban policy, in Catherine Stimpson, Elsa Dixler, Martha Nelson, Kathryn Yatrakis (eds) 1981 *Women and the American city.* London: University of Chicago Press.

Marriot Oliver 1989 *The property boom.* London: Abingdon.

Massey Doreen 1984 *Spatial divisions of labour: social structures and the geography of production.* London: Macmillan.

Massey Doreen, Quintas Paul, Wield David 1992 *High-tech fantasies: science parks in society, science and space.* London: Routledge.

Massingham Betty 1984 *Miss Jekyll: Portrait of a Great Gardener.* Newton Abbot: David & Charles.

Matrix 1984 *Making space: women and the man-made environment.* London: Pluto. See also WDS.

Mawhinney B 1995 *Transport: The Way Ahead.* London: Department of Transport.

Merrett Stephen 1979 *Owner occupation in Britain.* London: Routledge.

MHLG 1960 *The Control of Mineral Working.* (The Green Books), London: HMSO.

Millerson Geoffrey 1964 *The qualifying associations.* London: Routledge.

Mills C Wright 1959 *The power elite.* London: Oxford University Press.

Mishan E J 1973 *Cost–benefit analysis.* London: Allen & Unwin.

Montgomery John, Thornley Andy (eds) 1990 *Radical planning initiatives.* Aldershot: Gower.

Moore Robert 1977 Becoming a sociologist in Sparkbrook, in Colin Bell, Howard Newby (eds) *Doing sociological research.* London: Allen & Unwin.

Moore Victor 1995 *A practical approach to planning law.* London: Blackstone.

Morgan David, Nott Susan 1988 *Development control: policy into practice.* London: Butterworth.

Morgan Elaine 1974 *The descent of woman.* London: Corgi.

Morphet Janice 1983 Planning and the majority – women, paper given at the Town and Country Planning School, St Andrews, Scotland. London: RTPI.

Morphet Janie 1990 in Report of Summer School Proceedings 'Women and planning' *Planner* 76 (7): 58.

Morris A E J 1972 *History of urban form: prehistory to the Renaissance.* London: Godwin.

Morris Anne, Nott Susan 1991 *Working women and the law: equality and discrimination in theory and practice.* London: Routledge.

Morris Eleanor 1986 An overview of planning for women from 1945–1975, in Marion Chalmers (ed.) *New communities: did they get it right? Report of a conference of the Women and Planning Standing Committee of the Scottish Branch of the Royal Town Planning Institute, County Buildings, Linlithgow.* London: RTPI.

Morris Terence 1958 *The criminal area.* London: Routledge.

Mumford Lewis 1930 *The city.* Film for the American Institute of Planners by RKO, commentary by Mumford.

Mumford Lewis 1965 *The city in history.* Harmondsworth: Penguin.

Munro Bruce 1979 *English houses.* London: Estates Gazette.

Myerscough Cyril 1975 *Feet first: a pedestrian survival handbook.* London: Wolfe and the Pedestrians' Association for Road Safety.

Nadin Vincent, Jones Sally 1990 A profile of the profession. *Planner* **76** (3): 13–24.

Newby Howard 1982 *Green and pleasant land.* Harmondsworth: Penguin.

Newman Oscar 1973 *Defensible space: people and design in the violent city.* London: Architectural Press.

Norton-Taylor Richard 1982 *Whose land is it anyway?* Wellingborough: Turnstone.

OECD 1994 *Women and the City: Women in the City: Housing, Services and the Urban Environment.* Paris: OECD, Organisation for Economic Cooperation and Development.

OPCS (Office of Population Censuses and Surveys) 1983 *Census 1981: National Report – Great Britain* I, table 6, p. 15. London: HMSO.

OPCS 1995 (or annual) *Standard Occupational Classification, Registrar General.* London: HMSO.

OPCS 1995 (or annual) *Social trends.* London: HMSO.

Pahl Ray 1965 *Urbs in rure.* London: Weidenfeld & Nicolson.

Pahl Ray 1977 Managers, technical experts and the state, in M Harloe (ed) *Captive cities.* London: Wiley.

Pardo Vittorio 1965 *Le Corbusier.* London: Thames & Hudson.

Parker Morris Report 1961 *Homes for today and tomorrow.* London: Central Housing Advisory Committee.

Pearson Lynn 1988 *The architectural and social history of co-operative living.* London: Macmillan.

Pevsner Nikolaus 1970 *Pioneers of modern design.* Harmondsworth: Penguin.

Pickvance Christopher (ed.) 1977 *Urban sociology.* London: Tavistock.

Pinch Stephen 1985 *Cities and services: the geography of collective consumption.* London: Routledge.

Potter Stephen 1986 Car tax concessions; perk or problem? *Town and Country Planning* **55** (6): 169–76.

Potter Stephen 1989 A north–south divide in the new towns programme: biannual survey of new towns in Britain. *Town and Country Planning.* **58** (11): 296–302.

Power Anne 1987 *Property before people: the management of twentieth-century council housing.* London: Allen & Unwin.

Prince of Wales 1989 *A vision of Britain.* London: Doubleday.

Prizeman John 1975 *Your house; the outside view.* London: Hutchinson.

Punter John 1990 *Design control in Bristol, 1940–1990.* Bristol: Redcliffe Press.

Ratcliffe John 1981 *Introduction to town and country planning.* London: Hutchinson.

Ravetz Alison 1980 *Remaking cities.* London: Croom Helm.

Ravetz Alison 1986 *The government of space.* London: Faber.

Reade Eric 1987 *British town and country planning.* Milton Keynes: Open University Press.

Rees Gareth, Lambert John 1985 *Cities in crisis.* London: Arnold.

Reith Report 1946 *New Towns Committee: interim report; final report.* London: HMSO.

Rex John, Moore Robert 1967 *Race, community and conflict.* London: Institute of Race Relations.

Richardson B 1876 *Hygienia: a city of health.* London.

RICS (Royal Institute of Chartered Surveyors) 1989 *What use is a chartered surveyor in planning and development?* London: RICS.

Roberts Margaret 1973 *Town planning techniques.* London: Hutchinson.

Roberts Marion 1991 *Living in a man-made world: gender assumptions in modern housing design.* London: Routledge.

Roberts Patricia 1988 Women and planning history: theories and applications, paper given at Women in Planning History: Theories and Applications seminar of the Planning History Group. York: Institute of Advanced Architectural Studies.

Rodriguez-Bachiller Agustin 1988 *Town planning education: an international survey.* Aldershot: Avebury.

Rogers Barbara 1983 *52%: getting women's power into politics.* London: Women's Press.

Rowntree B 1901 *Poverty: a study of town life.* London.

RPG No. 3 (Regional Planning Guidance) 1995 *Strategic Guidance for London Planning Authorities.* London: HMSO.

RTPI (Royal Town Planning Institute) 1983 *Planning for a multi-racial Britain.* London: Commission of Racial Equality.

RTPI 1986 *The Royal Town Planning Institute distance learning course.* Bristol: Bristol Polytechnic and Leeds Polytechnic.

RTPI 1987 *Report and Recommendations of the Working Party on Women and Planning.* London: RTPI.

RTPI 1988 *Managing equality: the role of senior planners.* London: RTPI.

RTPI 1989 *Planning for Choice and Opportunity.* London: Royal Town Planning Institute.

RTPI 1991 *Traffic growth and planning policy.* London: RTPI.

RTPI 1995 *Planning for Women* PAN (Practice Advice Note) No. 12. London: Royal Town Planning Institute.

Rubenstein David 1974 *Victorian homes.* Newton Abbot: David & Charles.

Ryder Judith, Silver Harold 1990 *Modern English society.* London: Methuen.

Rydin, Yvonne 1993 *The British Planning System: An Introduction,* London: Macmillan.

Saunders Peter 1979 *Urban politics: a sociological interpretation.* Harmondsworth: Penguin.

Saunders Peter 1985 Space, the city and urban sociology, in Derek Gregory, John Urry 1985 *Social relations and spatial structures.* London: Macmillan.

SBP (Polytechnic of the South Bank) 1987 *Women and their built environment.* London: Polytechnic of the South Bank, Faculty of the Built Environment (now South Bank University).

Scarman Lord 1982 *The Scarman report: the Brixton Disorders, 10–12 April 1981.* Harmondsworth: Penguin.

Scarrett Douglas 1983 *Property management.* London: Spon.

Scott N K 1989 *Shopping centre design.* New York: Van Nostrand Reinhold.

Scott Report 1942 *Report of the Committee on Land Utilisation in Rural Areas.* London: HMSO.

SERPLAN (South East Regional Planning Council) 1988 *Housing, land supply and structure plan provision in the south-east.* London: SERPLAN (RPC 1070).

Service Alastair 1977 *Edwardian architecture.* London: Thames & Hudson.

Shoard Marion 1980 *The theft of the countryside.* London: Temple Smith.

Shoard Marion 1987 *This land is our land: the struggle for Britain's countryside.* London: Paladin.

Silverstone Rosalie, Ward Audrey (eds) 1980 *Careers of professional women.* London: Croom Helm.

Simmie James 1974 *Citizens in conflict: the sociology of town planning.* London: Hutchinson.

Simmie James 1981 *Power property and corporatism.* London: Macmillan.

Sjoberg Gidean 1965 *Pre-industrial city: past and present.* New York: Free Press.

Skeffington 1969 *People and planning.* London: HMSO.

Smith Mary 1989 *Guide to housing.* London: Housing Centre Trust.

Smith Neil, Williams Peter 1986 *Gentrification of the city.* London: Allen & Unwin.

Smith Susan 1989 *The politics of race and residence.* Oxford: Polity Press.

Spencer Anne, Podmore David 1987 *In a man's world: essays on women in male-dominated professions.* London: Tavistock.

Stacey Margaret 1960 *Tradition and change: a study of Banbury.* London: Oxford University Press.

Stapleton Timothy 1986 *Estate management practice.* London: Estates Gazette.

Stimpson Catherine, Dixler Elsa, Nelson Martha, Yatrakis Kathryn (eds) 1981 *Women and the American city.* Chicago: University of Chicago Press.

Stoker G and Young S 1993 *Cities in the 1990s: Local Choice for a Balanced Strategy.* London: Longman.

Strauss Anselm (ed.) 1968 *The American city.* London: Allen Lane.

Summerson John 1986 *Georgian London.* Harmondsworth: Penguin.

Sutcliffe Anthony 1974 *Multi-storey living: the British working-class experience.* London: Croom Helm.

Swenarton Mark 1981 *Homes fit for heroes.* London: Heinemann.

Tannahill Reay 1989 *Sex in history.* London: Hamish Hamilton.

Tawney R 1969 *Religion and the rise of capitalism.* Harmondsworth: Penguin.

Taylor Beverley 1988 Organising for change within local authorities: how to turn ideas into action to benefit women, paper given at Women and Planning: Where Next? conference. London: Polytechnic of Central London (Short Course Report, 16 March).

Taylor Judith 1990 Planning for women in Unitary Development Plans: an analysis of the factors which generate 'planning for women' and the form this planning takes. Unpublished MA thesis, Sheffield University.

Taylor Nicholas 1973 *The village in the city.* London: Temple Smith.

TCPA (Town and Country Planning Association) 1987 A place for women in planning. *Town and Country Planning* **56** (10).

TCPA 1993 *Planning for a Sustainable Environment,* London: Earthscan.

Telling J 1990 *Planning law and procedure.* London: Butterworth.

Tetlow John, Goss Anthony 1968 *Homes, towns and traffic.* London: Faber.

Thomas Keith 1988 *Development Control Distance Learning Package, Issues in Development Control:* Unit 4, *The home as workplace.* Oxford: Oxford Polytechnic in conjunction with the RTPI.

Thompson F, Michael L 1968 *Chartered surveyors: the growth of a profession.* London: Routledge.

Tönnies Ferdinand 1955 *Community and association.* London: Routledge.

Torre Susana (ed.) 1977 *Women in American architecture: a historic and contemporary perspective.* New York: Whitney Library of Design.

Tudor Walters Report 1918 *Report of the Committee on Questions of Building Construction in connection with the Provision of Dwellings for the Working Classes.* London: HMSO.

Uthwatt Report 1942 *Report of the Expert Committee on Compensation and Betterment.* London: HMSO.

Vallance Elizabeth 1979 *Women in the house.* London: Athlone Press.

Walker Derek 1996 *see* Greed (ed.) 1996, Vol. III in this series.

Watson Sophie, Austerberry Helen 1986 *Housing and homelessness: a feminist perspective.* London: Routledge.

Weber Max 1964 *The theory of social and economic organisation.* New York: Free Press.

WDS (Women's Design Service) 1995 current publications *It's not all swings and roundabouts: making better playspace for the under-sevens. Women and safety on housing estates. Thinking of small children: access, provision and play. Shoppers' creches: guidelines for child care facilities in public places. At women's convenience: a handbook on the design of women's public toilets. Built for women? Accessible Offices.* London: Women's Design Service.

WDS 1994 *Planning London: Unitary Development Plans.* London Women and Planning Forum, London: Women's Design Service, and check Broadsheet updates.

Wekerle Gerda, Peterson Rebecca, Morley David (eds) 1980 *New space for women.* Boulder: Westview Press.

WGSG (Women and Geography Study Group Institute of British Geographers) 1984 *Geography and gender.* London: Hutchinson.

Whitelegg Elizabeth, Arnot Madeleine, Bartels Else, Beechey Veronica, Birke Lynda, Himmelweit Susan, Leonard Diana, Ruehl Sonja, Speakman Mary Anne (eds) 1982 *The changing experience of women.* Oxford: Blackwell.

Whyte William 1981 *Street corner society.* Chicago: University of Chicago Press.

Wilson Des 1970 *I know it was the place's fault.* London: Oliphant.

Wilson Elizabeth 1980 *Only half way to paradise.* London: Tavistock.

Young Michael, Willmott Peter 1957 *Family and kinship in east London.* Harmondsworth: Penguin.

Young Michael, Willmott Peter 1978 *Symmetrical family: study of work and leisure in the London region.* Harmondsworth: Penguin.

Index

Abercrombie, Patrick 113
ad hoc 31–33
Advertisement control 170, 188
agricultural
  buildings 176
  land 179
  Revolution 174
Akroydon 89
American transportation planning 126
anomie 219
Architects and Surveyors Institute 53
Architectural styles 151
Area of Outstanding Natural Beauty
  176
Art Nouveau 163
Article '4' direction 170, 197

B1 business use 195
back to back housing 71
Barlow Commission 112, 134
Baroque style 151, 158
Bath 66, 160
Bauhaus 104
Beau Nash 160
Beeching cuts 127, 180
Bernini 158
Bethnal Green 85, 231
bicycles 97, 118, 202
Big Bang (deregulation of financial
  services) 43
Birmingham 69
blue land 204
Booth, Charles 230
Bourneville 98
Bristol Development Corporation 33
Broadacre City 73
Brundtland 187
Buchanan, Colin 127
building societies 89, 110
Burgess, Ernest 227
by-law housing 86

Cadbury, George 98
canals 68, 154
Capability Brown 174
cars 13–14, 44, 71, 106, 126–9, 209
  parking 106, 210, 258
caravans 188
CBD (Central Business District) 70, 227
Census 76
Central Government 20
Centre Point in London 123
Certificate of Lawful Use 192
Chandigargh 106
Channel Tunnel 54, 136
Chartered Institute of Building 53
chartered surveyor 43–50
Chicago School of Sociology 226
children 44, 105, 121, Chapter 12 (see
  creche)
cholera 83
CISC 42
City Challenge 143
City Grants 143, 166, 168
city state 94
  walls 103, 155
Civic
  Amenities 169
  pride 70, 162
  Trust 171
civil engineers 53
class Chapter 11 (see working)
classified road 99
co-operative housekeeping 96
Code of Professional Conduct 250
Coleman, Alice 223
Commission for Racial Equality 234
Common Agricultural Policy 179
communities 230
  of interest 222 (see neighbourhoods)
compensation and betterment 115
comprehensive development areas 115
Comte 219

concentric zones 227
concierge system 254
conditions in planning permissions 194, 248
conflict theory 234
conservation Chapter 9
conservatories 199
Corbusier 121, 254
cost benefit analysis 129
cost factor 40
Council for the Protection of Rural England 183
councillors 22, 56, 191
counties 27, 56
Country Landowners Association 183
Country Parks 178
Countryside Commission 172, 182
Covent Garden 159
Coventry 120
creches Chapter 12
crime 212
Crown Land 171
Cumbernauld 124
cybernetics 129
cycling 13, 127 (*see* bicycles)

defensible space 223
demolition 183, 253
Denington Report 131
densities 94, 205–8
Department of the Environment 21
derelict land 135, 183
detailed (full) planning application 184
development 31
  brief 36
  control Chapter 10
  process of 35
  Plan 26–30, 129, 191
disability 194, 203, 211
districts 28–30
dogs 183
domestic service 78
Dower Report 113
Dudley Report 113
Durkheim 219
dysfunctions 220

easements 204
Ebenezer Howard 46, 91
EC Directorates General 22, 25

education 46
Egypt 150
electronic mail 44
employment 256–9 (*see* class, and, working)
Enclosure Acts 174
English Heritage 166
enterprise 33
  culture 43
  zones (EZ's) 139
Environment Act 12, 31, 59, 187–8
environmental
  areas 128
  assessment 186
  determinism 60
  impact assessment (EIA) 186, 204
  protection 59
  watchdog 59
Essex Design Guide 200, 210, 255
Estate Agents, National Association of 53
ethnic issues 13, 50, 137, 227, 232–4
Europe 22, 31, 43, 54, 55, 136, 172, 179, 250
expanded towns 124
extensions 30, 197

feminism 76, Chapter 12 (*see* women, and gender)
feudal system 155
Florence 157
footprint 181
Forestry Commission 182
Frank Lloyd Wright 72
Friends of the Earth 183
full planning permission 194
Functionalism
  (architecture) 102–7, 149
  (sociology) 224
futurism 102

garages 199
Garden Cities 46, 90–8
Garden Festivals 140
Geddes, Patrick 102, 114
gemeinschaft (community) 242
General Development Order 30, 170, 195
General Improvement Areas 131
gender 74, 80, Chapter 12

Georgian 131, 158
gesellschaft 242
Gothic style 151, 156
Great Fire of London 83, 159
Greater London Council 29
Greater London Development Plan 29,
    113
Greek orders, Doric, Ionic and
    Corinthian 151, 153
green belts 94, 113, 172, 178
Green movement 59, 186–9
greenhouses 199
Gropius, Walter 104

ha-ha 174
Halifax school 89
Hampstead Garden Suburb 99
high rise 19, 99, 119, 254
Highways 194, 197
Hill, Octavia 91, 108, 243
Hobhouse Committee 113
homelessness 138
Homes for Heroes 108
hotels 131
house extensions 197–9
household formation 79
householder application 131, 191
housing 38, 83, 131, 138, Chapter 10
    Institute of 53
Howard, Ebenezer 46, 91

Incorporated Society of Valuers and
    Auctioneers 53
Industrial Development Certificates
    (IDCs) 135
Industrial Revolution Chapter 4
Inigo Jones 159
inner city 33, 136, 143, 227
Institution of Civil Engineers 53
Institution of Structural Engineers
    53

Jekyll, Gertrude 175
jerry built 71
journey to work 127, 246

Keeble 5

laissez faire 9, 56
Le Corbusier 102, 121, 254

leisure 131, 259
Letchworth 99
Lever 98
'life chances' 235
linear city 72
listed buildings 131, 166–7
local authority 26–8
London Borough 29
London
    County Council 104
    Docklands 33, 140
Lutyens 159, 163, 175

Malthus 85
Manchester 69, 85
Mawhinney 13, 118
medieval 155
metro land 110
Metropolitan
    County Councils 29
    District Councils 29
Michelangelo 157
Milton Keynes 125
minerals 185–6
Ministry for Agriculture, Fisheries and
    Food (MAFF) 24, 179
Ministry of Defence 24, 182
Model Communities 87
multiple nuclei concept 227
Mumford, Lewis 259
Municipal Corporations 82

Nash, John 160
National
    Coal Board 185
    Farmers Union 182
    Land Utilisation Survey 184
    Parks 32, 113, 176
    Trust 172, 183
nature conservation 179
neighbourhood 94, 105, Chapter 12
neo-marxism 236
network analysis 129
New Earswick 96
New Lanark 88
New Towns 32, 60, 113, 116,
    124–6
non-conformist 87
non-profit making 9, 56
non-statutory plans 33
Normans 151, 155

OECD 250
offices 44, 78, 107, 240
Office Development Permits 135–6
oil crisis 132
Ordnance Survey grid reference 190
out-of-town 259
outline permission 194
Owen, Robert 88

Park, Robert 226
Parker Morris 108
parking 106, 120, 198, 210, 258
Parthenon 153
partnership schemes 33, 120
Peabody Trust 85
Perry, Clarence 220
piazzas 157
planning
  agreements 37
  appeals 23
  applications 38, 191
  brief 37
  gain 37, 115, 191, 248
  obligation 37, 192
  permission, Chapter 10
playing fields 247
Pompidou Centre in Paris 164
poor law 84
population 1, 69, 78, 233
porch 197
Port Sunlight 98
post-modernist
  architecture 164
  sociology 238
pre-fabs 164, 252
Prince Charles 36, 147, 257
Property Boom 121, 132
Property Researchers 9
public conveniences 260
Public Health 83
pyramids 150

Quangos 32

Radburn 208, 220
Radiant City 105
railway 68, 72, 253
ransom strip 202
Regent's Park 148, 160
regional planning 25, 57, 109, 116, 133

register, planning 192
Reith Report 113
Renaissance 156
responsive environments 213
restrictive covenants 204
retail 128, 259 (*see* shopping)
  gravity models 128 (*see* shopping)
retired people 58, 122
Rex and Moore 235
Ribbon Development 110
Rio 187
Roehampton 121
Romans 154
Ronan Point 122
Rowntree, Joseph 98
Royal Institute of British Architects 53
Royal Institution of Chartered
    Surveyors 53
Royal Town Planning Institute 53, 102,
    248
rural issues 59, 172–85
  deprivation 180
  society 73
RSPCA 183

Saltaire 89
Sant' Elia 103
satellite dishes 197
Scott Committee 113, 176
Seagram Tower 106
Sears Building 106
Secretary of State 21
sector concept 229
set aside 181
shopping 120, 128, 259, Chapter 12 (*see*
    retail)
sick building syndrome 258
Simplified Planning Zones 139
Single Regeneration Budget (SRB) 33,
    58, 143
site analysis 201
Sites of Special Scientific Interest 179
slums 70, 118, 121, 131
social ecology 228
social engineering 220–3
socio economic groupings 76–8
Soria y Mata 72
South East 25
statutory undertakers 39, 171, 202
steel framed structures 103
Structure Plan 27, 38, 130, 201

suburbanisation 71, 244
sui generis 196
sunlight and daylight regulations 121, 208
survey-analysis-plan 102
sustainability 212
Swindon 71, 124
'systems' planning 129

threshold analysis 129
Tönnies 219
Town and Country Planning Association 46, 92, 102
townscape 147, 166
traffic calming 212
trees 194, 203
Tripp, Alker 128
Tudor Walters 108

ultra vires 249
under-utilised land 183
unemployment 109
Unitary Development Plans 28 (*see* structure plans, and development)
Unité d'Habitation 105
Unwin and Parker 91, 98

Urban Development Corporations 32, 136
urban managerialism 236
Use Classes Order 31, 195
Uthwatt committee 113

vandalism 122
Venice 157
vertical city 102–5
Victorian architecture 161
visibility splay 211

Weber, Max 224
Welfare State 113, 119
Welsh Development Agency 73
Welwyn Garden City 96
white land 178
William the Conqueror 155
women 68, 74, 123, Chapter 11
  workers 124
workers 67–8, 124, 176, Chapter 11 (*see* class, and, employment)
Wythenshawe 99

Young and Willmott 231

zone of transition 137, 227
zoning 43, 94, 110, 204